Can Christianity Survive in America?

Edited By Mike Willis

truth
BOOKS

ISBN 10: 1-58427-360-7

ISBN 13: 978-1-58427-3608

truth
BOOKS

Guardian of Truth Foundation
C E I Bookstore
220 S. Marion St., Athens, AL 35611
1-855-49-BOOKS or 1-855-492-6657
www.truthbooks.net

Table of Contents

Introduction
Mike Willis

The German philosopher, Friedrich Nietzsche (1844-1900) wrote, "Gott is tot" ("God is dead"). He did not mean by this that God as a being or person first existed and has subsequently died. What Nietzsche was saying is that God is no longer a viable source of any absolute moral principles to mankind. When one removes God from his belief system, there is no basis for moral judgments. The "death of God" idea is a way of saying that twentieth century (now twenty-first) men no longer believe in a cosmic order under divine control and moral governance.

Nietzsche's repulsive statement was subsequently presented in America by Thomas J. J. Altizer (1927 -), Emory University religion professor and key member of the Godless Christianity movement. A fair assessment of ongoing developments in much of America is that secularism is spreading to the point that some are already saying that we are living in Post-Christian America. God is less of a force in American politics and culture than at any time in recent memory. Research and media sources consistently report that Christians make up a declining percentage of the American population (Jon Meacham, "The End of Christian America," *Newsweek* [April 4, 2009]). Since 1990, the percentage of Americans who are self-identified as Christian has fallen from 86% to 76%. The same article related a conversation with R. Albert Mohler, Jr., president of Southern Baptist Theological University as follows:

> "A remarkable culture-shift has taken place around us," Mohler wrote. "The most basic contours of American culture have been radically altered. The so-called Judeo-Christian consensus of the last millennium has given way to a post-modern, post-Christian, post-Western cultural crisis which threatens the very heart of our culture." When Mohler and I spoke in the days after he wrote this, he had grown even gloomier. "Clearly, there is a new narrative, a post-Christian narrative, that is animating large portions of this society," he said from his office on campus in Louisville, Ky.

While liberals fear the advent of an evangelical theocracy, the truth is that Christians are now making up a declining percentage of the American population. The change that is occurring in American pluralism is not so much the blossoming of atheism as it is the birth of many gods. Meacham said, "The rising numbers of religiously unaffiliated Americans are people more apt to call themselves 'spiritual' rather than 'religious.' (In the NEWS-WEEK Poll, 30 percent describe themselves this way, up from 24 percent in 2005.)"

There are ominous signs that America's religious makeup is rapidly changing. Consider these developments.

Ominous Signs

1. A rising tide of secularism. A Pew Forum poll echoed the ARIS (American Religious Identification Survey) finding, reporting that the percentage of people who say they are unaffiliated with any particular faith has doubled in recent years, to 16 percent. In terms of voting, this group grew from 5 percent in 1988 to 12 percent in 2008—roughly the same percentage of the electorate as African-Americans (Meacham).

> Two thirds of the public (68 percent) now say religion is "losing influence" in American society, while just 19 percent say religion's influence is on the rise. The proportion of Americans who think religion "can answer all or most of today's problems" is now at a historic low of 48 percent. Many conservative Christians believe they have lost the battles over issues such as abortion, school prayer and even same-sex marriage, and that the country has now entered a post-Christian phase (Meacham).

The secularist mind set is an atheistic world view. The world came into existence through the random and chance development of matter. Atheistic evolution is the accepted explanation for how lifeless matter evolved into human life as we know it in the twenty-first century. With God removed from the world view, there are no absolute morals: morals are what works for the individual and have no implicit binding obligation on anyone else. There is no judgment at the end of life, so one is left to invent his own moral system, usually guided by hedonistic tendencies (what makes the individual happy at the moment). There is no logical reason for hope, so life is depressing with little reason to hope for anything ever to be better.

The secular world view is preached, not in the pulpits of the local churches, but through the media of movies, television, music (almost all genres, with the exception of religious music), literature (magazines, newspapers, books, epublications, etc.). The educational system is almost totally controlled by the secular world view which has eliminated God from the classroom. The creation narrative is replaced with atheistic evolution. Universal moral values as revealed in the Bible are replaced with a relativistic ethical system that approves sex outside of marriage, abortion to destroy babies so conceived, and welfare programs that have resulted in fathers being absent from the home, homosexual conduct, etc.

The secular philosophy is capturing the hearts of America's youth. It may not be logically expressed as a rejection of Christianity in favor of atheism, but it is shown by the number who question the creation narrative, the acceptance of sinful conduct as legitimate for that person (homosexuality, for example), a moral lifestyle that involves drugs, drinking, fornication, pregnancies outside the bonds of marriage, fathers absent from the homes and lives of their children, etc. On most occasions, sports and recreation take priority over religious activities when the two come into conflict with each other.

Who can deny that this wave of secularisim is spreading across our country? To see what it will produce, one can look at modern Europe with its beautiful cathedrals preserved as historical monuments but with few attending their worship services. The buildings are used for concerts but little used as places for professed Christians in Europe to join together for worship.

2. The worldliness that is spilling over into the churches. Most churches have experienced enough worldliness in its members first hand that they need no one to tell them about the cultural influence on the church. Among believers, many of their children dress like the world, listen to the music of the world, and watch the same movies and TV shows as non-Christians. Like their secular friends, they put sports and extra-curricular school activities before worship services. There is a growing ignorance of the Bible among this younger generation and little interest in learning the Bible. Young teenage boys conceive and young teenage girls bear children outside of wedlock. Most teens experiment with alcohol and perhaps also with recreational drugs. Pornography on the internet is spreading throughout the society and ensnaring many of our children. Filthy language is common on the Facebook pages and photographs of scantily-clad bodies are unashamedly displayed. Even the most degenerate dancing is widely viewed as acceptable and those who object to it are considered, at best, oddballs.

3. The aging of the church. As secularism spreads throughout the country we find fewer who are interested in learning about God. Churches are struggling to hold their own numerically. It is hard to baptize enough people to replace those who die, move away, or fall away. The end result is that the church is gradually aging. Unless something changes many of these congregations will be forced to close their doors because there are not enough members left to pay the utilities.

4. Lack of Bible studies. The secularism of our age means that this generation more nearly resembles that of Noah's day (Gen. 6), Sodom and Gomorrah (Gen. 19), and apostate Israel than it looks like Pentecost (Acts 2). There is less interest in Biblical studies. Many colleges and universities that were begun for the purpose of incorporating the Bible in its program of instruction or to train young men to preach have evolved into secular institutions with little interest in religious studies. Homes are centered around the TV rather than having a "family altar" in which the parents instructed their children in the word of God. The lethargic church is having trouble finding people committed enough to attend weekly services of worship each week, much less zealous enough to look for people to lead to Christ.

5. A powerful homosexual lobby. Although the percentage of homosexuals is probably in the 4% range (+/-), the influence of homosexuals upon politics, movies and TV, the legal system, etc. is astounding. The most likely character to be victimized by Hollywood is the homosexual; the one most likely to be presented in the most favorable light is not the preacher or doctor, but the homosexual. Think of such shows as "Will and Grace" and "The Real World." Christina Roush and Tawnia Simpson wrote,

> Because of the acceptance shown in these television shows, the casting of homosexuals in various TV shows has skyrocketed. Today there are around 22 television shows on major stations with a homosexual cast member as the main character of the show. This is proof that homosexuals are not only on their way to full acceptance, but also that people are willing to celebrate them for their openness and bravery ("Homosexuality in Television," http://www.bgsu.edu/departments/tcom/faculty/ha/tcom103fall2004/gp16/gp16.pdf accessed 6/30/2011).

Those who speak their convictions against homosexuality are accused of being homophobic, for which they can be summarily fired from their jobs – all in the name of creating a tolerant work environment, of course. Tolerant of whom? Certainly not those who believe that homosexuality is a sin against God! The homosexual community knows the power of the Hollywood media to reshape American thought and use it effectively.

6. A growing Islamic presence. As a matter of fact, several Eastern religions are growing in America, but since the events of September 11, 2001, America is more conscious of the Islamic threat. However, the growth rate of Islam in America comes primarily from two sources: large number of births in the Muslim population and immigration, but not from conversion. James Dretke wrote,

> . . . both Christian and Muslim sources assert that Islam is the fastest growing religion in the United States. The Yearbook of American and Canadian Churches 2000 gives the figure of 3,950,000 Muslims in America today. Islamic Horizons states that there are eight to ten million Muslims in North America. The most common figure cited (the statistic the United States government regularly uses) is about six million. The largest concentrations of Muslims are in California, New York, and Illinois — with an estimated 400,000 in the Chicago area.

> While specific figures may be debated, what cannot be debated is the phenomenal growth of Islam. According to United Nations statistics, the Muslim population in the United States grew by 25 percent between 1989 and 1998. In 1990 there were only about 50 Islamic schools in America. Today the number is over 200. Since about 1990 the number of "registered Islamic centers and mosques" has tripled to "more than 2,500" (Islam In America, "Islam Grows Into a Strong Presence in America").

I have not verified these statistics, but there can be little doubt that many Americans have developed a pluralistic view of all religions, not only an acceptance of all so-called Christian religions (regardless of whether or not what they believe and teach is aligned with historically Christian doctrine), but also an acceptance of non-Christian religions as well.

7. A church with a diluted message. The trend in preaching in America is moving away from Bible-based doctrinal preaching. Modern sermons are filled with anecdotes and examples that touch the heart, with catchy titles, and with non-judgmental lessons which address how to be happy on earth issues rather than matters pertaining to eternal salvation, judgment, heaven, and hell. Mega-churches are growing across America with a "come as you are" approach to ethical behavior; couples living together outside the marriage bonds are received into membership. Jesus' teaching on divorce and remarriage is ignored so that immoral conduct and no-fault divorce are about as commonplace among church goers as among the unchurched population.

Churches survey the community to find out what kind of church the community desires and then they work to create that model, thus allowing the pagan world to reshape Christianity rather than Christianity reshaping the pagan culture.

All of these are ominous signs in American culture that indicate America is rapidly changing from a population that predominantly professed Christianity and Christian values to a population that may call itself Christian, though it has obviously moved far away from historic Christian beliefs and morals, or is altogether secular.

What This Portends

The issue is this: Will Christianity survive in America? There is no question that Christianity will survive. The Lord Himself will preserve the seed of the kingdom, the word of God, which can be planted anew in the hearts of men. But the center of Christianity is undoubtedly shifting from America.

The center of Christianity at one time would unquestionably have been Jerusalem. Unlike the centers of some other religions, however, Christianity's center is constantly in a state of change. One can follow the different centers of Christian population through the centuries. At different times it has been Rome, Constantinople, North Africa, Egypt, Asia Minor, Great Britain, and America.

Andrew Walls said,

> What happened in each case was decay in the heartland that appeared to be at the center of the faith. At the same time, through the missionary effort, Christianity moved to or beyond the periphery, and established a new center. When the Jerusalem church was scattered to the winds, Hellenistic Christianity arose as a result of the mission to the gentiles. And when Hellenistic society collapsed, the faith was seized by the barbarians of northern and western Europe. By the time Christianity was receding in Europe, the churches of Africa, Asia and Latin America were coming into their own. The movement of Christianity is one of serial, not progressive, expansion (The Expansion of Christianity: An Interview with Andrew Walls, *http://www.religion-online.org/showarticle.asp?title=2052*; accessed 6/30/2011).

In an article about Walls, Tim Stafford wrote,

> The spread of the gospel is often presented as inexorable progress outward, like an inkblot, but Walls saw that time and again the real story was of ebb and flow. The loss of Christian territory happened not just

on the periphery but at the heartland. Jerusalem was the first heartland until the Romans leveled it, and the Jewish church all but ceased to exist. Then came Rome, until the northern Vandals sacked it; Constantinople, until Islam overran it; northern Europe, before Enlightenment skepticism cut its heart out. At each turning point, the gospel made a great escape, crossing over into an unknown culture just before disaster struck. History suggested that Christianity lives by this pilgrim principle (Tim Stafford, "Historian Ahead of His Time," *Christianity Today* [February, 2007], 89).

Western dominance of Christianity is dwindling, especially as America becomes more and more secular. Rob Mol wrote,

"The day of Western missionary dominance is over, not because Western missionaries have died off," says Scott Moreau, chair of intercultural studies at Wheaton College (Illinois), "but because the rest of the world has caught the vision and is engaged and energized."

Moreau says Americans must come to realize that "missions is a two-way street on every continent." Today's missionary is as likely to be a black African in Europe as a northern Indian in south India or a Korean in China. In addition, mission leaders are placing a new focus on Asia, where 60 percent of the global population lives. Samuel Hugh Moffett, the elder American statesman of Asian Christianity, told *Christianity Today* that Asia represents "the future for missions." Born in Korea to missionary parents and now professor emeritus at Princeton Theological Seminary, Moffett has spent his professional life studying Christianity in Asia. Between 1998 and 2005, he produced the two-volume History of Christianity in Asia, the recipient of many scholarly accolades. . . .

As the Western mission movement matures and slows down, majority-world missions are expanding. South Korea sends more than 1,100 new missionaries annually. That means Korea alone sends out as many new missionaries each year as all of the countries of the West combined" (Rob Mol, "Missions Incredible," *Christianity Today* [March, 2006], 30).

Undoubtedly, with the growth of secularism in American culture and the expansion of missions in many third world countries, the center of Christianity is rapidly shifting.

Conclusion

What is more in question than whether America will be the center of Christianity in the immediate future is whether or not Christianity can survive in America. This book identifies some of the things that pose a threat to the survival of Christianity in America and suggests some things that one can do to overcome those threats.

But another important issue than whether Christianity can survive in America is this: Can America survive without Christianity? And, if it survives, what will it look like? Will it follow the European model where cathedrals are maintained as historical monuments, places for concerts and other activities, but empty on Sunday morning? Or, will America go the way of other powerful, but ungodly, nations before us?

Sources Cited

Dretke, James. "Islam Grows Into a Strong Presence in America," taken from the web site of Islam in America (*http://www.arabicbible.com/ christian/islam_in_america.htm*, accessed June 30, 2011).

Meacham, Jon. "The End of Christian America," *Newsweek* (April 4, 2009). Accessed online at http://www.newsweek.com/2009/04/03/the-end-of-christian-america.html on 6/30/2011).

Mol, Rob. "Missions Incredible," *Christianity Today* [March, 2006], 28-34.

Roush, Christina and Tawnia Simpson, "Homosexuality in Television," (http://www.bgsu.edu/departments/tcom/faculty/ha/tcom103fall2004/gp16/gp16.pdf, accessedon 6/30/2011).

Stafford, Tim. "Historian Ahead of His Time," *Christianity Today* [February, 2007], 86-89.

Walls, Andrew, "The Expansion of Christianity: An Interview with Andrew Walls," *Portrayal of Homosexuality in the Media* (*http://www.religion-online.org/showarticle.asp?title=2052*; accessed 6/30/2011).

Christianity Can Survive in America

Jim Deason

Paul warned Timothy, "But realize this, that in the last days difficult times will come" (2 Tim. 3:1). The times of which the apostle spoke were dangerous, perhaps even violent times. Certainly they would be hard times, times of terrible stress. Though through the years and in any given geographical area God's people have experienced periods of relative peace, the truth is, walking with Christ has always been challenging.

We Live in Difficult Times

I believe we live in difficult times – times made difficult by many different things. Across the world, the religion of *Islam* gains strength and influence daily. *Hollywood* is spewing forth filth in the name of entertainment. The Biblical model for the *home* is under attack on many fronts. *Materialism* is a cancer that is eating at the heart of many Christians. *Sports* has become the God of our culture. *Secular education* is a dangerous threat to true Christianity. Subliminally and overtly, our children are

Jim Deason was born on June 30, 1953 in Jasper, AL. In his formative years he fell under the influence of gospel preachers like Jackie Richardson, Dwight Edwards, Art Thomas, and Hiram Hutto. These men helped to place within him a passion to preach. On May 4, 1973 Jim married the former Paige Adams, daughter of J. Wiley Adams, and they have three children: Melissa (David) Gipson of Bell Buckle, TN; David (Janet) Deason of Springville, AL; and Wiley (Mallory) Deason of Bentonville, AR. Seven grandchildren (Hannah, Emily, Julia, Joshua, Emma, Jay, and Caleb) light up his life. Jim has preached locally in Georgia, South Carolina, Alabama, and Tennessee and holds seven to eight gospel meetings each year. He has done foreign work in Almaty, Kazakhstan and Mariupol, Ukraine and has published Bob and Sandra Waldron's *History and Geography of the Bible* and Ferrell Jenkin's *The Early Church* in the Russian language. Jim is Vice-President of the Board and a regular contributor to *Biblical Insights*.

bombarded in our schools daily with humanism and evolution, philosophies which, at their root, are atheistic and godless. We face challenges from an *anti-Christian government*. Laws are passed and your tax dollars are used to support godless causes while many in our society bow at the altar of *political correctness*, unwilling to take a stand against evil and that which is clearly wrong.

How do New Testament Christians respond to it all? The truth is, some have no response at all. They are filled with *apathy*. As long as their daily routine is not interrupted, as long as they can make a living from week to week, most don't care! Others have so *diluted the gospel message* and made so many compromises with the world that they cannot recognize the compromises any more. Christianity, as described in the New Testament, cannot survive in hearts and lives like these – neither in America nor anywhere else.

Make no mistake, the kingdom of God still stands. We have received an unshakable kingdom (Heb. 12:28) which cannot be destroyed, a kingdom which "will itself endure forever" (Dan. 2:44). Yet, if you and I want to be a part of this kingdom, if we want to experience the rewards of citizenship in this kingdom, there are certain things we must recognize and do. If Christianity is to survive in America, if it is to live within our hearts, we need to do six things that are outlined for us in 2 Timothy 3:1-4:8.

1. Recognize the Characteristics of Difficult Times (2 Tim. 3:1-5)

> But know this, that in the last days perilous times will come: For men will be lovers of themselves, lovers of money, boasters, proud, blasphemers, disobedient to parents, unthankful, unholy, unloving, unforgiving, slanderers, without self-control, brutal, despisers of good, traitors, headstrong, haughty, lovers of pleasure rather than lovers of God, having a form of godliness but denying its power. And from such people turn away! (2 Tim. 3:1-5).

Paul's description of difficult times is vivid. Perilous times are characterized by men with despicable traits.

The **lover of self** is the narcissist who has an excessive interest in himself. Those who love self are by nature **lovers of money** or materialistic. A man who loves self and money is more than likely a **boastful** man who lays claims to having more power, ability, or money than he actually possesses. The **arrogant** man, contemptuous of others, usually manifests this in his language. Thus, he becomes a **reviler**, one who is abusively critical of others in order to build himself up.

Difficult times are characterized by children who are **disobedient to parents**. Would anyone argue that our age is characterized by disobedient children? Many are **ungrateful**, feeling they deserve everything that they have been given and rarely pausing to feel or express appreciation.

Times are difficult when men are **unholy** or profane, not merely in language but in life. The unholy man is also **unloving**; "without natural affection" in the KJV. This behavior is seen every day in the arrest reports in your local newspaper under the euphemism "domestic disturbances."

Perilous times are characterized by men who are **irreconcilable**. Have you ever known of a brother so bitter that he could not be appeased? Irreconcilable people are sometimes **malicious gossips** and it is easy to see why. The man who never wants to be reconciled will say virtually anything hateful and harmful about the object of his hatred.

Times are often made stressful by men **without self-control**. These are men who feel no restraint nor are they bound by any code of conduct. They are "loose cannons" ready to fire off with little or no provocation and without regard to the consequences. Such men are usually **brutal**. Like savage animals they attack and tear the object of their contempt to pieces. They become **haters of good**. They are **treacherous**, so self-absorbed and self-indulgent they would betray their mothers for personal profit. They are **reckless**, not taking notice of how their actions effect others around them. They are **conceited**, having a higher opinion of themselves than they ought (Rom. 12:3).

In difficult times men are **lovers of pleasure rather than lovers of God**. This is hedonism pure and simple. Look around you and what do you see? People whose lives are pleasure focused. Most church-going people in America might be categorized as **holding to a form of godliness, although they have denied its power**. These are difficult times.

Considering these characteristics of difficult times we need to make four observations:

- Though all of these characteristics may not be found in any one individual, it is easy to see that they are interrelated. Once one becomes a "lover of self," from that point the road is all downhill.

- Paul will observe later in this context that, "evil men and impostors will proceed from bad to worse" (1 Tim. 3:13). They do so by growing in these vices.

- This is our world, the world we live in. This is the world of Fox News and CNN. It is brought closer home on Channel 6 and 33. Then, when you pick up the local newspaper, you find names you recognize or people you know who have descended into the abyss of sin.

- Paul tells us to "avoid such men as these" (1 Tim. 3:5). "Do not be deceived, bad company corrupts good morals" (1 Cor. 15:33; cf. 1 Cor. 5:9-11).

2. Understand How Wicked Men Work
in Difficult Times (2 Tim. 3:6-9)

For of this sort are those who creep into households and make captives of gullible women loaded down with sins, led away by various lusts, always learning and never able to come to the knowledge of the truth. Now as Jannes and Jambres resisted Moses, so do these also resist the truth: men of corrupt minds, disapproved concerning the faith; but they will progress no further, for their folly will be manifest to all, as theirs also was (2 Tim. 3:6-9).

In difficult times, wicked men work secretly, entering into the seclusion of people's homes (2 Tim. 3:6). They love the cover of darkness and anonymity. They seldom emerge until they have gained a footing for their evil schemes, a following to their ungodly cause. They hate the exposure of their teaching to the light of truth.

Evil men prey on the weak (2 Tim. 3:6), especially those interested in the novel and being different. They rarely appeal to men who are sound in the faith and filled with a knowledge of God's word and the wisdom to apply it. It has amazed me how evil men always know where to go to gain sympathy for their rebellion. They find the people who are dissatisfied, always wanting to "think outside the box," and people who thrive on being different.

Wicked men oppose truth and those who teach it (2 Tim. 3:8-9). I have no idea regarding the identity of Jannes and Jambres because their names appear no where else in Scripture. Nevertheless, what we do know is that, like the Gentiles of Romans 1:28 and the apostates of Hebrews 6:6, the false teachers who faced Timothy and the Ephesian church were men who had rejected faith and were of such depraved mind that they were irretrievably bound up in their wickedness. These were tough times for Timothy and the church in Ephesus. They are the times of which sleepless nights are made. Never are strong, dedicated men needed more than in the effort to expose the works of evil, deceptive men.

3. Follow Paul's Pattern of Conduct
in Difficult Times (1 Tim. 3:10-13)

But you have carefully followed my doctrine, manner of life, purpose, faith, longsuffering, love, perseverance, persecutions, afflictions, which happened to me at Antioch, at Iconium, at Lystra--what persecutions I endured. And out of them all the Lord delivered me. Yes, and all who desire to live godly in Christ Jesus will suffer persecution. But evil men and impostors will grow worse and worse, deceiving and being deceived. (2 Tim. 3:10-13).

Jesus is our perfect pattern for conduct in difficult times (1 Pet. 2:21-23). Additionally, Paul encouraged others to follow his example (1 Cor. 4:16; 11:1; Phil. 3:17; 4:19; 1 Thess. 1:6; 2 Thess. 3:9). In Paul, Timothy had a mentor, an example of how men ought to behave themselves when facing difficult times.

Paul's life was an example of **teaching** sound doctrine (Acts 20:20, 24-27) and he encouraged Timothy to do the same (1 Tim. 4:6; 2 Tim. 4:2-3). His **conduct** was as a role model who knew others were watching (1 Thess. 2:10-11). He had a single **purpose** in life which all could see: "But I do not consider my life of any account as dear to myself, so that I may finish my course and the ministry which I received from the Lord Jesus, to testify solemnly of the gospel of the grace of God" (Acts 20:24).

Paul was an example in **faith**. He was dependable as a servant and messenger of God. In difficult times **patience** is especially important. Timothy observed how Paul was patient with both the weakness of others (1 Cor. 8:13; Rom. 15:1-2) as well as the trials of life. Such faith and patience came from a heart that **loved** both God and the souls of lost men. When times got tough and lesser men might have given up, Paul **persevered**. Timothy and all who knew the apostle could see it.

Times were difficult for Paul and Timothy just as they are sometimes perilous for people today. But as the Lord rescued Joseph from Pharaoh's prison, Daniel from the lion's den, and Paul from his persecutors, God will rescue us. He "knows how to rescue the godly from temptation" (2 Pet. 2:9).

4. Keep Our Focus on the Scriptures
in Difficult Times (2 Tim. 3:14-17)

But you must continue in the things which you have learned and been assured of, knowing from whom you have learned them, and that from childhood you have known the Holy Scriptures, which are able to make you wise for salvation through faith which is in Christ Jesus. All Scripture is given by inspiration of God, and is profitable for doctrine, for reproof, for correction, for instruction in righteousness, that the man of God may be complete, thoroughly equipped for every good work (2 Tim. 3:14-17).

While a child, Lois and Eunice taught Timothy to love the "sacred writing which are able to give you the wisdom that leads to salvation through faith which is in Christ Jesus" (2 Tim. 3:15). In early manhood, the apostle Paul served as a mentor to young Timothy. Many of us here today, like Timothy, were taught the Scriptures from our youth and how thankful we should be to those who set our feet on higher ground. Like Timothy, we were taught three very important principles regarding the Scripture:

- **The SOURCE of Scripture**, i.e., "all Scripture is inspired by God" (2 Tim. 3:16). The word "inspired" literally means "breathed out by God." As God said to Jeremiah, "Behold, I have put My words in your mouth" (Jer. 1:9). This principle is fundamental to faith because, "faith comes from hearing, and hearing by the word of Christ" (Rom. 10:17).

- **The BENEFIT of Scripture**, i.e., "all Scripture is . . . profitable" (2 Tim. 3:16). It is profitable for teaching (what's right), reproof (what's not right), correction (how to get right), and training in righteousness (how to stay right).

- **The SUFFICIENCY of Scripture**, i.e., "that the man of God may be adequate, equipped for every good work" (2 Tim. 3:17). There is no need for anything else; no need for further revelation. God's word has been once and for all time revealed to the saints (Jude 3). And we were taught in both word and song, "Whatever you do in word or deed, do all in the name of the Lord. . ." (Col. 3:17).

The point to be made here is this: You can never take your focus off God's word. Like Mary at the feet of Jesus (Luke 10:38-42), we dare not let anything take priority over His instruction, especially in perilous times!

5. Maintain the Work of Preaching in Difficult Times (2 Tim. 4:1-5)

I charge you therefore before God and the Lord Jesus Christ, who will judge the living and the dead at His appearing and His kingdom: Preach the word! Be ready in season and out of season. Convince, rebuke, ex-hort, with all longsuffering and teaching. For the time will come when they will not endure sound doctrine, but according to their own desires, because they have itching ears, they will heap up for themselves teachers; and they will turn their ears away from the truth, and be turned aside to fables. But you be watchful in all things, endure afflictions, do the work of an evangelist, fulfill your ministry (2 Tim. 4:1-5).

Sometimes when things are difficult and dangerous, when our lives are filled with stress, we are tempted to give up and quit. Indeed, the road to the cross is littered with the carcasses of men who have felt the burden too heavy. However, in difficult times Paul charged Timothy to **"preach the word"** – not human opinion or pop psychology, but the word. Do the work, don't shirk it or be distracted from it. It is the most important work among men—a charge to a task made solemn by the very presence of God. The apostle reminded Timothy to **"be ready in season, out of season."** As a soldier ready for a battle or a guard constantly alert, be prepared for the onslaught of the enemy because he is coming. It is not a matter of *if* but *when!* Get your shield up and have your sword ready (Eph. 6:10-17). He commanded the young man to **"reprove, rebuke, exhort,"** i.e., to use every appropriate measure to keep men's hearts focused on God's instructions and the way God wants them to live. Sometimes error must be exposed and men convicted of their sinful actions. At other times, people just need a word of encouragement and exhortation to keep up the good fight. In every action use great **"patience and instruction."** In essence, love the souls of men. Spend your life helping folks go to heaven. This is not a sprint, this race is a marathon.

Paul understood that the time would come in Timothy's experience when men would not "endure sound doctrine" (2 Tim. 4:3-5). These would be dif-ficult, stressful days in the young preacher's life. Many do not want to hear sermons on marriage, divorce, and remarriage. Some wink when preachers preach on social drinking or immodesty. Sermons on the exclusive nature of the Lord's church or doctrinal sermons on denominational doctrine are sometimes frowned upon lest some visitor be offended. As long as we preach sermons one could preach in any denominational church in town, people are happy. But the moment you preach a militant gospel of truth, get ready because difficult days are coming.

6. Fill Our Hearts with Hope in Difficult Times (2 Tim. 4:6-8)
The good thing about preaching and living the gospel in difficult times is

that a Christian can always realize that he is not living for earthly rewards. Our reward is out of this world! While here, there is a fight to be fought, a race to run, and a faith to be kept. If we are sacrificed on the altar of service to God, so be it. There is a "great crowd of witnesses surrounding us" (Heb. 12:1) who have run the race before us and are cheering us on. Victory crowns awaited Paul and Timothy and they await me and you as well.

Charles Pollock put everything in perspective in the beautiful words of an old hymn entitled, *Above the Bright Blue*:

> There's a beautiful place called heaven,
> It is hidden above the bright blue.
> Where the good, who from earth ties are riven,
> Live and love an eternity through.
>
> Above the bright blue, the beautiful blue,
> Jesus is waiting for me and for you.
> Heaven is there, not far from our sight,
> Beautiful city, of light.

"But realize this, that in the last days difficult times will come" (2 Tim. 3:1). They are here. Yet, we are not of those who wring their hands in worry. Instead, we are a people of faith who believe along with Isaiah, "Behold, God is my salvation, I will trust and not be afraid; For the Lord God is my strength and song, And He has become my salvation" (Isa. 12:2). God's kingdom will forever stand.

Christianity Can Survive . . .

The Threat of Hollywood

Leon Mauldin

Introduction

Romans 1 portrays the world of the first century, a culture in a downward spiral of degradation. Paul speaks of those who knew God, but failed to glorify Him (v. 21). They were not thankful to Him who is the Giver of every good and perfect gift (v. 21; cf. Jas. 1:17). They were lifted up with pride as they professed to be wise but became fools (v. 22). But man is a worshipful being; when one does not reverence the proper object (God), he will fill the vacuum with a sinful substitute (idolatry) (v. 23).

Leon Mauldin and his wife Linda have three children (Alysha [Montgomery], Micah, and Seth) and six grandchildren. Their son Seth and his wife Summer preach in Lincoln, NE. Leon has preached since 1972 in the states of Georgia, Tennessee, and Alabama, and is currently in his 22th year of work with the Hanceville church of Christ in Hanceville, Alabama. Leon serves as one of four elders.

During most of his first thirty years of preaching, Leon had the opportunity to make use of the medium of radio, especially enjoying the Q&A format. Some representative questions and answers may be found at *www.goodfight.com*. Click on *Short Answers to Tough Questions*.

God has also opened doors for several preaching trips to foreign countries, including the Czech Republic, Hungary, Norway, Russia, Ukraine, Belgium, and Canada.

Leon is one of the authors of *Discovering God's Way*, Bible class curriculum edited by Bob Harkrider, and also writes the back page for the monthly *Biblical Insights*.

Leon has been doing History and Geography of the Bible presentations since 1993. He has had the opportunity to make numerous trips to the Bible lands for research and photography, and directs annual tours with brethren to the Bible lands. He makes use of the photos in teaching as well as in publications. You can see some of the photos and info at Leon's Message Board at *http:// bleon1.wordpress.com*.

These foundational choices set the stage for the behavior and subsequent consequences with which Paul continues. First there is the sin of homosexuality, which is directly tied in to "exchanging the truth of God for the lie" and their false system of worship (vv. 24-25). This conduct is described as "vile passions," "against nature," "shameful," and "error."

When people refuse to have God in their knowledge, darkness takes over the hearts, and there are many disastrous consequences:

> God gave them over to a debased mind, to do those things which are not fitting; being filled with all unrighteousness, sexual immorality, wickedness, covetousness, maliciousness; full of envy, murder, strife, deceit, evil-mindedness; they are whisperers, backbiters, haters of God, violent, proud, boasters, inventors of evil things, disobedient to parents, undiscerning, untrustworthy, unloving, unforgiving, unmerciful; who, knowing the righteous judgment of God, that those who practice such things are deserving of death, not only do the same but also approve of those who practice them (vv. 28-32).

Increasingly the world of our day is becoming like that of the first century. The solution is Jesus Christ. The answer is His Word. That was the answer then, and it is the answer now.

Hollywood and the Prevailing Worldview

In his timely book, *The Battle for the Mind,* Tim LaHaye references the processes of societal change of the past two centuries which are certainly impacting the culture and worldview of our day:

> During the last 200 years, humanism (man's wisdom) has captivated the thinking of the Western world. After conquering Europe's colleges and universities, it spread to America, where it has developed a stranglehold on all public education. Recognizing as they did the strategic nature of both education and the communications field in waging their battle for the minds of mankind, the humanists gradually moved in, until they virtually controlled both. Almost every major magazine, newspaper, TV network, secular book publisher, and movie producer is a committed humanist, surrounding himself with editors and newscasters who share his philosophy and seldom permit anything to be presented that contradicts humanism, unless forced to by community pressure (LaHaye, 25-26).

Raymond Bailey has not overstated the case when he said, "The mass media are the most important single force shaping modern culture . . . no intelligent person can ignore it" (Bailey, 4).

Our lesson will focus on what has undeniably been a tremendous influence in shaping the worldview that prevails today: Hollywood with its various media. But we wish to do more than look at the problem; we want to show how Christianity can survive the threat of Hollywood. We want to see how we can become "more than conquerors through Him who loved us" (Rom. 8:38).

By the word *Hollywood* we are talking about a world-view that emanates from the media. We are referencing underlying philosophies and attitudes that tremendously impact culture. Further, we are not saying that Hollywood is the only influence that shapes the world in which we live, but is certainly is a powerful one. Michael Medved observed in his *Hollywood vs. America,*

> . . . it's important to remember that the term "Hollywood" most often describes an industry, not a place. Of the ten major movie production companies, only one of them, Paramount, is actually located within the geographic boundaries of the sadly seedy district of Los Angeles that is officially designated "Hollywood." The rest of them are scattered throughout Southern California, while maintaining important "branch offices" in New York.

> Their business is by no means limited to making motion pictures: all of the "majors" are connected to massive entertainment conglomerations that own everything from television networks to theme parks, from book publishers to gigantic record companies. Partially as a result of this concentration of show business resources, the dividing lines that once separated the various entertainment endeavors have never been so easily blurred. Distinguished movie directors regularly devote their talents to creating "music videos"; these productions in turn are featured on a round-the-clock television network devoted to promoting new hit records. In past years, major motion picture stars tried to avoid appearing on television, except for occasional high-profile specials; today, even the most critically acclaimed figures in the movie business will attempt serious and ambitious projects for TV. While some distinctions in emphasis and style still apply to the different branches of the business, it is now more appropriate than ever before to discuss "Hollywood" as one all-encompassing industry, united by common interests and common attitudes (Medved, 15).

How pervasive is Hollywood's influence? By 1953, only half of American homes owned a television set. By 1991, 98% of American homes were equipped with TV, in many cases with several sets. Even when you protect your children from inappropriate material, they will eventually be with other children who have received full exposure.

Hollywood's influence is not limited to America. Our movies are shown internationally. Travel overseas and you will see American TV programming dubbed in the local language.

I approach our topic, not troubled about any one single movie, one television program, or one popular song. "It is, rather, the hundreds of thousands of regularly repeated messages, the sheer weight of this material as it piles up over months and years of daily consumption, that should give us pause" (Medved, xxiv). It is the cumulative impact of this material which has played a major role in shaping societal values and perceptions. Anyone who would question this obvious and inevitable media effect is dismissed as a "right-wing extremist," a "fundamentalist," or a "religious fanatic."

In the landmark work, *Watching America*, by Lichter, Lichter, and Rothman, they ask the question, "Why does all this matter?" and then go on to answer,

> Because it [television] is on our minds and in our lives so continuously. During the past four decades, television has transcended its role as mere entertainment to become a potent force shaping everyday life. The average American now watches more than four hours of TV each day and the average household keeps a set on more than seven hours a day. The full force of television's impact is rarely felt in a single program or even a single season. It is the long-term result of exposure to an artificial reality so pervasive it has become a major part of the social environment (3).

This viewing of hours of television day after day is considered normal behavior. If beginning at age five you watch TV only three hours per day, by the time you retire (age 65) you will have clocked 63,000 hours—that's 7.19 years! A Christian seeks to maximize his time, to redeem the time (Eph. 5:17; cf. John 9:4).

Measuring the Impact of Hollywood

Medved quotes Dr. Jennings Bryant of the University of Alabama as declaring that "some of the most durable and important effects of watching television come in the form of subtle, incremental, cumulative changes in the way we view the world" (Medved, 245). It is Hollywood's influence that has helped shape that worldview that we want to address in this lecture. In short, Hollywood's worldview is one of materialism, existentialism, individualism, hedonism, and secularism. It is a mindset that views sin as normal and righteousness to be strange.

Satan, Our Adversary. One should remember that we wrestle not against flesh and blood (Eph. 6:10-13). Our real adversary is Satan. There is a very real ongoing battle for our hearts, minds, and souls.

To that end, Satan has exploited Hollywood and the media for his destructive purposes. Gallagher quotes Frank Mankiewixz and Joel Swedlow, authors of *Remote Control*:

> Satan uses the world's system obviously and boldly. He works through our schools, universities, and governments, but most overtly through the media. And the most powerful tool of the media is television. It should be obvious to us today that Satan is using television in a mighty way. We are surrounded by strategic warfare that is calculated to immobilize Christians. . . (Gallagher, 184).

Increase of Violence. Concern over television crime and violence is not new. In 1961, Senator John Pastore of Rhode Island headed a committee to address television violence. In 1968, five days after the assassination of President Kennedy, President Johnson established the National Commission on the Causes and Prevention of Violence. He asked the committee to address the question, "Are the seeds of violence nurtured through the public's airwaves, the screens of neighborhood theatres, the news media, and other forms of communication from our leaders that reach the family and reach the young?" In its concluding report the commission says, "It is reasonable to conclude that a constant diet of violent behavior on television has an adverse effect on human character and attitudes. Violence on television encourages violent forms of behavior, and fosters moral and social values about violence that are unacceptable in a civilized society" (*http://www.firstamendmentcenter.org/about.aspx?id=19525*).

It would surely be an understatement to say that Hollywood's featuring of violence has only grown worse since the concerns of five decades ago! As Robert G. DeMoss, Jr. said, ". . . children around the country are waking up to a culture that teaches them to equate violence with a good time." He quotes a high school senior who said, "When I watch someone getting beat up, it just makes me feel good inside" (DeMoss, 10). There are no indications that he was atypical in this.

Hypocritical Denial of Accountability. When someone acts out behavior portrayed and glorified by Hollywood (brutal violence, sexual crime, murder, or attempted assassination, etc.), the media insists that they, by their programming, have no power whatsoever to influence the public.

They have absolutely no responsibility in shaping attitudes, perceptions, or actions. These are the same network executives who demand lavish payment for brief moments of advertising! "In short, the industry's position is both flagrantly dishonest and lavishly illogical" (Medved, 252). (Consider the money spent for advertising during Super Bowl 2011—a 30 second Super Bowl ad cost about $3 million! All ad spots had sold out months in advance.) Such is the hypocrisy of Hollywood.

Consider the ability of an advertiser to position its product in your mind. "You deserve a break today at _____." "When E. F. Hutton speaks, people _____." "M-m m-m good, m-m m-m good, That's what _____ soup is, m-m m-m good." Consider the fact that the average American consumes more than 32,000 commercials per year. "By and large, advertising is a fantasy world that plays upon our needs, fears, wants and desires, promising miracle cures for what ails us" (DeMoss, 24).

Hollywood's advertising uses the bandwagon approach—everyone's doing it, and so should you. They make skillful use of image projection, such as the former tobacco commercials which feature the rugged cowboy Marlboro man on his horse with beautiful western scenery. Many are swayed by testimonials, in which famous persons place their stamp of approval on various products.

Desensitization. One result of Hollywood's overwhelming accumulation of violent imagery is that of desensitization. It is increasingly difficult to frighten or disgust an audience. In the movies, there is a *pattern* of featuring the bizarre, the hideous, and the perverse. There is an obvious delight in challenging conventional beliefs and norms.

God-given barriers are removed as one has frequent and repeated exposure to programming featuring sexual intimacy; altered moral judgment results. For example, Medved references a report by Dr. Bradley S. Greenberg of Michigan State University which concluded that "adolescents take in some three thousand to four thousand references to sexual activity in movies and television each year." Dr. Greenberg went on to report that, if a teenager views one hour per day of MTV, he thereby adds 1,500 more video-sex experiences per year (Medved, 245-246). Recent statistics indicate that MTV enters 387 million homes worldwide!

The end result of such *entertainment* is that God-given inhibitions to inappropriate sexual expression are dismantled. Many have bought the lie that being a virgin until married is not possible, and further, not even desirable.

In the Los Angeles riots of 1992, according to press accounts, many looters got the idea to participate in the looting by watching other looters on TV, as the images communicated the idea of looting as common behavior, as justified behavior, with a miniscule likelihood of police interference. Television can make outrageous behavior look routine.

Loss of Appetite. My friend Raymond Harville (deceased) used to make the observation that not only is pornography wrong in itself, but it is like junk food—it destroys your appetite for good, nourishing food. That appropriately sums up what has happened. The problem with the Hollywood agenda is not only that so much is wrong with the programming itself—indeed a steady diet takes away the hunger and thirst for righteousness.

Sensory Organ Malfunction. This results in eyes that cannot see, ears that do not hear, and hearts that do not understand, like that of those to whom Isaiah was sent (Isa. 6:8-10). We are made by God to be "imaging beings." What we revere we resemble, as did ancient Israel, who became like the gods which they created (Ps. 135:15-18; cf. 2 Kings 17:15). (G. K. Beale thoroughly develops these concepts in his excellent work, *We Become What We Worship.*)

Unrealistic view of life. Regarding commercials, Bailey quotes Leroy E. Kennel, author of *Ecology of the Airwaves:*

> What do TV commercials teach us about life? What do they do to us as individuals? At times, commercials are openly deceptive. They make claims which cannot be substantiated. They divert attention from the nature of a product by developing a clever jingle to go with it or by showing a deceptively conceived picture to accompany it. . . .
>
> Television advertisements also create a climate of excessive materialism. They nurture a preoccupation with things. Their underlying message is that the more things one possesses, the better one will enjoy life (Bailey, 4).

The world of Hollywood is a *pretend* world. Knowing this can even help in your Old Testament word studies. For example, Proverbs 13:7 states, "One pretends to be rich, yet has nothing; another pretends to be poor, yet has great wealth" (ESV, cf. NET). The *NET* textual note on the phrase *pretends to be rich* states, "The Hithpael of *'āshar* ('to be rich') means 'to pretend to be rich' (BDB 799); this is the so-called 'Hollywood Hithpael' function which involves 'acting' or pretending to be something one is not" (NET Bible notes).

Many take very seriously that pretend world. Look at all the Hollywood gossip and scandal featured in the magazines at the checkout at your grocery stores and supermarkets. Apparently those magazines and newspapers sell! I remember many years ago doing some visitation while conducting a gospel meeting in north Alabama. The local preacher and I called on one of their older members. That sister said, "I don't want to get close to anyone, and I don't want anyone to get close to me." On her coffee table in her living room was a copy of *Soap Opera Digest.*

The Values of the Programmers. It is appropriate to ask, "What values are spread by today's movies, television, and music?" Consider the men behind the tube, the "creative leaders" in the media. Surveys have shown that 43% favor a complete restructuring of America's basic institutions. Only 8% believe women would be better off staying at home and rearing families rather than having outside careers. 97% believe a woman has the right to decide for herself whether to have an abortion. 80% do not regard homosexual relations as wrong. 86% support the rights of homosexuals to teach in public schools. A majority (51%) does not regard adultery as wrong (Lichter, 15-16). Bear in mind that these statistics were reported in 1991; the situation has not improved! But consider how these are the obvious values reflected by media in their various forms.

Clearly there is a Hollywood agenda. Director Mick Garris (*Critters 2: The Main Course,* and *Psycho IV: The Beginning*) also directed *Sleepwalkers* which features an incestuous sex theme along with vampirism and cannibalism. In *Sleepwalker's* press kit, Garris proudly stated, "Our theme on this project was to take Norman Rockwell and send him straight to hell" (quoted in Medved, 167).

Attitudes Toward Sexual Activity. The Lichter work quotes a National Institute of Mental Health report, "entertainment television has become an important sex educator" (26) and Lichter then goes on to observe, "Meanwhile, in challenging onetime taboos from extramarital sex to homosexuality, television entertainment increasingly transmits Hollywood's perspectives rather than middle America's" (*ibid.*).

Hollywood promotes the joys of fornication. The message is that we can sleep around with no harmful results. Extramarital sex is taken for granted as a normal form of recreation without moral or emotional consequences. Michael Robinson summarizes the situation as "lots of sex, very little remorse" (Lichter, 33). With increased competition, programmers find themselves in a "race to be racy" (DeMoss, 50).

Consider Hollywood's treatment of homosexuality. The Alliance for Gay Artists began giving out awards for "sensitive and honest depictions of gays and lesbians." One screenwriter quoted in the Lichter work stated, "You can handle homosexuality—as long as you handle it in a lovely, tolerant fashion that will not upset the gay liberation lobby" (Lichter, 37). Robinson concluded that primetime's favorite "innocent victim . . . was clearly the misunderstood, harassed homosexual" (*ibid.*)

The Family Under Attack. There is a brazen assault on the traditional (biblical) family, as the media promotes extramarital sexual activity, homosexuality, and denunciation of parental authority, especially that of the father. "Father Knows Best" is hopelessly antiquated; the prevailing media thinking is that *kids know best*. Medved suggests that in today's climate, *Father Knows Nothing* "would stand a far better chance" (Medved, 148). Kids talking back is *cute*—that's the message of such programming as *The Simpsons, Beavis and B. . .*, etc.

Medved makes this common sense observation regarding the current collapse of the family:

> The "general goofolas" who shape much of the popular culture are by no means single-handedly responsible for this sad situation, but they do make a significant contribution to the ongoing confusion. Their antifamily messages—promoting promiscuity, maligning marriage, encouraging illegitimacy, and undermining parental authority—may not make it impossible to maintain a solid marriage or to raise decent kids, but they certainly make it harder than it has to be (157).

Wiersbie observes in his comments on 1 Peter 3:1, "When Christian couples try to imitate the world and get their standards from Hollywood instead of from heaven, there will be trouble in the home. But if both partners will imitate Jesus Christ in His submission and obedience, and His desire to serve others, then there will be triumph and joy in the home."

Attack on Religion. There is a pattern of attacking religion, especially Christianity (e.g., *The Last Temptation*, which lost an estimated $10 million).

If religion is not being attacked, it is obviously omitted. Medved illustrates this with three 1991 big-budget Hollywood films—*Dying Young* (with Julia

Roberts), *The Doctor* (with William Hurt), and *Regarding Henry* (starring Harrison Ford). Each of these films had the theme of patients facing dreadful illnesses and lengthy hospitalizations, with life and death hanging in the balance. "At no point in these proceedings, however, did the main characters, or any of their friends or family members, turn for even one moment to the power of prayer, or ask to see a member of the clergy, on in any way invoke the name of God" (Medved, 73). In contrast, *Newsweek* reported that 78 % of the country prays "*at least* once a week under ordinary circumstances," and as is known from experience, "you will find precious few atheists on operating tables" (*ibid.*).

My family physician observed that doctors actually see very little death. When one dies (in the context of hospitalization, etc.), there are generally family members present, and often a preacher.

Passion for Profanity. Hollywood has an infatuation with foul language. This is even true for PG movies, which some have suggested should stand for *profanity guaranteed.*

Cheapening of Human Life. We are living in what some refer to as a *Culture of Death.* Many Americans have been convinced "that some lives are less worth living than others, that in fact some lives are not worth living it all. The result is that abortion, infanticide, euthanasia, and assisted suicide are exceedingly common. In some cases they are protected by law, but they are all forms of murder—violations of the sixth commandment" (Ryken, 139).

Other Effects. Any listing of the impact of Hollywood's messages on our society and our children must be incomplete. The tendency to a short attention span is a by-product of rapidly changing scenes (every few seconds or sometimes within a second). We have not discussed the role of music, or the influence of groups such as 2 Live Crew with albums such as *As Nasty as They Wanna Be.*

Winning the Victory
Not Conformed But Transformed. In the song "Am I a Soldier of the Cross?" the question, "Is this vile world a friend to grace, to help me on to God?" is a rhetorical question. The world of our day is not a friend to grace, and it never has been. Accordingly we are reminded,

> I beseech you therefore, brethren, by the mercies of God, that you present your bodies a living sacrifice, holy, acceptable to God, which is your reasonable service. And do not be conformed to this world, but be trans-

formed by the renewing of your mind, that you may prove what is that good and acceptable and perfect will of God (Rom. 12:1-2).

Control TV Programming. One answer is to throw out the television set. At the end of 1990, columnist Cal Thomas announced his resolution to quit watching the networks altogether. "They have not only abandoned my values, they now have sunk to the sewer level, dispensing the foulest of smells that resemble the garbage I take to the curb twice a week" (Thomas, quoted in Medved, 5).

What is certain is that the TV must be controlled. Gallagher warns that

> . . . the home must be carefully guarded. Television, as we have already discussed, is a way the enemy can bring a lustful atmosphere right into your living room. The best approach is to get rid of it. At the very least, the man should limit how often he views television and be extremely selective in which shows he views. Other items within the home which must be seen as potential traps are magazines, catalogues, and newspapers. One does not necessarily have to cut them out completely, but at least be careful as to what is in the house. The internet is also a possible trap of the enemy. Pornography sites on the web are by far the largest money-makers through internet commerce. It is important to ruthlessly root out anything in the home which the devil might use in a time of weakness. The person who is going to get the victory over lust must do everything within his power to minimize the enemy's ability to affect him spiritually. Sacrificial decisions such as these are what Jesus was referring to when He spoke about tearing out eyeballs and cutting off one's hands (Gallagher, 261-262).

Disciples Indeed. It is not enough to cast out the demon, only to leave the "house" empty (Matt. 12:43-45). This balance is seen in Romans 13:14. The man of sin must be put to death, but we must put on the Lord Jesus Christ. We must make *disciples* who are constantly becoming more like Jesus (Luke 6:40; Rom. 8:29; Eph. 4:22-24).

Teach Biblical Love. We will never understand true love from Hollywood. We must teach the qualities of love set forth in 1 Corinthians 13:4-8. There is a crying need for older sisters to teach the young women the character traits of Titus 2:3-5. There is the need for older men to provide wisdom and leadership. In our teaching, we need not only to condemn what is wrong but also to stress what is honorable and pleasing to God (Heb. 13:4; Prov. 5:15-23; 1 Cor. 7:3-5).

Get Back to the Divine Plan regarding Primary Sources of Infor-

mation and Influence. That, of course, begins with the home (Deut. 6:4-6; Eph. 6:1-4). It just won't do for us to habitually say to our children, "Just leave me alone and go watch TV for a while." In the world, the entertainment culture has become the chief babysitter by default. That has to stop if we are serious about victory in this spiritual warfare. We need to stop just letting the TV play continuously, "just to have a noise in the house."

The Medved's cite a study founded by the National Institute of Child Health and Human Development which found "more than half of infants under age one receive care by someone other than their mothers, and most mothers return to work in their child's first three to five months" (Medved and Medved, 189-190).

How does this square with texts such as 1 Timothy 2:15, and Titus 2:3-5? If we are to have more Timothy's, we must have more Lois's and Eunices's. If we want to have *Good Homes in a Wicked World* (to borrow from brother Irven Lee) we must invest ourselves in giving both quality and quantity time.

The theme of the book of Leviticus is that of holiness to the Lord. God's people do not follow the practices of Egypt or Canaan; they keep His judgments (Lev. 18:3-4; 19:2). This must be taught from infancy (2 Tim. 2:15). As a result we are empowering our children to distinguish between the unclean and the clean (cf. Ezek. 22:26) and accordingly to make the right choices.

Role of the Church. We must be disciples who demand sound doctrine, with shepherds feeding the flocks entrusted to them. We must keep before us the picture of Ephesians 4:11-16, where the ongoing work is equipping the saints, growing up in all things into Him who is the head—Christ. We need each other. Timothy was to flee youthful lusts, and pursue righteousness, with those who call on the Lord out of a pure heart (2 Tim. 2:22). Make friends of God's children!

The Fear of the Lord Is to Hate Evil. An intense hatred of what is evil is essentially linked with the fear of the Lord (Prov. 8:13). "Therefore all Your precepts concerning all things I consider to be right; I hate every false way" (Ps. 119:128, cf. v. 104). We are to "abhor what is evil. Cling to what is good" (Rom. 12:9). Brother Homer Hailey said frequently, "With the same intensity with which you love the good, you hate the evil." If one does not hate that which is evil, the underlying problem is that he does not truly love what is good. May our prayer be, "Lord teach me to love what you love, and hate what you hate."

Many of our denominational friends are concerned about the growing indifference toward sin. Gallagher stated,

> Unfortunately, a sinister and flippant attitude has crept into the Church. Our perspective of the horrible nature of sin has become so distorted by humanism. . . .By and large the Church is quite comfortable with the very thing that this holy Being hates: SIN (Gallagher, 288).

We must make a covenant with our eyes. Job did this (Job 31:1). David learned by experience the importance of resolving to "set nothing wicked before my eyes" (Ps. 101:3). Jesus taught this principle in the Sermon on the Mount (Matt. 5:28).

The Need for Sensible thinking. There must be the ability to discern between good and evil. Christians don't laugh or enjoy it when their values are attacked, mocked, or undermined by popular culture. A Christians desires to honor and please the Lord with the choices he makes. "A critical thinker understands that Hollywood's attack upon his mind is a slow, insidious process—a clear sense of right and wrong keeps him from wallowing in a limbo of gray confusion" (DeMoss, 89).

We should bear in mind that the basic plot of most programming celebrates one or more of the sinful behaviors listed in Galatians 5:19-21, and remember "that those who practice such things will not inherit the kingdom of God." "It is inconsistent for a critical thinker to laugh at and enjoy the very thing which prompts God's anger. The more we become Christ-like, the more we will perceive these expressions as direct attacks upon our values and priorities" (DeMoss, 93).

Our Source of Strength. Remember that without Jesus we can do nothing (John 15:5; Phil. 4:13; Eph. 6:10). Our strength is in the One who made heaven and earth (Ps. 121). "If My people who are called by My name will humble themselves, and pray and seek My face, and turn from their wicked ways, then I will hear from heaven, and will forgive their sin and heal their land" (2 Chron. 7:14).

We've been chosen for a high calling, a heavenly calling, a holy calling to be salt and light to a lost and dying world. "Trust in the Lord with all your heart, And lean not on your own understanding; In all your ways acknowledge Him, And He shall direct your paths" (Prov. 3:5-6). "Hear,

O Israel: The Lord our God, the Lord is one! You shall love the Lord your God with all your heart, with all your soul, and with all your strength. And these words which I command you today shall be in your heart. You shall teach them diligently to your children, and shall talk of them when you sit in your house, when you walk by the way, when you lie down, and when you rise up. You shall bind them as a sign on your hand, and they shall be as frontlets between your eyes. You shall write them on the doorposts of your house and on your gates" (Deut. 6:4-9).

If we do these things, with God as our helper, we will not only survive, but be "more than conquerors through Him who loved us" (Rom. 8:37).

Bibliography

Bailey, Raymond. "The Mass Media and the Church," *Review and Expositor,* Volume 81 (1984): 1, p. 4.

Beale, G. K. *We Become What We Worship.* Downers Grove: InterVarsity Press, 2008.

DeMoss, Robert G., Jr. *Learn to Discern.* Grand Rapids: Zondervan, 1992.

Duguid, I. M. and R. K. Hughes (2006). *Numbers: God's Presence in the Wilderness.* Preaching the Word (58–59). Wheaton, IL: Crossway Books.

Gallagher, S. (2000). *At the Altar of Sexual Idolatry.* Dry Ridge, KY: Pure Life Ministries.

Lichter, Linda, Robert Lichter, and Stanley Rothaman. *Watching America.* New York: Prentice Hall Press, 1991.

Medved, Michael. *Hollywood vs. America.* New York: HarperCollins Publishers Inc., 1993.

Medved, Michael and Diane Medved. *Saving Childhood.* New York: HarperCollins Publishers Inc., 1998.

The NET Bible First Edition Notes. Biblical Studies Press, 2005.

Ryken, P. G. *Written in Stone: The Ten Commandments and Today's Moral Crisis.* Wheaton: Crossway Books, 2003.

Wiersbe, W. W. *The Bible Exposition Commentary* (Electronic Edition). Wheaton: Victor Books, 1996.

Christianity Can Survive . . .

The Threat of Sports Mania

Alton E. Bailey

"Mania" is defined by Joseph P. Pickett (*American Heritage Dictionary* Fourth Edition, Boston and New York, Houghton Mifflin Company, 2006, p. 1062) as "an excessive, intense, enthusiastic, interest or desire in something. It is abnormal behavior." The synonyms for "mania" are "insanity" and "madness." We get the word "maniac" from the root word "mania"!

Introduction

A part of my undergraduate degree from Auburn University is in Recreation. Sports and recreation is a multi-billion dollar business annually in our great nation. Sports facilities cost millions of dollars to build and to operate. Medical doctors, lawyers, certified public accountants, and other professional people are employed by the sports network to take care of in-

Alton E. Bailey was born May 5, 1947 to Pierce and Agnes Bailey in Cullman County, Alabama. He grew up on a farm. He played high school sports. He and his wife, Diana have two grown children: Marty, their son, and their daughter Melissa, who is married to Colby Junkin who preaches at Piney Chapel Church of Christ near Decatur, Alabama. Melissa and Colby have one son (Ben), who is Alton and Diana's only grandchild. Alton served in the U.S. Navy during the Viet Nam War, serving two tours of duty in Viet Nam. After serving honorably in the Navy, Alton was released in 1970. He attended college and graduated from Auburn University in 1974 with his BS degree in Health, Physical Education and Recreation. He completed his Masters Degree in1978 from Jacksonville State University in Traffic Education. He attained a Master Degree certification in School Administration in 1993 from Alabama A&M University. Alton coached high school and junior high football and baseball for seventeen years. He retired from public education as an assistant high school principal. Also he served as the elementary principal. Alton has been a full time preacher since 1996. He and his wife, Diana, are involved in foreign work. They travel to Belize, South Africa, and England. Bobby Graham introduced Alton to the Belize work. George Harris introduced him to the work in South Africa. Alton is an elder and the preacher at Sugar Creek Church of Christ in Hayden, Alabama.

juries, lawsuits, taxes, and other needs created by the sports and recreation activity.

How do you behave at a ball game? Do your children see you act unbecomingly at a sports event? Parents are their children's reputation until their children have had time to develop their own reputation. As a parent, do you set the example that you would want your child to follow at a ballgame? If you see the parents of your child's friend acting as a fanatic at a ballgame, does other discomfort come to your mind concerning them? Would you allow your child to stay the night at the home of that parent? A person's *reputation* is what other people think he is. His *character* is what he really is. For example, Philip wanted Jesus to show the Father to the Apostles (John 14:8-9). Jesus said to Philip in John 14:9, "Have I been with you so long, and yet you have not known Me, Philip? He who has seen Me has seen the Father, so how can you say, 'Show us the Father?'" Fathers, can your children say that about you? What kind of character do you have? Would you want someone to say to your child that he is just like his father? Would you want someone to say to your child that they could see his father in him? Parents are to set examples for their children at sports events as well as sother occasions (Prov. 22:6). Yelling and screaming at the officials and the coaches are not becoming of a parent, but especially of a Christian parent. Would you want someone to say about your child that he is a "chip off the ole block" concerning your example at a sports event?

We are living in the "vapor" part of our existence (James 4:13-15). James says that our life upon this earth is like a vapor. It will appear for a little while and then vanish away. Over ninety-nine per cent of our existence will be on the other side of our earthly existence. It will be in eternity. How we conduct ourselves on this side of eternity will determine where we will spend our existence in eternity. We have two options of where we will spend eternity, Heaven or Hell. If we miss Heaven, our life upon this earth is a total failure. Sports mania may lead someone to be eternally lost.

The church will survive sports mania. But, will you abstain from sports mania? Does a ball game cause you to become angry when your favorite team loses (Eph. 4:26)? Do you take that anger to bed with you? Would you miss worship to attend a sporting event? Would you allow your child to miss worship to participate in a sporting event? Do our actions teach our children where our priorities are?

Many American athletes and sports fans fit the *American Heritage*

Dictionary's definition of "mania." As a coach, I have stood between some fans and the referees after a game to keep an altercation from happening.

In high school sports, the referees must come to the game in one automobile for protection. They must park their car inside the football field's gate. As a coach, once we were forced to back the school bus to the door of our locker room and load the players through the emergency exit for protection from some irate fans after our close victory. Some professional football coaches wear bullet proof vests during their games. Why? They want to be protected from fans who are overcome by sports mania. Many players must hire security guards to protect themselves and their families. Many players verbally attack the game officials if they lose. Many coaches use abrasive language towards the officials if a penalty goes against their team.

Sports mania is alive in our great nation. The love for sports is much more prevalent than the love for God in America! We are a nation for sports. Wouldn't it be wonderful to have as much excitement in teaching and living the life of a Christian as exists in participating and watching sporting events in our nation?

Sports Can Be a Good Teacher in Life

In competitive sports, one must give his best. The same is true as a Christian. Paul said in Colossians 3:23, "And whatever you do, do it heartily, as to the Lord and not to men." Life is a marathon; it is not a sprint. We will not go through life without committing a sin from time to time, but we can win over sin through Jesus (1 John 1:8-10). In sports, we have a rule book. In Christ, we also have a rule book — God's word, the Bible. We must play by the rules to be crowned a champion. Recently, Reggie Bush lost his Heisman Trophy because he did not follow the rules. While at USC, he received gifts and benefits that were in violation of the NCAA rules. Paul said in 2 Timothy 2:5, "And also if anyone competes in athletics, he is not crowned unless he competes according to the rules." With God, we must play by His rules, if we are to be crowned with everlasting life. Paul said in 2 Timothy 4:7-8, "I have fought the good fight, I have finished the race. I have kept the faith. Finally, there is laid up for me the crown of righteousness, which the Lord, the righteous Judge, will give to me on that Day, and not to me only but also to all who have loved His appearing."

In competitive sports, one must be focused on the task at hand. He cannot have his mind concentrating upon other things. In its strategy, football is similar to warfare. We must plan our strategy and work our plan. In sports, coaches call this their game plan. Paul said in 2 Timothy 2:4, "No one en-gaged in warfare entangles himself with the affairs of this life, that he may please him who enlisted him as a soldier." When I was in Viet Nam, the Navy did not want us to focus on the things back home. If we did, someone may get killed. In competitive sports, one must focus upon his assignment. God has given us an assignment to serve Him in this life (Matt. 6:33). We must comply with His rules. We must be focused upon what we are doing. If we don't, Satan will win. Christians are in competition with Satan for our souls.

Team sports will teach us to work together. As a player, you may make your block in football, but if your teammate misses his block, the opposing team may make the tackle. If this happens, the play fails. In football, every-one cannot be the quarterback. But, without the lineman, the quarterback would fail. In a congregation, everyone cannot be an elder or the preacher. But, without the congregation, there would be no need to have elders or a preacher. Paul teaches, in 1 Corinthians 12:12-31, that everyone is important and everyone must work together within a congregation.

Sports Mania Is on the Increase in America

In 1 Timothy 6:10, Paul said, "For the love of money is a root of all kinds of evil." Large sums of money are involved in American sports. The more money that is involved in sports, often times, the more obnoxious and unruly the coaches, players, and fans become. Division one college and professional football coaches are paid multi-million dollar contracts per year. Many professional athletes are paid millions of dollars per year to perform. One hundred thousand seat stadiums are built to provide for the fans to watch the games. Television contracts pay the universities millions of dollars to show the game on TV. The thirty-second TV commercial at the Super Bowl football game will cost over one million dollars. Millions of dollars are gambled per game in sports. With the money that is involved in sports, it is no surprise that great pressure is placed upon the coaches and players to win. At a major university in my home state, the head football coach is paid over $4 million per year in wages. The President of the same university is paid $500,000 per year in wages. Can we see the priority of sports over academics?

I coached high school and junior high football for seventeen years in Alabama. Great pressure is placed upon the coaches and players to win. Football was the talk of the community. A high school coach could be a successful coach and a poor classroom teacher and keep his job in the school system. But, an excellent classroom teacher and a poor coach would be terminated. Sports mania shows the priority in our communities. Sports fans tend to glorify the coach over other faculty members. Have you ever seen players lift their coach upon their shoulders and take the coach onto the field after a major victory? Why do they do this? They are glorifying their coach. They are showing others that their coach was instrumental in their victory. They are showing others that their coach has priority in their lives. Wouldn't it be wonderful if mankind would lift God upon their shoulders signifying that God is instrumental in man's victory over sin? By doing this, mankind would be glorifying God! By doing this, mankind would show others that God has priority in their lives. By doing this, mankind would show the world that God is man's champion!

Sports Can Cause Mood Changes

Sometimes we are happy. Sometimes we are sad. Sometimes mood depends upon the progress during a game and the outcome of the game. If a person's team gets beat, sometimes a person becomes angry. After watching on TV their team lose, I have known of sports fans destroying their TV in anger. I have known of family members to get into a fight with each other when their favorite teams play each other. These are signs of sports mania. Paul said in Colossians 3:8, "But now you yourselves are to put off all these; anger, wrath, malice. . . ." Do you want to hurt someone if he is a fan of your opposing team? As a coach, some of my closest friends were coaches whom I coached against.

There is a difference between *happiness* and *joy*. *Happiness* is based upon what is happening at the present time. For example, as a coach, when we would win a game, we were happy. When we would lose, we were sad. *Joy* is based upon something deeper, more mature, something longer lasting. For example, I coached football for several years. We won some games; we lost some games. Overall, it was an enjoyable career. It reminds me of Jesus. In Hebrews 12:2, the writer records in the New King James Version, "Looking unto Jesus, the author and finisher of our faith, who for the joy that was set before Him endured the cross, despising the shame, and has sat down at the right hand of the throne of God." How could it be joy to endure the cross? Because Jesus knew what it would accomplish by Him going to the cross. He knew man's salvation could be provided by God by His great sacrifice. Jesus was not happy while He hung upon the cross but His sacrifice brought Him joy. Also, it pleased the Father. In Isaiah 53:10, the prophet said, "But the Lord was pleased to crush Him, putting Him to grief." So, we know it grieved Jesus to die upon the cross but it brought Him joy.

How Is Addiction to Sports Affecting the Local Congregation?

Sports mania within a congregation will affect Christianity in different ways. The addiction to sports will affect the attendance in the local congregation. Where is your priority? Do you miss the assembly to watch a football game on television? Do you miss the assembly to watch your child play in a sport during a Gospel Meeting? Do you allow your child to miss the worship assembly to play or watch a ballgame? Do you spend more time in front of your television watching sports than you do Bible reading God's word? Where is most of your furniture facing in your living room? Is it facing the TV? It is not a sin to have a television. But, Satan can use the television to help us sin. When we miss the worship assembly to watch a ballgame on the television, we sin. It is recorded in Hebrews 10:24-25, "And let us consider one another in order to stir up love and good works, not forsaking the assembling of ourselves together, as is the manner of some, but exhorting one another, and so much the more as your see the Day approaching." How can we exhort someone if we are not at the assembly? How can we be exhorted if we are not in the assembly? How can we consider someone of our congregation if we are not in the assembly? Are we putting God's Kingdom first in our lives (Matt. 6:33)?

Addiction to sports affects one's study of God's word. It takes time for personal study of God's word. It is hard work. Paul told Timothy in 2 Timothy 2:15, "Be diligent to present yourself approved to God, a worker who does not need to be ashamed, rightly dividing the word of truth." It takes time to study God's word with someone else. Paul told Timothy in 2 Timothy 2:2, "And the things that you have heard from me among many witnesses, commit these to faithful men who will be able to teach others also." It takes time to watch sports on television. Which is more enjoyable to you—watching a sporting event or teaching someone the Gospel of Jesus? Which is more exciting to you—seeing someone become a Christian or seeing your favorite team win their sporting event? Do you spend as much time studying God's word each week as you do studying the sports page in your local newspaper? It is more exciting and enjoyable to watch someone obey the Gospel of Jesus than to watch from the sideline, as a coach, your team win a game. When someone obeys the Gospel, Satan just got beat. Our victory over Satan is much more important than our favorite team's victory over their opponent. At the Judgment, will it be important which team won the Super Bowl? Do you know the statistics of your favorite team, but you can't take a sheet of paper and write down what someone must do to become a Christian? What example are you leaving your children (Prov.

22:6)? When they are growing up, they know us better than anyone else, except one's wife. By your actions, are you teaching your children that sports is more important than studying God's word and doing His work?

Addiction to sports affects the concentration of one's thoughts at the worship assembly. During the worship, is your body tired from staying up late the night before watching a sports event instead of getting your needed rest to worship the God of Heaven the next morning? During the worship, are you thinking about Saturday's game and its result? During the worship, are you thinking about your friends coming to your house to watch Sunday afternoon professional football? Jesus said in Matthew 26:41, "The spirit indeed is willing, but the flesh is weak." God wants our minds to be focused upon Him at the worship assembly. When you partake of the Lord's Supper, where is your mind? Is it upon things of this world or upon our Savior who died for the world?

Addiction to sports affects us in not attending a Gospel Meeting, not visiting the sick, not helping the needy, and not doing other works that we should be doing for the Lord. What treasures are you laying up, earthly or eternal? Jesus said in Matthew 6:19-20, "Do not lay up for yourselves treasures on earth, where moth and rust destroy and where thieves break in and steal; but lay up for yourselves treasures in heaven, where neither moth nor rust destroys and where thieves do not break in and steal." God created this world for us to use (Gen. 1:26). He didn't create the world for us to fall in love with it (1 John 2:15-17). What will it matter a thousand years from now which team won the Super Bowl? What will matter a thousand years from now is if you and I died in relationship with God. We must realize that our works will follow us. John said in Revelations 14:13, "their works follow them."

Addiction to sports may affect some brethren's contribution for the Lord's work. When we earn a certain amount of money each week, we must purpose in our hearts what we will give to the Lord on the first day of the week (2 Cor. 9:7; 1 Cor. 16:1-2). Do you spend the Lord's portion of your wages upon a sporting event? Does a sporting event reduce the amount that you will give to the Lord? If you answer yes to either of these two questions, you have your priorities mixed up!

In some liberal congregations, addictions to sports mania by the members have affected the elders' decision in implementing sporting events to please the congregation. It reminds me of the people in the days of Moses and Aaron, who sat down to eat and to drink, and rose up to play (Exod. 32:6). While Moses was in the mountain (Exod. 32), the people assembled around Aaron for him to make a molten calf to be their god. Today, some congregations have assembled around their elders for the elders to make a sporting event to be their god. Some congregations use sports to attract people to their congregation. The congregation will build a gymnasium to house the social and sporting events. Brethren, we must remember that the Gospel is the power of God to draw people to the assembly, not a sporting event (Rom. 1:16)!

Some Sports Celebrities Are Poor Role Models

When I coached, I told our athletes to show their character: don't be one! I told our players to be role models for other students. I told them that elementary students look to them as an example. Paul told the Corinthians in 1 Corinthians 11:1, "Imitate me, just as I also imitate Christ." Could someone use you as an example to follow? I told our athletes that, when they were on the football field, they not only represented themselves in their manner of conduct, but also they represented God, their family, their school, and their coaches. I told them that, when they were off the football field, they should not run with a skunk lest they smell like a skunk. Paul told the Corinthians in 1 Corinthians 15:33, "Evil company corrupts good habits." When you leave the church building, are you be the same Christian as you are inside the building? We can't mock God and get away with it (Gal. 6:7)! I told our players that the only ones who they could control are themselves. They could not control other players or the officials. They must discipline themselves on each play. Paul told the Corinthians in 1 Corinthians 9:27, "But I discipline my body and bring it into subjection. . . ." We must discipline ourselves in living the life of a Christian. We must have a check up from the neck up concerning our lives (2 Cor. 13:5).

Being a good role model in sports is developed. Being a good role model in Christianity is developed. Being a poor role model in sports is developed. Being a poor role model in Christianity is developed. Neither a good nor bad role model is inherited. Jesus said in Matthew 7:13-14, "Enter by the narrow gate; for wide is the gate and broad is the way that leads to destruction, and there are many who go in by it. Because narrow is the gate and difficult is the way which leads to life, and there are few who find it." Being a good role model takes more effort than being a poor role model. Much of the talent in sports is hereditary. A person's body frame or much of his speed is inherited from both of his parents. Becoming a Christian is learned (Rom. 10:17). It is not inherited from our parents. In sports, our work habits are learned. Also, in Christianity, our work habits are learned. Many of us remember Pete Rose. He was an outstanding professional baseball player. He was spoken of as "Mr. Hustle." But, he is most remembered as the player who cheated by gambling. As of now, he has not been added to the professional Baseball's Hall of Fame. Why did Pete Rose want to gamble? He knew that it was against the rules. The desire of being covetous overpowered him (1 Cor. 610). Most of us remember Barry Bonds. He was a great professional baseball player who took steroids. He knew that steroids were against the rules of professional baseball. Why did he take the steroids? Did he want to become stronger than other professional baseball players? Was cheating the answer? Tiger Woods is one of the most well known professional athletes of today. He was overcome with the sin of fornication. He lost his marriage. He lost much of his time with his children. There are some sins in the New Testament that God has told us to flee from: fornication and covetousness are two of them. These are two of the sins Tiger Woods and Pete Rose were involved in.

What is the primary purpose a farmer puts a pasture fence next to a busy highway? Is the primary reason for the fence to restrict his cattle or protect his cattle? Yes, the fence restricts them, but the primary reason for the fence is to protect them from the dangers of the automobile traffic on the highway. It is for their good. What is the primary reason that God restricts us through His word? The primary reason for God's word is to protect us against sin. It is for our good. Obeying the rules in sports and in God's word is for our good.

God's word determines whether a sports celebrity is a good role model or not. The world's standards are different from God's standards. For example, a sports celebrity may be a homosexual. People led by the world's standard would condone homosexuality. They would say that a person has his/her right to make his/her own sexual preference. Paul said in 2 Corinthians 4:4, "Whose minds the god of this age has blinded, who do not believe, lest the light of the gospel of the glory of Christ, who is the image of God, should shine on them." God hates the sin of homosexuality. The world believes that it doesn't matter what sexual orientation a person is as long as he/she is a good athlete.

What Can Christians Do to Overcome the Threat of Sports Mania in Its Competition with the Gospel?

Sports mania is not unique to the twenty-first century. During the first century, the Romans enjoyed sports. They built large coliseums. Thousands of people watched sporting events. Christians were sometimes the victims in these sporting events. Christianity was threatened. But the Gospel survived the first century. The Gospel will survive the twenty-first century. We need to remember that, as long as Satan is in the world (Job 1:7), there will be a threat towards the Gospel. Satan knows that the power of God for man's salvation is contained in the Gospel (Rom. 1:16). Satan knows that God's hand is not so short that He cannot save (Isa. 59:1), but Satan also knows that God has placed Himself within a box and God will not save man outside of man's obedience to the Gospel. Satan knows what Genesis 3:15 means. God said, "And I will put enmity between you and the woman, and between your seed and her seed; He shall bruise you on the head, and you shall bruise Him on the heel." Satan knows that, when God raised Jesus from the dead, it was the crushing blow to Satan's head as was prophesied in Genesis 3:15. As a coach, very seldom did we have someone quit the team alone. He wanted someone to quit with him. The same principle is true with Satan. He knows that he is going to Hell. He wants to take as many people with him as he can. He uses sports mania to help him overcome people. He knows that America is a nation with a voracious appetite for recreation. So Satan uses sports and its influence to cause many Christians to be weak in their service to God. How? When Christians spend more time involved in sports than they are involved in the work of the Lord, they show God their priorities. They are making sports their god. The God of Heaven is a jealous God (Exod. 20:5). He does not want anything to be put ahead of Him.

By being an example to those of the world, Christians can overcome the threat of sports mania. When I was a coach, I attended worship. Sports did not interfere with my worship. Action speaks louder than words. We can be a light unto the world. Jesus said in Mathew 5:16, "Let your light so shine before men, that they may see your good works and glorify your Father in heaven." When I was a coach, I never used curse words. I used proper language in front of our players and our coaches. By our example, we will show the world that God is more important than sports. When I was a coach, I always wore modest clothing. I did not want attention focused on me. As preachers, we should not seek attention for ourselves (2 Cor. 4:7). Sports may have its place in our lives. But, God should have first place in our lives. As parents, we need to show by our example that sports are not to have the ultimate place in our life. Do you use the officials as a scape goat? Do you fuss about the play the coach called? Our children see and hear us. They know us well.

Teaching the Gospel is a way to overcome the threat of sports mania. Sports have gone into the entire world: so should the Gospel. The Gospel is to be prevalent throughout the world. The Christians of the first century took the Gospel to the world. Jesus told the Apostles in Matthew 28:19-20, "Go therefore and make disciples of all the nations, baptizing them in the name of the Father and of the Son and of the Holy Spirit, teaching them to observe all things that I have commanded you; and lo, I am with you always, even to the end of the age." Speaking of the Gospel, Paul said in Colossians 1:23, ". . . which was preached to every creature under heaven, of which I, Paul, became a minister." Teaching the Gospel will occupy our minds with things that are eternal.

Participating in a sporting event is exciting. Participating in a home Bible study across the kitchen table is more exciting. When someone obeys the Gospel, Satan is defeated! Are you stronger in your knowledge of the Scriptures than you are in the knowledge of your favorite sport? In Hebrews 5:12 the writer records, "For though by this time you ought to be teachers, you need someone to teach you again the first principles of the oracles of God; and you have come to need milk and not solid food." It is sad when a Christian knows more about his favorite team than he knows about God. He can name coaches and players. He can write down each player's position, his statistics, his weight, and height. But, he cannot write down on a sheet of paper, the scriptures that shows what a person must do to be saved. At the Judgment, do you think it will be important to have a favorite team? At the Judgment, do you think it will be important to be a Christian? Where should we put our priorities?

Conclusion

Sports mania existed in the first century. A remnant of a coliseum is standing today in Rome to verify this. The Gospel of Jesus survived the first century. The Gospel of Jesus will survive the twenty-first century. The Gospel of Jesus will survive all obstacles that are placed in its path. God is more powerful than man. God's word is more powerful than man's word. We must let God be true and every man a liar (Rom. 3:4). We must let God rule in our lives and not sports!

Sports mania is of this world and the things of this world are not eternal (1 John 2:17). Being a Christian leads to eternal life (1 John 5:13). The choice is ours to make. Do not let sports mania separate you from God throughout all eternity.

Christianity Can Survive . . .

The Threat of Secular Education

David Arnold

This topic on surviving secular education reminds me of my early child-hood in the summers of 1933 through 1935. My father was a salesman for Frank Rambo's Motor Company in Fayetteville, Tennessee. When the Great Depression became deeper in 1933, he rented a twelve-acre farm with abundant rich soil for $10.00 a month in Ethridge, Tennessee, which was my mother's home town. My father continued to live in Fayetteville, sell a few cars, and come home to the farm at every opportunity.

We *survived* the Depression because of all the food that was produced on this small farm. My brothers ten and twelve years old in 1933 learned to work on the farm and continued to do so for three summers. Following our father's death in 1936, they worked for farmers to provide funds for

David Arnold was born on January 17, 1930. He graduated from Lawrence County High School in Lawrenceburg, TN in 1948, David Lipscomb College in 1952 (degree in Bible, mathematics, and speech), and Louisiana State University (M.A. and the course work for the Ph.D., speech pathology and audiology). He taught public speaking and developed a program in speech and hearing at Middle Tennessee State College (University) from 1962 to 2001.

David married Janice Morris of Lawrenceburg in 1952 and to this union were born David Morris Arnold and Mary Lee Arnold Barnes. Janice has been of great importance to David in that she is a dedicated Christian and excellent student of the word of God.

David worked with the McRae Road Church in Camden, SC (1952-1958), during which time two other churches were established in Camden and Bethune resulting from Bible Correspondence Courses and tent meetings. He moved to Gonzales, Louisiana where he and Janice assisted in establishing the Southside Church. While at Murfreesboro, he has helped establish five churches. David began his sixty-third year of preaching on January 16, 2011 and trusts that he will have other years to teach the wonderful and saving word of God!

the family and my mother worked at a shirt factory from 1937 to 1942. At thirteen I learned the work ethic by mowing yards for fifteen cents an hour with a *reel-push mower*, delivering newspapers and doing other work until I was eighteen years of age.

This may not directly relate to my topic, but it surely taught me lessons on *surviving* difficult circumstances.

WWII and Its Effect on Faithfulness

The men who went into the armed forces in the early years of World War II often ended their service not having the same religious beliefs as they had before the War.

In the 1940s twelve young men were baptized into Christ in the Little Shoal Creek at Ethridge, Tennessee just before they went into the service of their country. Few were faithful to the Lord through World War II. Marriages failed during this time because of the pressures of the war and because some had married denominationalists. Some left the faith. Most of those who had been converted went to WW II without having heard regular preaching. Gospel meetings lasting two weeks were the most concentrated preaching and teaching which they had received. Most of the preaching in these meetings was on what is termed "first-principles" with seldom a deeper lesson into the depths of the word of God. No wonder that the faith of these young men was weak. Sunday mornings at the Ethridge Church had consisted of what was then called the Sunday School in which the Gospel Advocate "quarterlies" were used, but not very well taught. During this time there was no regular preaching on Sunday mornings.

From a positive aspect of military service during WW II many men from other areas remained faithful to the Lord, preached the gospel in other countries, and established churches. The same was done during the Korean and Viet Nam wars and possibly others. Credit and com-mendation should be given to those men and women who were faithful in times of conflict.

The Threat of Secularism Experienced

Humanism and secularism, beginning with John Locke and Jean-Jacques Rousseau, have pervaded public education. This was in contrast with the early days of this country when Harvard, Yale, William and Mary, and Princeton, the oldest of American Universities, were founded with an em-phasis on biblical studies.

To make the threat or danger of educational secularism apparent, consider the plethora of indoctrination of humanistic secularism.

The influence of John Locke:

The fundamental principles of Locke's philosophy are presented in *An Essay Concerning Human Understanding* (1690), the culmination of twenty years of reflection on the origins of human knowledge. According to Locke, what we know is always properly understood as *the relation between ideas*, and he devoted much of the *Essay* to an extended argument that all of our ideas—simple or complex—are ultimately *derived from experience*. The consequence of this *empiricist* approach is that the knowledge of which we are capable is *severely limited* in its scope and certainty. Our knowledge of material *substances*, for example, depends heavily on the secondary qualities by reference to which we name them, while their real inner natures derive from the *primary qualities* of their insensible parts.

John Locke (1632-1704)

Nevertheless, Locke held that we have no grounds for complaint about the limitations of our knowledge, since a proper application of our cognitive capacities is enough to *guide our action* in the practical conduct of life. The *Essay* brought great fame, and Locke spent much of the rest of his life responding to admirers and critics by making revisions in later editions of the book, including detailed accounts of human *volition* and moral freedom, the *personal identity* on which our responsibility as moral agents depends, and the **dangers of religious enthusiasm** (Emp. mine, DA). One additional section that was never included in the *Essay* itself is *Of the Conduct of the Understanding* a practical guide to the achievement of useful beliefs about the world. The bachelor philosopher's notions about childrearing appeared in *Some Thoughts concerning Education* (1693) (*Britannica Internet Guide Selection:* Locke*)*.

Locke was one of the most influential philosophers of the Seventeenth Century to emphasize that human knowledge was based on experience and that religious enthusiasm was dangerous. The writings of John Locke appear to have been of great influence on Jean Jacques Rousseau who popularized Lock's philosophy.

The influence of Jean Jacques Rousseau:

As a brilliant, undisciplined, and unconventional thinker, Jean-Jacques Rousseau spent most of his life being driven by controversy back and forth between Paris and his native Geneva. Orphaned at an early age, he left home at sixteen, working as a tutor and musician before undertaking a literary career while in his forties. Rousseau sired but refused to support several illegitimate children and frequently initiated bitter quarrels with even the most supportive of his colleagues. His autobiographical *Les Confessions* (*Confessions*) (1783) offer a thorough (if somewhat self-serving) account of his turbulent life.

Rousseau first attracted wide-spread attention with his prize-winning essay *Discours sur les Sciences et les Arts* (*Discourse on the Sciences and the Arts*) (1750), in which he decried the harmful effects of modern civilization. Pursuit of the arts and sciences, Rousseau argued, merely promotes idleness, and the resulting political inequality encourages alienation. He continued to explore

Jean-Jacques Rousseau (1712-1778)

these themes throughout his career, proposing in *Émile, ou l'education* (1762) a method of education that would minimize the damage by noticing, encouraging, and following the natural proclivities of the student instead of striving to eliminate them.

Rousseau began to apply these principles to political issues specifically in his *Discours sur l'origine et les fondements de l'inégalité parmi les hommes* (*Discourse on the Origin of Inequality*) (1755), which maintains that every variety of injustice found in human society is an artificial result of the control exercised by defective political and intellectual influences over the healthy natural impulses of otherwise noble savages. The alternative he proposed in *Du contrat social* (*On the Social Contract*) (1762) is a civil society voluntarily formed by its citizens and wholly governed by reference to the general will [Fr. *volonté générale*] expressed in their unanimous consent to authority.

Rousseau also wrote *Discourse on Political Economy* (1755), *Constitutional Program for Corsica* (1765), and *Considerations on the Government of Poland* (1772). Although the authorities made every effort to suppress Rousseau's writings, the ideas they expressed, along with those of Locke, were of great influence during the French Revolution. The religious views expressed in the "Faith of a Savoyard Vicar" section of Émile made a more modest impact (*Britannica Internet Guide Selection: Rousseau*).

One must only peruse the Durant's Volume 10 to become aware of Rousseau's influence in our world (Will and Ariel Durant, Vol. 10).

Dinesh D'Souza, in *What's So Great About America,* wrote of Rousseau stating:

> Rousseau was a deeply strange man. It had been said of him that he labored under the illusion that changes within his own life mirrored the great transformations of Western civilization. . . .In fact, Rousseau was a champion of radical freedom. We can see this by focusing on a central element of Rousseau's thought—the one that pertains to the "new morality" of the 1960s.

> By insisting that each of us has an original way of being human, Rousseau is articulating the idea of individuality. But he is doing a lot more than that. Rousseau insists that in determining the unique course of one's life, the self is sovereign. . . .Rousseau argues that in deciding what to become, whom to marry, how to live, I should not go by the dictates of my parents, or my teachers, or my preachers, or even God. I should decide for myself alone. . . .

> As the Savoyard Vicar puts it in Rousseau's Émile, "I do not derive these rules from the principles of high philosophy, but I find them written by nature in Ineffaceable characters at the bottom of my heart." Here Rousseau is giving expression to the idea of authenticity, of being true to oneself.

> It is a massively important idea. **Before Rousseau, no one believed that each human life should follow its own distinctive moral course, nor did anyone think of giving the inner self—the voice of nature with us—final authority in determining that course** (Emp. mine, DA). Rousseau's view emerged in resistance to an earlier view, according to which morality was a matter of costs and benefits (D'Souza, 141-143).

The influence or John Dewey (1859-1952):

It is not evident that John Locke and Jean Jacques Rousseau had great influence on John Dewey, but his philosophy of education is similar to that of these men.

> John Dewey was a leading proponent of the American school of thought known as *pragmatism,* a view that rejected the dualistic epistemology and metaphysics of modern philosophy in favor of a naturalistic approach that viewed knowledge as arising from an active adaptation of the human organism to its environment. On this view, inquiry should not be understood as consisting of a mind passively observing the world and drawing from this ideas that if true correspond to reality, but rather as a process which initiates with a check or obstacle to successful human action, proceeds

to active manipulation of the environment to test hypotheses, and issues in a re-adaptation of organism to environment that allows once again for human action to proceed. With this view as his starting point, Dewey developed a broad body of work encompassing virtually all of the main areas of philosophical concern in his day. He also wrote extensively on social issues in such popular publications as the *New Republic,* thereby gaining a reputation as a leading social commentator of his time (*Internet Encyclopedia of Philosophy*).

John Dewey

James Neill, Ph.D., in an article on John Dewey, "Philosophy of Education—The Modern Father of Experiential Education," wrote of Dewey:

Dewey is lauded as the greatest educational thinker of the 20th century. His theory of experience continues to be much read and discussed not only within education, but also in psychology and philosophy. Dewey's views continue to strongly influence the design of innovative educational approaches, such as in outdoor education, adult training, and *experiential therapies.*

In the 1920's / 1930's, John Dewey became famous for pointing out that the authoritarian, strict, pre-ordained knowledge approach of modern traditional education was too concerned with delivering knowledge, and not enough with understanding students' actual experiences.

Dewey became the champion, or philosophical father of experiential education, or as it was then referred to, progressive education. But he was also critical of completely "free, student-driven" education because students often don't know how to structure their own learning experiences for maximum benefit (Neill).

The philosophers John Locke, Jean Jacques Rousseau, and John Dewey developed liberal concepts which pervade the schools and colleges of today. One is not guided by religious principles, but each person's character develops in relation to the environment while doing one's own experiential learning.

Go to *http://www.americanhumanist.org/Who_We_Are/About_Humanism/Humanist_Manifesto_I* and note that John Dewey signed the 1933 Humanist Manifesto I which was basic to the advance of secularism in the schools. Also search Google for Human Manifesto II and III. In Humanist Manifesto II the supernatural is rejected under the heading "Religion." It is no wonder that secularism has become the basic philosophy in the public schools of America.

Conservatism in Schools

Some schools established in the south in the mid-nineteenth century taught the classical languages of Latin and Greek along with reading, writing, and mathematics. Headmasters of these schools were often preachers of the gospel who taught the Bible in the schools.

In 1908, J. M. Stribling, a rather wealthy Christian and banker in Lawrenceburg, Tennessee, built the building for the Lawrence County High School with the condition that the Bible would be taught in the school. He paid the teacher's salary and the Bible was taught for several years. Later, because of some complaints, this teaching ceased and Mr. Stribling reportedly sold the building to the county for one dollar. One of the early teachers was Professor E. O. Coffman, a gospel preacher. He was later appointed as principal from about 1920 to 1950 and under his oversight his influence was such that the school was very conservative with no school dances or other questionable activities.

Conservatism was replaced in Lawrence County as schools became more secular after 1950. This was true of other schools in Tennessee and was even more radical in some states.

How Are Christians to Survive in the Humanistic-Secular Schools and Universities of the Present Age?

Note that I have changed the direction of this lecture to focus on Christians rather than on Christianity. If children and young people are to survive the threat of secular education, there must first be in-depth education in creation and other Old Testament teachings and in-depth study of the New Testament to establish an abiding faith in God's word!

My wife, Janice, and I have been blessed to have membership in the Wyndham resorts. We invited about thirty dedicated-knowledgeable Christians to the Wyndham Fairfield Glade Resort seven miles NE of Crossville, Tennessee. During the first full week of September, 2009 and again in 2010, we met for five days of singing spiritual songs, praying, and studying God's wonderful word. The first year the theme of the meetings was Evangelism and the second year the theme was Righteous Living. In an introductory lesson, it was stressed that we are blessed of God if we (1) live righteously, (2) study the word deeply; not cursorily, (3) teach/preach the word enthusiastically and (4) pray the Lord of harvest to send reapers into the fields white unto the harvest. Each man is encouraged to make a ten minute presentation to the other men, which is then followed by a 45 minute discussion of the topic. This format was followed in the women's meetings.

Many of those attending these in-depth studies indicated that they were greatly benefited by this approach of Christians' singing, praying, and studying together over several days. These meetings were generated by an evangelist, doing the work of an evangelist, endeavoring to strengthen understanding of God's word and relationships with other Christians.

Local churches need to provide in-depth teaching in addition to that which consists of current sermons and Bible classes. We must not give up these effective means of teaching, but, brothers and sisters, we need to be motivated to teach God's word faithfully, enthusiastically, and fervently. We must not wait for the lost to come to us but must go to them and we must be sure that young people in the local churches have knowledge of the facts of Genesis chapter 1 and other information of the Old Testament. Some of you are likely thinking, "But we do this where I attend or am a preacher or an elder!" Great! Let us all be more diligent to do so.

Young people, who do not have a deep understanding of God's word, will lose their faith because of the false doctrines of humanistic secularism and macro evolution. Christians can survive secular education, but this will be true only with correct knowledge to enable them to reject and refute secularism. Secularism has often seemed to creep into those schools which were established by Christians in more recent years. David Lipscomb would be appalled to see the present practices at David Lipscomb University. He would wish he had held the position of Tolbert Fanning who is reported to have said that a school should begin and end with the man who founded it.

Recently the threat of secularism has resulted from the teaching of macro or general evolution in the schools from kindergarten through colleges and universities. Children are bombarded with the theory of macro evolution, which *belief system* denies the existence of a divine-supernatural force. This weakens or destroys faith in God and His word. The theory is based on assumptions and not on facts.

It is my judgment that macro or general evolution does more to destroy the faith of children and youths than any other single error or false teaching. As parents, teachers, elders, and preachers, we should build our libraries with books and other media which support the Genesis account of creation. We must teach the Biblical accounts as facts in the home and see that Bible class teachers, elders, and preachers where we worship do the same. Home schooled children have an advantage of not hearing macro evolution taught as fact. They need to be made aware of the teaching and answers should be given to enable them to reject the theory of macro or general evolution which is a belief-system.

The Editorial staff of *Forerunner*, a college newspaper, discussed the concepts of macro versus micro evolution as follows:

Macro vs. Micro Evolution

Charles Darwin sparked a revolution in scientific thought with the pub-lication of his book, *The Origin of Species*, in 1859. With his concept of evolution by natural selection, Darwin attempted to render invalid the biblical idea that "every living thing produces life after its own kind."

In the first half of *Species*, Darwin cited evidence for "micro-evolution," or changes on a small level between species. His discovery of the several different types of finches on the Galapagos Islands with similar charac-teristics, derived from a common ancestor, comprised his evidence for micro-evolution. The 14 different species of finches vary according to plumage, size (from the size of a sparrow to that of a large blackbird), beak morphology, behavior and environmental habitat. They were each very different, yet closely related.

From this observation, Darwin then extrapolated his explanation for the origin of life forms from a common ancestor, or "macro-evolution." He used the evidence from the first half of his book on micro-evolution to suggest that the same mechanism could produce all life forms. However, this concept of macro-evolution is not supported by modern scientific evidence. Although we can explain and understand the mechanism behind micro-evolution, we still can only theorize about possible explanations for macro-evolution – since it has no scientifically valid occurrences.

The "Evolution" of Poodles and Chihuahuas?

The concept of micro-evolution – or diversification of species – is a fact of nature. Species do vary and change, but only on a small scale. We have many examples of Darwin's finches and even the breeding history of dogs which supports the notion of micro-evolution.

Micro-evolution was first understood when George Mendel demonstrated the variation within species based on genetic mechanisms. By Mendelian genetics we see the various dog species, which range from the St. Bernard to the chihuahua (sic). The concept of micro-evolution is widely accepted today and supports the biblical notion of life reproducing after its own "kind." In other words, it is accepted in scientific circles that all the different types of dogs most likely descended from a common canine ancestor.

Evolutionists, however, have expanded the model to suggest the origin of the universe, the origin of life from non-life, the origin of amphibians from fishes, the origin of birds from reptiles, and so on. Scientists have many theories of the mechanisms behind macro-evolution, but none of them have any direct evidence. The theories are merely extrapolations from what can be seen on the smaller scale.

This extrapolation is scientifically unjustified. The underlying logic behind this premise is similar to plotting the fastest times man has run the mile over the years, and then predicting that someday man will run a two or three-minute mile. Anyone realizes that there are limits to valid extrapolation. Likewise, Darwinian macro-evolution is undergoing tremendous scrutiny in scientific circles because of the lack of evidence (Rogers). *Reprinted by permission from: The Forerunner International, P.O. Box 362173, Melbourne FL 32936-2173.*

We should note that some students or teachers of evolution and creation do not use the terms *macro* and *micro* evolution. I continue to use the terms in this paper as some scientists tend to use them, but remember there are issues with respect to evolution when using them. *Macro* evolution is used by those scientists who believe that through the process of mutation over millions or billions of years, mankind and other living creatures came into existence from non-life with no designer or Supreme Being. *Micro* evolution is used to refer to the obvious changes in animals through selective breeding, or changes in location over time, as in the case of dogs as discussed above.

Sarfati, a young-earth creationist who works with *Answers In Genesis* in Australia, writes,

These terms, which focus on "small" versus "large" changes, distract from the key issue of *information.* That is, particles-to-people evolution requires changes that *increase* genetic information, but all we observe is *sorting* and *loss* of information. We have yet to see even a "micro" increase in information, although such changes should be frequent if evolution were true. Conversely, we do observe quite "macro" changes that involve *no* new information, e.g., when a control gene is switched on or off (Sarfati, 223-224).

On January 15, 2011, I had a telephone conversation with my twenty-year old Grandson, Taylor Arnold Barnes, a doctoral student in Physical

Chemistry at the California Technological University. He stressed that Natural Selection (micro evolution) is deleterious to information which is passed on to an animal; therefore, there is no way to breed Chihuahuas so as to produce St. Bernards or wolves because much of the information of the original canine or wolf stock has been deleted.

I noted in my association with scientists while teaching at Middle Tennessee State University that some concluded that they had superior knowledge to those of us who believe in a super-natural power which created all things. In speaking with one, relative to the general theory of evolution, I said, "We all have the same information." He denied this. My response was that those who are not evolutionists can certainly have the intelligence to understand the writings of the evolutionists. He, of course, was not willing to accept my thoughts. This compares to the proceedings in a court of law in deciding a case. Through the process of discovery, the prosecution and defense develop a body of information which must ultimately be shared by each side in the law suit. Both prosecution and defense have the same information. Each interprets it according to his/her responsibility in the case. In a similar way evolutionists and creationists have the same information. Each must interpret that information. The evolutionist concludes that all things came forth from non-life and through various mutations animals and mankind came into being. The creationist believes that "In the beginning God created the heavens and the earth!"

Can Creationists Be Scientists?
by Dr. Jason Lisle, Ph.D., astrophysics, AiG–USA speaker and researcher.
First published in Answers Update–USA April 2005

It has been often said that "creationists cannot be real scientists."

Several years ago, the National Academy of Sciences published a guidebook entitled *Teaching about Evolution and the Nature of Science.*[1] This guidebook states that evolution is "the most important concept in modern biology, a concept essential to understanding key aspects of living things."

In addition, the late evolutionist Theodosius Dobzhansky once made the now well-known comment that "nothing in biology makes sense except in the light of evolution."[2]

But is a belief in "particles-to-people" evolution really necessary to understand biology and other sciences? Is it even helpful? Are there any technological advances that have been made because of a belief in evolution?

Although evolutionists interpret the evidence in light of their belief in evolution, science works perfectly well without any connection to evolution. Think about it this way: is a belief in molecules-to-man evolution necessary to understand how a computer works, how planets orbit the sun, how telescopes operate, or how plants and animals function? Has any biological or medical research benefited from a belief in evolution? No, not at all.

In fact, the Ph.D. cell biologist (and creationist) Dr. David Menton, who speaks at many conferences, has stated, "The fact is that, though widely believed, evolution contributes nothing to our understanding of empirical science and thus plays no essential role in biomedical research or education."[3]

Nor has technology arisen due to a belief in evolution. Computers, cellular phones and DVD players all operate based on the laws of physics which God created. It is because God created a logical, orderly universe and gave us the ability to reason and to be creative that technology is possible. How can a belief in evolution (a belief that complex biological machines do *not* require an intelligent designer) aid in the development of complex machines which are clearly intelligently designed?

Technology has shown us that sophisticated machines require intelligent designers—not random chance. Science and technology are perfectly consistent with the Bible.

So it shouldn't be surprising that there have been many scientists who believed in biblical creation. In my own research field of astrophysics, I am reminded of several of the great minds of history. Consider Isaac Newton, who co-discovered calculus, formulated the laws of motion and gravity, computed the nature of planetary orbits, invented the reflecting telescope and made a number of discoveries in optics.

Consider Johannes Kepler, who discovered the three laws of planetary motion, or James Clerk Maxwell who discovered the four fundamental equations that light and all forms of electromagnetic radiation obey. These great scientists believed the Bible.

Today as well, there are many Ph.D. scientists who reject evolution and instead believe that God created in six days as recorded in Scripture. Consider Dr. Russ Humphreys, a Ph.D. nuclear physicist who has developed (among many other things) a model to compute the present strength of planetary magnetic fields[4] which was able to predict the field strengths of the outer planets. Did a belief in the Bible hinder his research? Not at all.

On the contrary, Dr. Humphreys was able to make these predictions precisely because he started from the principles of Scripture. Dr. John Baumgardner, a Ph.D. geophysicist and biblical creationist, has a model of catastrophic plate tectonics, which the journal *Nature* once featured (this model is based on the global Genesis Flood).

Additionally, think of all the people who have benefited from a Magnetic Resonance Imaging (MRI) scan. The MRI scanner was developed by the creationist Dr. Raymond Damadian[5] who has been featured twice in *Creation* magazine.

Clearly, creationists can indeed be real scientists. And this shouldn't be surprising since the very basis for scientific research is biblical creation. The universe is orderly because its Creator is logical and has imposed order on the universe. God created our minds and gave us the ability and curiosity to study the universe. Furthermore, we can trust that the universe will obey the same physics tomorrow as it does today because God is consistent. This is why science is possible.

On the other hand, if the universe is just an accidental product of a big bang, why should it be orderly? Why should there be laws of nature if there is no lawgiver? If our brains are the by-products of random chance, why should we trust that their conclusions are accurate? But if our minds have been designed, and if the universe has been constructed by the Lord as the Bible teaches, then of course we should be able to study nature.

Yes, science is possible because the Bible is true (Lisle).

References and Notes
1. The claims made in this guidebook have been refuted in Dr. Jonathan Sarfati's powerful book *Refuting Evolution*.
2. *The American Biology.*
3. A testimony to the power of God's Word.
4. *www.creationresearch.org/crsq/articles/21/21_3/21_3.html.*
5. Super-scientist slams society's spiritual sickness!

The references above were included as found in the article (Lisle).

The Age of the Earth
A Caveat!

This author will be referencing the works of various scientists but does not necessarily endorse their life-styles or behaviors. They are referenced as authorities or scholars of the documents which they have produced!

Since macro evolution may be a primary reason for children and teenagers to lose their faith, special attention needs to be given to this false theory by **parents, Bible class teachers, elders, and preachers**. John F. Ashton's book, *In Six Days: Why Fifty Scientists Choose to Believe in Creation,* includes short articles by scientists in biology, mechanical engineering, biochemistry, medical research, physical chemistry, mathematical physics, genetics, organic chemistry, horticulture science, inorganic chemistry, botany, theoretical chemistry, medical physics, geophysics, zoology, astronomy, meteorology, medical research, orthodontists, geology, geography, architectural engineering, hydrometallurgy, forestry research, physics, informational science and agricultural science (Ashton, 9-384).

Many of the articles have "Endnotes" to provide other sources supporting the creation as having occurred in six literal days.

The "paperback" back cover of the book states:

> Why would any educated, self-respecting scientist with a PhD advocate a literal interpretation of the six days of creation? Why, indeed, when only one in three Americans believes "the Bible is the actual word of God and is to be taken literally, word for word" according to a recent Gallup poll.

> Science can neither prove nor disprove evolution anymore than it can creation. Certainly there are no human eyewitness accounts of either. However, certain factors are present today which are capable of swaying one's beliefs one way or the other.

> In this book are the testimonies of fifty men and women holding doctorates in a wide range of scientific fields who have been convinced by the evidence to believe in a literal six-day creation (Ashton).

Ken Ham's book, *The Great Dinosaur Mystery Solved,* is an important resource refuting macro evolution. In his introduction, Ham states: "a true Christian philosophy **STARTS** (emphasis—Ham) with the time-line of history as given in Scripture. Once a person understands this, he or she will find it easy to be able to give many answers to a variety of questions, including dinosaurs" (Ham, *The Great Dinosaur Mystery Solved*, 10).

Bert Thompson, Ph.D., is imminently qualified to discuss the age of the Earth. He holds the master's degree and doctorate in microbiology from Texas A&M. He holds a professorship in the College of Veterinary Medicine at Texas A&M and serves as Coordinator of the Cooperative Education Program in Biomedical Science.

Thompson discusses the age of the earth, the day-age theory, the gap theory, and other miscellaneous old-earth theories, and he provides scientific and biblical refutation of the theories (Thompson, *The Bible and the Age of the Earth*).

Tony Campolo and William Willimon introduce their book, *The Survival Guide for Christians on Campus,* with two quotations from their acquaintances. The first is from a dentist who said:

> I used to be a dedicated Christian. Then, like a lot of people, I went to college. I took a couple of religion courses that did more to destroy my religion than to teach me anything about it. Those professors asked some tough questions about the Bible and made me see that it's mostly just a bunch of myths and ancient fables. That was the beginning of the end of my faith (Campolo and Willimon, 1).

In chapter one, "How Do I Know If I'm A Christian?", Campolo and Willimon (Tony and Will) discuss "The Value of a Support Group" (Campolo and Willimon, 16-22).

This concept is elaborated in chapter 3: Do I Have To Go To Church To Be A Good Christian? This material is typically denominational in concept with a wide variety of concepts introduced (*Ibid*. 53-81).

Campolo and Willimon suggest that even in church-related schools the Bible is not taught as the inspired word of God, but that it's filled with myths. Thus, a "Christian Education" is no assurance that students will be taught truth. This is particularly so of some of the oldest religious schools founded in this country. Graduate Schools of Religion are often filled with rank liberals, having little or no faith in Scripture as the word of God.

"Will" had a conversation with a student who indicated being a "Christian" on the college campus was a struggle. The conversation:

> "So you are in a campus Bible study?" Will asked,
>
> "Yep," the student answered. "I love my Bible study group. We meet every Wednesday in the basement of the dorm."
>
> "You were big into Bible study in high school?"
>
> "No. I grew up Episcopalian. I don't think we do that sort of stuff."
>
> "Well," Will continued, "I find it interesting that, though you have not been in a Bible study group before, you come here to college and get into Bible study. Why is that?"

He looked at Will as if he were dumb, then said, "Dr. Willimon, have you ever tried to be a sophomore and a Christian at the same time? It's not easy" (*Ibid.* 2).

The authors stress the importance of studying with others to aid the student to grow in faith. They say that Jesus did not work alone (*Ibid.* 5-6).

Even though the authors emphasize *The Apostle's Creed,* they do give emphasis to obeying Christ's teaching as found in the Bible, emphasizing that it is a "truthful message of God." They indicate that doubts will arise, but that associations with other "Christians" will help students overcome their doubts (*Ibid.* 9-34).

Campolo and Willimon continue to write about the growth of students in reading and understanding the Bible. The book is written, however, with a denominational "slant." It is a good reference for one who is seeking to assist college students in keeping their faith, but it would be better used as a guide for the teacher rather than as a guide directly for the student.

Warning and Critical Information

Perhaps this part of my lecture is the most important. The focus for many years has been our children are lost to the faith in college. In reality, research indicates they are "already gone" before they enter college according to Ken Ham and Britt Beemer.

Ken Ham moved from Australia to the United States in 1987 thinking that to do so would be advantageous for his children's spiritual lives. You may be familiar with Dr. Ham through having read his books on the fossils of a young earth and of his Creation Museum in Petersburg, Kentucky across the river from Cincinnati, Ohio.

In his recent book, *Already Gone—Why Your Kids Will Quit Church and What You Can Do to Stop It,* he addressed the issues relating to the closing of church buildings and the loss of children to the Lord prior to their years in college.

In the introduction to his book, Ham tells of having entered a large church building in London with seats for more than 3000 persons, yet on a Sunday morning he was ushered into a foyer where thirty chairs were set up for the elderly folk who were present for worship. He considered his being there for a funeral; not a funeral of a person but of an institution, the church. He concluded that within months it was likely that the older generation would shut and lock the doors of the meeting place where the "resounding anthem of the great hymns of our spiritual forefathers will never again echo in its passages" (Ham, *Already Gone,* 9-10).

Ham adds a reference from the Victorian Society, No. 26, November 2007, *http://www.victoriansociety.org.uk/publications/redundant-churches-who-cares/,* as follows:

> Since 1969, 1,500 churches in England have heard that final *thud* as their doors were shut after their final service after hundreds of years of active life. It should be noted that the primary purpose of the Victorian Society is to preserve the architecture of the Victorian and Edwardian buildings in England and Wales. There appears to be little interest in the preservation of "worship" in these buildings (Ham, *Already Gone,* 10-11).

In my work in Lithuania in 1998, I observed that some of the large church buildings were being used for secular, rather than religious, purposes. Many others of you who have worked overseas have likely observed the same situation in other countries.

Ham continues with a discussion of the redundant churches (buildings), in that so many are no longer used for worship, he writes that the buildings are being used for other purposes. A fund has been setup to preserve the "historical and archaeological interest or architectural quality, together with their contents" according to *http://www.opsi.gov.uk/si/si1994/Uksi_19940962_en_1.htm.*

Summarizing his concepts of the redundant buildings, Ham says,

> The decline of the Church has followed the plummeting spirituality of a nation that has lost its roots—its foundation. England, the country that was once a cornerstone of western Christianity, is now, by and large, a wasteland of lost souls where the word "God" has many different definitions, with so few these days who would even think of "God" as the Creator God of the Bible (Ham, *Already Gone,* 11-12).

After indicating that "only 2.5 percent of the population is attending Bible-based churches," and providing pictures of redundant churches being used for secular purposes, Ham writes, "Empty churches now stand in the cities and the countryside as monuments to the triumph of the new religion of secular humanism" (Ham, *Already Gone,* 12-17).

Far more important than the redundancy of church buildings in the United Kingdom, is the evidence in a study of George Barna, a respected pollster.

Based on interviews with 22,000 adults and over 2,000 teen-agers in twenty-five separate surveys, Barna unquestionably quantified the serious-ness of the situation: six out of ten twenty-somethings who were involved in a church during their teen years are already gone. Barna Research Online, "Teenagers Embrace Religion but Are Not Excited About Christianity," January 10, 2000, *www.Barna.org* (Ham, *Already Gone*, 23).

Ham declares, "Despite strong levels of spiritual activity during the teen years, most 20-somethings disengage from active participation in the Christian faith during their young adult years—and often beyond that." Consider these findings:

Nearly 50% of teens in the United States regularly attend church-related services or activities.

More than three-quarters talk about their faith with their friends.

Three out of five teens attend at least one youth group meeting at a church during a typical three-month period.

One-third of teenagers participate in Christian clubs at school. *http://www.lifeway.com/lwc/article_main_page/0,1703,A%253D165951%2526M%253D201117,00.html* (Ham, *Already Gone*, 23).

Most are leaving church in their twenties.

61% of today's young adults who were regular church attendees are now "spiritually disengaged." They are not actively attending church, praying, or reading their Bibles.

20% of those who were spiritually active during High school are maintain-ing a similar level of commitment.

19% of teens were never reached by the Christian community, and they are still disconnected from the Church or other Christian activities (Ham, *Already Gone*, 24).

After these data were published, the Southern Baptist Convention's re-search revealed "that *more* than two-thirds of young adults who attended a Protestant church for at least a year in high school stopped attending for *at least* a year between the ages of 18 and 22 (Ham, *Already Gone*, 24).

Britt Beemer who designed the Barna studies concluded that of "those who no longer believe that all of the accounts and stories in the Bible are true: 39.8% first had doubts in middle school, 43.7% first had their doubts in high school (and) 10.6% had their first doubts during college" (Ham, *Already Gone*, 32).

These data evidence that our emphasis is erroneous in concluding that college is the time and place when doubts cause young adults to lose their faith.

Of those twenty-somethings who are planning on returning to church, 76.4% said they "believe all the books of the Bible are inspired by God," 92.1% said they "believe in creation as stated in the Bible," 91.3 % "believe in the creation of Adam and Eve in the Garden of Eden" and 59.5% said they "believe all the accounts/stories in the Bible are true/accurate" (Ham, *Already Gone*, 63).

It appears that the *location of the church meeting house* is not the most important factor in the growth of a church, at least with respect to the retention of youths. Clearer teaching must be provided that all of the universe was created in six days and that all of the land animals were created on the sixth day prior to the creation of man—Adam. This factual teaching provides young children and youths with confidence that the Bible is true.

The account of creation is not just a "story," but it teaches the fact that the universe was created in six days as Moses recorded. Middle school children and teenagers must be well grounded in evidences that the Bible is God's revelation to sinners beginning with the facts of creation. Evidence for a young earth should be provided to counteract the teaching of macro or general evolution which is being taught from pre-kindergarten through high school. When students believe their teachers are always correct in what they teach, it is no wonder that inadequate teaching by the parents, Bible class teachers, elders, and preachers leads to doubts in the minds of these vulnerable youths.

Conclusion
Even though I have read or perused several books with considerations of survival in college, it is my judgment that college, as such, is not the primary problem. The college chosen is a major issue. Based on the research of the Barna Group, as reported by Ken Ham and Britt Beemer, it is my judgment that the reasons a majority of middle school and high school students have become disillusioned with their faith is that they have not been adequately taught by their parents, Bible class teachers, elders, and preachers. Their doubts beginning at a very young age have caused them to leave their "faith" by the end of their high school experience. The research evidences that they have determined to continue their lives as twenty-somethings separated from all religious activities. About 61% of young adults have made the decision

to abandon their faith before entering college. A marked minority, 10.6% leave their "faith" after beginning college.

Twenty percent of 2,000 twenty-somethings maintained the faith which they practiced in middle and high school. Another 19% of the 2,000 adults in the study had never practiced religion. These with the 61% who left their faith are the composition of the 2,000 twenty-somethings who were interviewed.

Based on the research and personal observations, it is imperative that children are taught the Genesis **facts** of the six-days creation of all things, including those creatures identified by science as the dinosaurs. Instead of teaching Bible "stories," Bible **facts** should be taught. Adam and Eve were human beings, created by God on the sixth day following the creation of the land animals. Moses, Abraham, Isaac, and Jacob were people who believed in God and obeyed His will. Apparently these accounts are not being sufficiently taught as **facts**, so young children and high school students may have concluded that the Bible is just a book of stories and myths. They have no foundation to build their faith in God's word or to maintain their faith in the Bible, therefore, they have no faith in the Father, Son, and Holy Spirit.

Admittedly, the children taught in churches of Christ were only 3.45% of the twenty-somethings researched, so such children and youths may have more factual teaching than those in denominations. Yet how many of us would say we have done adequate work in preparing our children for enduring faith in God and in His word? A basic problem of those in the Lord's church may well be that parents are not doing their own religious teaching of their children, but "turn them over" to Bible class teachers in the local church, many of whom may be unqualified to do the necessary teaching.

Bibliography
Ashton, John F. *In Six Days—Why Fifty Scientists Choose to Believe in Creation.* Green Forest, AR: Master Books, Inc., 2000.

Bomar, Chuck. *99 Thoughts for College-Age People.* Lake Forest, CA: Simply Youth Ministry, 2008

Britannica Internet Guide Selection. http://www.philosophypages.com/ph/lock.htm.

Britannica Internet Guide Selection. http://www.philosophypages.com/ph/rous.htm.

Campolo, Tony and Willimon, William. *The Survival Guide for Christians on Campus*. West Monroe, LA: Howard Publishing Co., 2002.

D'Souza, Dinesh. *What's So Great About America*. New York: Penguin Books, 2002.

_____. *What's So Great About Christianity*. Washington, DC: Regnery Publishing, Inc., 2007.

Durant, Will and Ariel. *The Story of Civilization X, Rousseau and Revolution*. New York: Simon and Schuster, 1967.

Ham, Ken. *The Great Dinosaur Mystery Solved! A Biblical View of These Amazing Creatures*. Green Forest, AR: Master Books, 1998.

Ham, Ken & Beemer, Britt. *Already Gone—Why Your Kids Will Quit Church and What You Can Do To Stop It*. Green Forest, AR: Master Books, 2009.

Ham, Ken, General Editor. *The New Answers Book 1—Over 25 Questions on Creation/Evolution and the Bible*. Green Forest, AR: Master Books, 2006.

_____. *The New Answers Book 2—Over 30 Questions on Creation/Evolution and the Bible*. Green Forest, AR: Master Books, 2008.

Internet Encyclopedia of Philosophy—A Peer-Reviewed Academic Resource. *http://www.iep.utm.edu/dewey/#H2*.

Jackson, Wayne. *Fortify Your Faith*. Montgomery, AL: Apologetics Press, Inc., 2001.

Kullberg, Kelly Monroe. *Finding God Beyond Harvard—The Quest for Veritas*. Downers Grove, IL: Intervarsity Press, 2006.

Lisle, Jason. *http://www.answersingenesis.org/us/newsletters/0405lead.asp*.

Locke, John. *Britannica Internet Guide Selection*. *http://www.philosophypages.com/dy/zt.htm#165*.

_____. *Stanford Encyclopedia. Supplement to John Locke The Influence of John Lock's Works*. *http://www.philosophypages.com/dy/zt.htm#16*.

Neill, James. *Wilderdom—a project in natural living and transition*. *http://www.wilderdom.com/experiential/ExperientialDewey.html*.

Rogers, Jay, Director. Editorial Staff, The Forerunner, America's Campus Newspaper. *Macro vs. Micro Evolution*. *http://www.forerunner.com/forerunner/X0737_Macro_vs._Micro_Evol.html*, Published December, 2007.

Sarfati, Jonathan. *Refuting Evolution 2.* Green Forest, AR: Master Books, Inc., 2002.

Smith, Abbie. *Can You Keep Your Faith in College?* Colorado Springs, CO, 2006.

Thompson, Bert. *Rock-Solid Faith How to Build It.* Montgomery, AL: Apologetics Press, Inc., 2000.

_____. *The Bible and the Age of the Earth.* Montgomery, AL: Apologetics Press, Inc., 2000.

_____. *The Global Flood of Noah.* Montgomery, AL: Apologetics Press, Inc., 1986, Revised Edition, 1999.

_____. *The History of Evolutionary Thought.* Fort Worth, TX: Star Bible & Tract Corp., 1981.

Thompson, Bert and Jackson, Wayne. *The Case for the Existence of God.* Montgomery, AL, 1996.

Williams, Jon Gary. *The Other Side of Evolution.* LaVergne, TN: 1970.

Christianity Can Survive . . .

The Threat of Materialism
David Flatt

Can Christianity survive in America? The answer to this question is conditional. Of course, God has assured His people that His Church will not be overthrown by any force the Devil would use against Her. Jesus assured the apostles of this fact: "And I say also unto thee, That thou art Peter, and upon this rock I will build my church; and the gates of hell shall not prevail against it" (Matt. 16:18). When all else fails, death is the last and greatest instrument the Devil can use against God's people. Jesus proclaimed this powerful weapon, hell or death, could not destroy His Church.

These affirming words of Jesus were put to the test and proven early in the history of the Church. Severe persecution faced much of the Church during the first century. However, God, through His divine revelation, sought to reassure Christians of His promise to save them. If Christians were questioning the continuation of Christianity and their personal salvation, Christ reassured them of His irrevocable promises through the disciple whom He loved: John.

David Flatt was born on July 5, 1985 in Akron, Ohio. He was raised by two godly parents, David and Kathy. They taught him and his younger brother, Ryan, the truth. From an early age, David expressed an interest in preaching. During high school, he was closely mentored by Lewis Willis for two years. Throughout high school and college, he preached by appointment. In addition to his work as a preacher, David graduated *magna cum laude* from Kent State University. He earned a bachelor of science in the field of education with a minor in history. Following graduation in 2008, David married Elizabeth Woodford. Elizabeth has proven to be an indispensable help to David in his life and work as a preacher. Currently, David preaches for the Thayer Street Church of Christ in Akron.

In the book of Revelation, a divine panorama passed before the eyes of the apostle John. Towards the middle of his vision, he viewed a most beautiful scene in which a radiant, pregnant woman in a wilderness was presented before him. After giving birth to the Messiah, she found protection from the Devil. While protected in a place prepared for her by God, the Devil could not harm her (Rev. 12). The remainder of John's revelation described the assaults of the Devil used against the woman in the wilderness, the Church. Though the Devil would use powerful weapons and tactics, the Church would survive. In the end, the glorious bride of Christ would be eternally united with Him in Heaven, while the Devil and his servants would be punished eternally in a lake of fire and brimstone. Make no mistake, the Church can and will survive.

While the Church will survive, the Church or Christianity surviving in America is a slightly different proposition. Christianity's survival relates to a particular time, place, society, and culture. The Bible documents the early history of Christianity existing in the world. As such, the inspired writers have left us with a record of Christianity existing in particular times, places, societies, and cultures. Essentially, the divine record is cautionary. To be brief, Christianity certainly grew and thrived in various places. However, Christianity has essentially disappeared in many of the places in which it once thrived.

Perhaps the best example of a place in which Christianity existed but later disappeared is Ephesus: a city in modern-day Turkey. Of all the places in which Christianity was planted in the first century, the Bible documents Christianity in Ephesus more than any other place in the world at that time. About a fifty year history of this church is documented (A.D. 50-96). The origin of Christianity in Ephesus begins in Acts chapters eighteen through twenty. Christianity grew in Ephesus with the diligent work of their elders, the apostle Paul, Priscilla and Aquila, and Apollos. The Ephesian brethren became some of the most committed Christians we can read about in the Bible. They taught the Gospel to the point of disrupting an economy driven by idolatry.

After Paul left the brethren, Timothy worked with the Ephesians. Both of the letters Paul wrote to Timothy were written while he was working with the Ephesians. Also, from what is recorded in the letter Paul wrote directly to the Ephesians, we can deduce they were mature Christians. Some of the most profound truths relating to God's eternal desire to redeem humanity are described by Paul in this letter. The book of Ephesians certainly would

not be described as *Christianity 101*. This letter is more of a graduate studies course in Christianity: the meat of the word.

The last we hear of the church at Ephesus is in the book of Revelation.
In the first of seven letters to churches throughout Asia, Ephesus was
described as having left their first love. They were commanded to repent.
If they refused, their candlestick would be removed from the presence of
Christ. Their fellowship with Christ would be broken (Rev. 2:1-4). Did these
brethren repent? Did they go back to serving Christ as fervently as they had
in their early history? The Bible does not reveal this information.

Instead, history has left the record of Christianity in Ephesus. The down-
fall of faithful brethren in Ephesus began as early as A.D. 115.[1] From what
little is known historically, they seemed to have changed the organization
of the Church by developing a pastoral type arrangement for the eldership.[2]
One elder seemed to have been in charge over a plurality of other elders.
This type of neo-eldership is not described in the New Testament. For a time,
a perverted form of Christianity, an incipient form of Catholicism, existed
in Ephesus as late as A.D. 431.[3] Currently, Ephesus, modern-day Turkey,
has outlawed the practice of Christianity. Islam is the national religion. The
well-known Hagias Sophia, was formerly an Orthodox patriarchal basilica,
but was later transformed into a mosque, as Islam spread in the country. On
1 February 1935, it was opened as a museum.

Something changed in Ephesus. The people changed. The people and
their commitment to the word of God changed. Their perception of life and
God changed. The Devil was able to use his deception to cause people to
turn from the truth. No other explanation can be given as to why Christianity disappeared from Ephesus.

Ephesus serves as a cautionary tale for us as we seek to preserve and
perpetuate Christianity in our country. The reality of the work of the Devil
has not changed: "Be sober, be vigilant; because your adversary the devil,
as a roaring lion, walketh about, seeking whom he may devour" (1 Pet.

---

[1] Ethan R. Longhenry, (2008). *Churches of the New Testament*. DeWard Publishing
Company: Chillicothe, Ohio, 78.

[2] "The Epistle of Ignatius to the Ephesians," *Early Christian Writings*. Retrieved
from *http://www.earlychristianwritings.com/text/ignatius-ephesians-roberts.html*.
Accessed 10 November 2010.

[3] *Ibid.*

5:8). Who is the Devil working to destroy? In the book of Revelation, the Devil actively pursued the radiant woman in the wilderness: the Church. He wants Christians. He does not need to pursue the atheist, the apathetic, the fornicator, the workaholic, or the false teacher. He already has those. The Devil only wants those who have committed themselves to faithful service to God.

The Threat of Materialism

As Peter warned of the reality of the work of the Devil, he admonished his readership to be sober and vigilant. Someone who is sober and vigilant is someone who is able to think clearly for the purpose of protecting himself. As Christians, we must think clearly for the purpose of keeping ourselves pure from sin (Jas. 1:27). We must use truth to understand the world in which we live. Truth informs us of how God perceives the world and the means through which the Devil uses the world to afflict the Church. Sadly, far too many times we have failed to think clearly as God's people. Fear of being made to feel uncomfortable has prevented us from making necessary application of truth in our lives. We have allowed the influences of the Devil to come into our homes and congregations. A particular threat or weapon the Devil has effectively used against us, and the cause of Christianity in our country, is materialism.

The concept of materialism can be broken down into two schools of thought. The first relates to the concept of everything in the world consisting of physical matter. All we have and know is physical matter. There is nothing beyond the physical, tangible world. This view eliminates any notion of a spiritual world or afterlife. The second relates to identity, personal fulfillment, and social status being measured in terms of economics. [4] Therefore, the aforementioned criteria can only be gained by the acquisition of material goods. We are well familiar with this view of materialism and will primarily focus on it in the balance of this writing.

Materialism permeates our society. Our society teaches that happiness and success are determined by material wealth. This can be evidenced through the philosophy of the American Dream. The American Dream is inspirational and designed to bring hope. Through the lens of the American Dream, we hope for the day we will become rich. The American Dream is a modern evolution of a previous world view: Manifest Destiny. This ideology is a religious perspective. Essentially, this belief states God has destined us to

---

[4] *Op. cit.*

become independent, wealthy, and successful. This belief was the driving force of westward expansion of the United States.[5]

The American Dream has greatly shaped our outlook on life. From a very young age, children are taught materialism is the measure of happiness and success. In 2007, UCLA did a study which showed seventy-five percent of their freshmen class said it was essential or very important to be financially well-off.[6] What does it mean to be *financially well-off?* Does this mean if our bank accounts reach a certain amount we will be content? Where did these freshmen, who are now in the work-force and possibly starting families of their own, come to the conclusion that it was essential or very important to be financially well-off? Perhaps they learned this from their families and the world around them.

Most people believe that happiness and success are determined by our wealth, our houses, our cars, the number of vacations we take each year, and other superficial criteria. In this view of happiness and success, both are contingent upon material objects. Material objects are genuinely believed to bring us a sense of accomplishment. If we do not gain the material objects the world teaches we need, we cannot be happy or successful. This belief is the polar opposite of what Solomon expressed: *"He that loveth silver shall not be satisfied with silver; nor he that loveth abundance with increase: this is also vanity"* (Eccl. 5:10).

We will never become satisfied physically or spiritually through the acquisition of material goods. While there is nothing sinful with wanting to be happy and successful, this is not the means by which God has described happiness and success being achieved. As will be described later, the teaching of Jesus did not focus on the acquisition of material wealth in any way, shape, or form. However, much teaching done in the name of Christianity in our country preaches financial success will come if we obey Jesus. A new, materialistic form of Christianity has become commonplace in our country.

In his book, *Radical: Taking Back Your Faith from the American Dream,* David Platt presents a critique of the culture of mainstream Christianity in

---

[5] Link Hullar & Scott Nelson (2001). *The United States: A brief narrative history.* Harlan Davidson, Inc.: Wheeling, Illinois.

[6] Martha Irvine (2007). "Today's youth more focused on being wealthy, polls find." *Akron Beacon Journal* (23 January 2007). Retrieved from *http://www.ohio.com/mld/ohio/news/nation/16523989.html.* Accessed 26 January 2007.

America. Preacher for the Church at Brook Hills in Birmingham, Alabama, a mega church, Platt believes we have Americanized the Gospel. Instead of worshipping God, we have developed a form of Christianity in which we worship ourselves.[7] This is partly evidenced by multi-million dollar church buildings, hundreds of thousands of dollars worth of cars in church parking lots, and worship services/productions that entertain the audience rather than exalt God. Contrasting the American Dream and the Gospel, Platt stated the following in an interview:

> I believe that the gospel and the American Dream have fundamentally different starting points. The American Dream begins with self, exalts self, says you are inherently good and you have in you what it takes to be successful so do all you can, work with everything you have to make much of yourself. The gospel's starting point is completely different. The gospel begins with God, the reality that we were created to exalt his name to the ends of the earth. . . . And from those starting points flow two different trajectories for how life looks, how success looks like, what satisfaction in life looks like. And if we miss the starting point – either self and the American Dream or God and the gospel – then that changes everything from then on out.[8]

Essentially, Platt believes Christianity in our country has drastically changed the purpose and intent of Jesus' message. The materialistic corruption of Christianity noticed by Platt has been the result of the materialistic influences of the world diluting the minds of people who are interested in serving God.

Materialism has become a plague to Christianity. Many have even become attracted to Christianity with the hopes of becoming financially blessed. The actual message of Jesus stands in stark contrast to the materialistic expectation of many modern practitioners of the faith. Instead of financial gain, Jesus taught painful loss would be experienced by those seeking to do His will: "For whosoever will save his life shall lose it: and whosoever shall lose his life for my sake shall find it" (Matt. 16:25).

---

[7] David Platt (2010). *Radical: Taking back your faith from the American Dream.* Multnomah Books: Colorado Springs, Colorado (13).

[8] The *Christian Post* Interview: David Platt on the American Dream, Radical Christianity. Conducted 15 May 2010. Retrieved from *http://www.christianpost. com/article/20100515/interviewdavid-platt-on-the-american-dream-radical- christianity/page2.html.* Accessed 02 November 2010.

As God's people, we are influenced by our culture. We chase the al-mighty dollar as fiercely as anyone else. We pursue material wealth at the expense of our families, friends, brethren, churches, and our personal spiritual growth. Sadly, some will pursue material wealth at the expense and sacrifice of their souls.

Evidence of Materialism in the Church

We could consider evidence of materialism impacting the world, but this would be of little value to us. We need to identify evidence of materialism negatively impacting the Church and the preservation of Christianity in our country. Consider the following evidence of materialism impacting our churches:

Divorce: Divorce among Christians has become a common occurrence in the Church in our country. An older generation of Christians can remember a time in which divorce rarely occurred in their congregations or even among their communities. Sadly, such is not the case anymore. Statistics do not have to be cited to prove this point. Most could make a list of Christians they personally knew in their congregations who have divorced.

There are many reasons why divorce occurs. On any list of the most com-mon reasons why divorce occurs, financial reasons can always be found. Too many Christians have unrealistic financial expectations. If a married couple cannot have the biggest house, newest car, nicest clothes, send their children to the most prestigious college, they believe they cannot be happy. Some couples have put unnecessary financial strains on themselves at the expense of their marriages and families. Even if their marriage does not end in divorce, their diluted perception of what is important in life impacts their spirituality and the spirituality of their children in devastating ways. This happening at the family level impacts the local church: a unit largely comprised of families.

Lack of involvement in the Church: Materialism can be evidenced in Christianity in American by the lack of involvement Christians have with their local churches. Essentially, too many Christians are overwhelm-ingly concerned with materialistic pursuits. How many Christians in our congregations can only attend one service on Sunday because they work? How many Christians are unable to attend mid-week Bible studies because they are busy with work? How many Christians are too busy to attend their congregation's Gospel meetings? How many Christians are too busy to at-tend Gospel meetings at other congregations? How many high school and college age Christians are too busy pursuing their education to participate in the above mentioned activities of the local church? How many men are too busy seeking to fulfill materialistic goals instead of preparing themselves to one day serve as deacons and elders? How many parents do not encourage their sons to become preachers because it is not as lucrative as some business position? How many parents do not encourage their daughters to become godly homemakers and mothers? How many reading this are still unconvinced Christianity is not threatened by materialism?

Materialistic pursuits of local churches: The recent history of the Church in our country, post-World War II, illustrates the extent to which materialism has impacted Christians. The economic prosperity that followed the end of World War II provided many Americans with great opportunity. Employment increased. As a result, disposable income of families and individuals increased. Christians, and by extension local churches, prospered financially. For example, in 1940, the average disposable personal income level was $77.8. By 1950, the level had risen to $210.1.[9] This statistic represents the amount of money families had to spend at their discretion after taxes.

This increase in financial wealth was noticed by leaders in the Church. Of course, during the 1950s and 1960s, the Church suffered major division. Issues of institutionalism were debated. Not only did local churches begin to financially support various colleges and orphans homes, they began to embark on major building construction projects. This was partly done to gain broader acceptance in the religious culture of America. After all, the other "churches" in town had beautiful, architecturally attractive buildings.

Richard T. Hughes documented this shift in his book, *Reviving the Ancient Faith*. Hughes describes the efforts of once prominent church leader M. Norvel Young to call on congregations to modernize their facilities. Well known throughout the country as a preacher, Young wanted congregations to construct large, attractive buildings located in respected places in town. He encouraged congregations to build facilities with nurseries, offices, educational areas, large fellowship rooms with cooking facilities. In 1957, he and James Marvin Powell authored a book entitled, *The Church is Building*. Their book described how brethren should go about constructing their

---

[9] U.S. Census Bureau. Personal Income and its Disposition. *http://www.census. gov/compendia/statab/2007/tables/07s0657.xls - 2007-10-30*. Accessed 6 October 2010.

new buildings.[10] In this book, Young and Powell reported one thousand new church buildings had been constructed since 1940 and were valued at $147 million.[11] Clearly, materialism impacted the Church during this time.

We do not live in the 1950s. The *Institutional Movement* has come and gone. What lessons can be learned from this movement's materialistic, superficial approach to Christianity? While we may be able to recognize fixed Biblical patterns that were violated by the institutional church, the spirit of the movement can be seen among faithful brethren to certain degrees. Serious and honest introspection is needed as to how we are attempting to present ourselves to our country and the world.

While we may like and appreciate nice, attractive church buildings, are they needed for Christianity to grow and survive in America? The question is not about choosing vinyl siding over brick. The question relates to our motivations for such projects. Aside from needing a place to worship, do we believe a nicer building will attract more people? Do we believe a new, attractive place to worship will give us greater social acceptance by the community? Do we feel pressure to compete with the materialistic culture of Christianity in America?

We need to be cautious as to how we go about presenting Christianity to the world. Literally, millions of dollars of the Lord's money has been spent to construct places for congregations to worship. There is nothing sinful about building a place to worship. Any construction project, albeit new construction or remodeling, costs large amounts of money. However, we should take into consideration the impact a building project will have on our spirituality. Our spirituality is not dependent on a building. Spiritual growth is not and cannot be measured by materialistic standards. The ability for us to spread Christianity in our communities is not dependent on a structure. People cannot be converted to a structure simply because a structure cannot save anyone. Paul clearly stated, "God that made the world and all things therein, seeing that he is Lord of heaven and earth, dwelleth not in temples made with hands; neither is worshipped with men's hands, as though he

---

[10] Richard T. Hughes. *Reviving the Ancient Faith: The story of churches of Christ in America* (244-250). Wm. B. Eerdmans Publishing Company. Grand Rapids, Michigan, 1996.

[11] David Edwin Harrell, Jr. *The Churches of Christ in the 20th Century: Homer Hailey's Personal Journey of Faith* (157). University of Alabama Press. Tuscaloosa, Alabama, 2000.

needed anything, seeing he giveth to all life, and breath, and all things" (Acts 17:24-25). People can only be converted to Christ. This process takes place through genuine obedience to the Gospel (Rom. 1:15-17).

Jesus' View of Materialism

Jesus is the author of Christianity. The whole system of faith rests upon Him, His blood, and His doctrine. The only means by which pure Christianity can survive the threat of materialism in America is by appealing to Jesus. Jesus spoke extensively about the threat of materialism. Materialism stands in direct opposition to spirituality. In His teaching, Jesus informed how humanity could become spiritual. Only by becoming spiritual can we find contentment, peace, joy, and salvation. These and all other spiritual blessings available in Jesus are not in the slightest way dependent on gaining material objects.

The greatest dissertation on Christianity ever given came from Jesus. During the second year of His public ministry, Jesus found Himself at the pinnacle of His fame and notoriety. While on a mountain in Galilee a great crowd anxiously gathered to listen to His uniquely insightful words. His words were unexpected, radical, and challenging. The sermon describes the nature and essence of the kingdom of God and the character of citizens of this eternal, spiritual kingdom. A great portion of His sermon considered materialism.

In the sixth chapter of Matthew, Jesus revealed the perception which citizens of His kingdom must have about material goods:

> Lay not up for yourselves treasures upon earth, where moth and rust doth corrupt, and where thieves break through and steal: But lay up for yourselves treasures in heaven, where neither moth nor rust doth corrupt, and where thieves do not break through nor steal: For where your treasure is, there will your heart be also. The light of the body is the eye: if therefore thine eye be single, thy whole body shall be full of light. But if thine eye be evil, thy whole body shall be full of darkness. If therefore the light that is in thee be darkness, how great is that darkness! No man can serve two masters: for either he will hate the one, and love the other; or else he will hold to the one, and despise the other. Ye cannot serve God and mammon (Matt. 6:19-24).

In this section of His sermon, Jesus drew the great contrast between the material world and the spiritual kingdom. Contextually, Jesus identified material wealth as being a self-constructed barrier which hinders us from the soul saving love of God. He instructed His followers not to consume their lives pursuing material wealth or objects. Material objects do nothing to profit the soul. Material objects are not lasting. They lose their appeal. They are unable to satisfy. They deteriorate and decay. Instead, Jesus instructed His followers to consume their lives by pursuing spiritual qualities. These qualities, such as the beatitudes of chapter five, will profit our soul's salvation.

After stating this command, Jesus illustrated the point He was trying to make. Light comes into the body through the eye. If light does not come into the body, the body is in darkness. Jesus is preaching about the effect of perception. If our perception of what is of the single greatest importance in our life is on materialistic gain, we live in utter spiritual darkness. Following this illustration, Jesus emphatically stated we cannot serve two masters. Jesus revealed truth which many either do not believe or struggle to accept. Many believe we can serve two masters. We sometimes believe we can strike some kind of a balance of service. We can pursue material satisfaction and spirituality at the same time. Jesus dispelled this delusion of the Devil. We cannot serve God with all of our hearts while pursuing riches. Pursuing riches and God is symptomatic of a divided heart.

As Jesus came to the end of this part of His teaching, He instructed the audience what they were to pursue in the place of material goods. Jesus stated, "But seek ye first the kingdom of God, and his righteousness; and all these things shall be added unto you" (Matt. 6:33). Jesus defined the single most important goal, purpose, and pursuit of humanity. We are to seek first the kingdom and righteousness of God.

Seeking first the kingdom and righteousness of God implies sacrifice. In order to serve God acceptably, we must be willing to sacrifice anything and everything in pursuit of Him. For one rich young man, his wealth was too great a sacrifice to make to follow Jesus (Mark 10:17-31). After asking what he needed to do to inherit eternal life, Jesus told him, "One thing thou lackest: go thy way, sell whatsoever thou hast, and give to the poor, and thou shalt have treasure in heaven: and come, take up the cross, and follow me. And he was sad at that saying, and went away grieved: for he had great possessions" (Mark 10:21-22). This man being wealthy was not sinful. His unwillingness to part with his wealth was sinful. He was unwilling to sacrifice for the purpose of totally and completely devoting himself to God. He had greater love for his possessions than he had for Jesus.

Finally, on another occasion in which Jesus spoke to a large audience of people, Luke recorded more of His important teaching related to materialism (Luke 12). A man listening to Jesus was impressed by His ability to pass judgment, His authority, or both. This was evidenced in the request made by the man: "…Master, speak to my brother, that he divide the inheritance with me" (Luke 12:13). This man wanted what was owed to him. Jesus responded to the man's request by stating, "Man, who made me a judge or a divider over you?" (Luke 12:14). Jesus was not interested in this man's request or his inheritance. Instead, Jesus began to warn the crowd against materialism: "Take heed and beware of covetousness: for a man's life consisteth not in the abundance of the things which he possesseth" (Luke 12:15). Jesus addressed the character of the materialistic: they are covetous. Covetousness also can be used to describe the motivation behind the pursuit of materialistic gain. Jesus' teaching certainly stands in contrast to what the world teaches about the measure of happiness, success, and achievement.

After stating these truths, Jesus illustrated His doctrine with a parable. He described a man who had become financially stable, if not wealthy. After the man had achieved such great success, he decided he needed bigger barns to store his goods. After deciding to build larger barns, he determined to retire and enjoy the fruits of his labor for the rest of his life. Not only did he trust exclusively in his wealth to sustain the remainder of his life, the man did not express gratitude to the source of his blessings: God. In a moment of what this man must have perceived as happiness, God said to him, "Thou fool, this night thy soul will be required of thee: then whose shall those things be, which thou hast provided?" (Luke 12:20). While this may have sounded harsh to those to whom Jesus was teaching, Jesus concluded by making a profound spiritual point. Jesus applied this parable by stating, "So is he that layeth up treasure for himself, and is not rich toward God" (Luke 12:21). Material goods are spiritually profitless and those who believe otherwise are fools.

What Can We Do?
Having identified the threat of materialism, we must consider what we can do to overcome this danger. Simply wringing our hands about the danger and threat of materialism will do little to solve this problem. Consider the following actions we can take to prevent Christianity from being damaged or even lost in our country by the threat of materialism.

1. *Live by the teaching of Jesus.* "But seek ye first the kingdom of God, and his righteousness; and all these things shall be added unto you" (Matt. 6:33). In another passage, an inspired author wrote, "But without faith it is

impossible to please him: for he that cometh to God must believe that he is, and that he is a rewarder of them that diligently seek him" (Heb. 11:6). The word "diligently" describes the quality of our seeking. Diligently seeking God entails a willingness to sacrifice anything and everything that will hinder us from the love of God.

To help analyze the quality of our diligent pursuit of God, we should reflect on our life goals. There is not a Christian in the kingdom of God who could not spiritually benefit from rethinking the goals of his life. The goals of one's life indicate what is of the utmost priority to him. The pursuit of materialistic goals has led to the sacrifice of one's Christianity. Jesus taught, "If any man will come after me, let him deny himself, and take up his cross daily, and follow me" (Luke 9:23). Jesus expects His followers to daily deny or disown their selfish ambition and replace it with His ambition for us.

2. Invest in the word of God. Paul wrote, "All scripture is given by inspiration of God, and is profitable for doctrine, for reproof, for correction, for instruction in righteousness: That the man of God may be perfect, thoroughly furnished unto all good works" (2 Tim. 3:16-17). We make all types of financial investments. Investing in the word of God is the greatest investment we could ever make. In order to gain what it has to profit, we must invest our lives in learning and applying its message. People driven by materialism invest in the wrong places, in the wrong things.

3. Devote ourselves to prayer. Prayer is a demonstration of our dependence on God. Materialistic people are people who believe in themselves and their own ability. To be a profitable citizen in the kingdom of God, we cannot trust in ourselves. Instead, we must exclusively trust and rely on God to provide for us. The writer of Hebrews stated, "Let us therefore come boldly unto the throne of grace, that we may obtain mercy, and find grace to help in time of need" (Heb. 4:16). Materialism blinds our eyes from seeing our spiritual needs.

4. Learn contentment. Perhaps this is the most difficult challenge for us as Christians living in such a materialistic society. Paul expressed how he was able to learn contentment: "Not that I speak in respect of want: for I have learned, in whatsoever state I am, therewith to be content. I know both how to be abased, and I know how to abound: everywhere and in all things I am instructed both to be full and to be hungry, both to abound and to suffer need. I can do all things through Christ which strengtheneth me" (Phil. 4:11-13).

Paul suffered a great deal for the cause of the Lord. Through his sufferings, he learned how to find joy and contentment, neither of which were dependent on material goods. Rather than try to find ways to gain material goods, Paul learned to live with what he had and primarily focused on growing spiritually. Our natural inclination is to focus on gaining material goods at the expense of our spirituality. This was not Paul's approach to serving God and should not be ours either.

Another passage in the book of Hebrews stated, "Be ye free from the love of money; content with such things as ye have: for himself hath said, I will in no wise fail thee, neither will I in any wise forsake thee. So that with good courage we say, The Lord is my helper; I will not fear: What shall man do unto me?" (Heb. 13:5-6). Imagine reading this passage while living in abject poverty. Our spiritual growth and salvation are not dependent on our material goods. A person in poverty has the same potential for spiritual maturity as a person who is wealthy.

Collectively, these four actions will lead to spiritual growth. Personal spiritual growth affects every relationship in which we are engaged. Marriages will grow stronger. Families will become established on God and His word. Local churches will become brighter beacons of light to a world in spiritual darkness. Souls will be strengthened and saved when we commit ourselves to the work of the Lord. These pursuits will require personal, material sacrifice. Are we willing to bear the cost?

Conclusion

On one occasion, Jesus spoke to a large crowd of people on the sea shore. From a boat, He spoke of the ways in which people would react to the word of God in their lives. To illustrate this, Jesus spoke of a man who planted seed (Matt. 13). The seed represented the word of God and the various soils upon which the seed was planted represented different people and the influences in their lives. Some seed was planted on ground overtaken by thorns. While the seed blossomed for a time, eventually the seed was choked by the thorns. The thorns represented riches and the anxieties of life. Imagine the collective effect riches and the anxieties of life could have on a group of Christians in a given location. Could not materialism cause Christianity to disappear in America? If not, why not? We must take this weapon of the Devil seriously. We must use God's word in our lives to protect our salvation and ensure pure Christianity is preserved for the next generation.

Bibliography

Earnhart, Paul. *Invitation to a Spiritual Revolution: Studies in the Sermon on the Mount.* Floyd Knobs (IN): Gary Fisher, 1998.

Harrell, David Edwin, Jr. *The Churches of Christ in the 20th Century: Homer Hailey's Personal Journey of Faith.* Tuscaloosa: University of Alabama Press, 2000.

Hughes, Richard T. *Reviving the Ancient Faith: The story of churches of Christ in America.* Grand Rapids: Wm. B. Eerdmans Publishing Company, 1996.

Hullar, Link & Scott Nelson. *The United States: A brief narrative history.* Wheeling (IL): Harlan Davidson, Inc., 2001.

Irvine, Martha. "Today's youth more focused on being wealthy, polls find," *Akron Beacon Journal* (23 January 2007). Retrieved from *http://www. ohio.com/mld/ohio/news/nation/16523989.html.* Accessed 26 January 2007.

Knight, Kevin. "Council at Ephesus," *The Catholic Encyclopedia.* Retrieved from *http://www.newadvent.org/cathen/05491a.htm.* Accessed 05 November 2010.

Longhenry, Ethan R. *Churches of the New Testament.* Chillicothe (OH): DeWard Publishing Company, 2008.

Materialism—What Matters? All About Philosophy.org. Retrieved from *http://www.allaboutphilosophy.org/Materialism.html.* 02 November 2010.

Middleman, Udo W. *The Market Driven Church.* Wheaton (IL): Crossway Books, 2004.

Platt, David. *Radical: Taking back your faith from the American Dream.* Colorado Springs: Multnomah Books, 2010.

The *Christian Post* Interview: David Platt on the American Dream, Radical Christianity. Conducted 15 May 2010. Retrieved from *http://www.christianpost.com/article/20100515/interviewdavid-platt-on-the-american-dream-radical-christianity/page2.html.* Accessed 02 November 2010.

"The Epistle of Ignatius to the Ephesians." *Early Christian Writings.* Retrieved from *http://www.earlychristianwritings.com/text/ignatius-ephesians-roberts.html.* Accessed 10 November 2010.

U.S. Census Bureau. Personal Income and its Disposition. *http://www. census.gov/compendia/statab/2007/tables/07s0657.xls-2007-10-30.* Accessed 6 October 2010.

Christianity Can Survive . . .

The Threat of Islam

Andrew Roberts

Rehearsing numerous terrorist activities of Muslim militants is unnecessary. Who would deny that various Islamic sects read and practice the teachings of the Qur'an fundamentally? This leads to violence. Since Al-Qaeda hijackers used airplanes as guided missiles on the World Trade Center and the Pentagon (September 11, 2001), over 16,500 deadly terror attacks have

Andrew Roberts was born December 30, 1978 in Indianapolis, IN. He married his high school sweetheart, Julie (McColgin) on June 8, 2001. They have two daughters, Erin Elizabeth (5) and Olivia Claire (2).

Andrew graduated from Indiana State University in 2000 with a B.S. in Communication Studies. In 2001, he completed a year-long preaching internship with the Brownsburg church of Christ (Brownsburg, IN). In 2002, Andrew began serving as an evangelist with the Jackson Heights church of Christ (Columbia, TN).

In 2004, Andrew's Bible class workbook on Islam and Christianity was published, *Night and Day: A Comparative Study of Christianity and Islam.* Since then, he has written another adult Bible class workbook (*The Lion Is the Lamb: A Study of the King of kings, His glorious kingdom, and His promised return* [2008]) and two class workbooks for teenagers: *The Purity Pursuit* (2005) and *The Gospel and You* (2009). Additionally, Andrew's articles have appeared in *Biblical Insights* magazine.

Andrew has been able to encourage several younger preachers, facilitating both summer and year-long preacher training programs at Jackson Heights church since 2004. Andrew has done gospel meeting work in Alabama, Georgia, Illinois, Indiana, Kentucky, Tennessee, and Virginia. He has made two evangelistic trips overseas to the Commonwealth of Dominica and he hosted a daily radio broadcast for five years, *The Bible Way.*

been perpetrated around the world.[1] Thousands upon thousands of lives have been taken in the name of Allah's cause – recently. *Threatened,* is perhaps a mild word to capture the emotional reaction of American Christians to the rising profile and popularity of Islam in the West.

Yet, the survival of Christianity is not threatened by potential persecution, martyrdom, or the possibility of going underground in some nations. Through the ages, Christ's followers have faced scourging in synagogues (Matt. 10:16-17), lions in coliseums, and papal inquisitions. Christianity is still here. As Tertullian observed, "The blood of the martyrs is the seed of the church" (*Apologeticus,* chapter 50). Persecution might threaten the physical well-being of *a Christian,* but it cannot eradicate Christianity.

The greatest threat of Islam is that precious souls are being indoctrinated with a false religion. It is not just people in faraway lands that submit to Islam, but the rapid growth of Islam in the West means that our communities, neighbors, and families will interact with Muslims and deal with Islamic influences. Are Christians ready to explain the faith and contend for Christianity in a society that holds no allegiance to, or has little knowledge of, the Bible? Whether we personally feel that a man-made religion is altruistic or dangerous and deadly, Christians cannot abandon anyone to errant faith-systems. Love for our neighbor compels us to offer everyone the opportunity of the gospel (2 Cor. 5:14-20).

Christianity can survive the threat of Islam. After all, "the gates of hell" cannot prevail against Christ's church (Matt. 16:18, KJV). But is the Bible mandate merely to *survive,* or are Christians to "make disciples of every nation," "warning every man and teaching every man" the gospel of Jesus Christ (Matt. 28:19-20; Mark 16:15; Col. 1:28)? Survival might be all that Christians can hope for if the Islamic challenge is met by fearful, double-minded, or apathetic brethren. But if Christians will take courage, put Christ first, and care for their fellow man, they won't have to travel great distances to the mission field of Islam, the field is coming to them.

The Trouble of Frightened Disciples
Christianity can survive the threat of Islam but there is danger if disciples are frightened. Fearful saints are often silent and hidden saints. How can

---

[1] *www.thereligionofpeace.com.* Accessed 12/13/10. This website monitors international news outlets to collect, report, and offer analysis on militant Muslim activities around the globe.

Christianity survive the threat of Islam if disciples, crippled by fear, fail to take the gospel to Muslim neighbors?

Paul reminded the young minister Timothy, "For God has not given us a spirit of fear, but of power and of love and of a sound mind" (2 Tim. 1:7). While Christians can take courage from reading such assurances, many find themselves intimidated by the idea of talking to Muslims about religion. Two common reasons account for this fear:

1. Many Christians feel ignorant as to what Muslims believe and are unprepared to answer. Islam seems foreign and unknown to many believers in the United States. The unknown is intimidating.

2. There is a fear of violent reprisal for broaching spiritual subjects with Muslim acquaintances. Maybe brethren in the U.S. don't know a lot of Muslims personally; the Muslims that they see on nightly television news reports are murdering people and blowing up buildings and cars. Masked Muslim men are filmed chanting verses of the Qur'an and hoisting assault rifles in the air. These images coincide with the stories of soldiers, Jews, Christians, even other Muslim sects being attacked.

It is time to move from fear to faith.

Christians are more prepared than they realize to evangelize Muslims. Solomon's words are true, "there is nothing new under the sun" (Eccl. 1:9). The more Christians learn about Islam, the more they will be struck by the similarities it shares with other false faith-systems that brethren know about and have been contending with for decades.Obviously the names and dates differ, but there are tremendous echoes in religious error.

The Qur'an Is A Latter-Day Revelation

For instance, Christians have known groups that follow a latter-day revelation. Islam does, too! Islam claims that Allah has revealed his religion, Islam,[2] to two other groups of people before the Arabians: Jews and Christians.[3] The Qur'an asserts that Allah gave the Bible – the Old Testament and the New Testament.

---

[2] "Islam" means "submission." It does not mean "peace." Islam is the religion of submission to the one God Allah in accordance with the teaching of Allah's prophet, Muhammad. A Mulism is one who submits.

[3] The Qur'an speaks of "People of the Book." These are people groups that received scripture from Allah in the past, but corrupted it or rejected it. Specifically, the People of the Book are Jews and Christians.

He has verily revealed to you this Book, in truth and confirmation of
the Books revealed before, as indeed He had revealed the Torah and the
Gospel (Surah 3:3).[4]

But Allah could not safeguard his word. Satan has tampered with those
holy books and he used Jews and Christians to do it.

We have sent no messenger or apostle before you with whose recitations
Satan did not tamper (Surah 22:52).

The Muslim contention is that Allah was revealing Islam to the Jews
through prophets like Adam, Noah, Abraham, *Ishmael*, and Moses – meaning the Old Testament Israelites were actually Muslims. But after a while
the Jews corrupted Islam and so Allah sent Jesus Christ to teach the Jews,
along with the rest of the world, Islam (Surah 5:42-47). But then the followers of Jesus corrupted Islam and created Christianity. This required Allah
to select Muhammad to be his final mouthpiece, the Seal of the Prophets.
The Qur'an is to be accepted as the final word of Allah to Muslims and
the rest of the world, superior to his previous and corrupted revelation, the
Bible (Surah 22:52-53).

O people of the Book, Our Apostle has come to you, announcing many
things of the Scriptures that you have suppressed, passing over some others. To you has come light and a clear Book from God (Surah 5:15).

Twenty-first century Christians have heard similar charges against the
Bible's integrity. The Mormon church, particularly, come to mind. How
long have they been peddling their latter-day revelation on Christian's
doorsteps? What do brethren say to Mormons? Eventually they point out
their inconsistency and fallacious attitude toward Scripture. How can Mormons (or Muslims) be so sure that their holy book is sound? If the Bible
is corrupted, how can they be certain their book is not corrupted? If their
god has allowed his word to be tampered and wrecked in the past, why
couldn't it happen again?

There is no reason to fear the Qur'an. English translations are easily
procured. Anyone can read it and comprehend its precepts (Surah 12:1-3).
They will find that it is not Scripture. It falls far below the bar of Inspira-

---

[4] *Surah* means revelation. The Qur'an is composed of 114 *Surahs*. Each one has
a name and multiple verses. Muhammad orally recited the Qur'an, piece meal,
over a 22 or 23 year period. Quotations from the Qur'an are given with the
Surah number and verse number. They are taken from Ahmed Ali's *Al-Qur'an: A
Contemporary Translation*.

tion. It is mired with pointless repetitions, threats, mistakes, and contradictions. In fact, one of the first apostates of Islam was a scribe working with Muhammad, writing down the supposed revelations that comprised the Qur'an. One *hadith*[5] recounts that 'Abdollah b. Abi Sarh (the scribe) actually made suggestions to Muhammad to make improvements on the words of the Qur'an – and the prophet consented!

> On a number of occasions, he had, with the Prophet's consent, changed the closing words of verses. For example, when the Prophet had said, "And God is mighty and wise" (*'aziz, hakim*), 'Abdollah b. Abi Sarh suggested writing down "knowing and wise" (*'alim, hakim*), and the Prophet answered that there was no objection. Having observed a succession of changes of this type, 'Abdollah renounced Islam on the ground that the revelations, if from God, could not be changed at the prompting of a scribe such as himself. After his apostasy, he went to Mecca and joined the Qorayshites (Dashti, 98).

The Qur'an's numerous internal contradictions confuse Islamic doctrine on a variety of issues. Three examples make the point and show how the Qur'an can "teach it both ways":

* Either Allah created the world in six days (Surah 10:3), or Allah created the world in two days (Surah 41:9, 12).

* Either Christians (and Jews and Pagans) can enter Paradise so long as they do good deeds (Surah 2:62), or Christians are damned because they are Christians and not Muslims (Surah 9:30; 98:6).

* Either Islam is tolerant and there is no compulsion in religion (Surah 2:256), or Islam is exclusive and Muslims are to militantly persecute unbelievers – that is, non-Muslims, until they die, convert, or flee the land (Surah 47:4-11).

The Islamic Doctrine of Abrogation
How do Muslims accept a book that is consistently inconsistent con-

---

[5] *Hadith* are collections of the activities and sayings of Muhammad. They are not considered inerrant or the word of Allah, like the Qur'an. These were oral traditions and stories of the prophet's life that were collected and written hundreds of years after his death. While the *hadith* writings are not believed to be inspired, they are incredibly authoritative. Muslims use the *hadith* to aid in interpreting the Qur'an and they are a large component in the mandates of *Shariah* Law.

cerning matters of faith and practice?[6] Islam's defense for Muhammad's confusion and contradictions throughout the Qur'an is the doctrine of *naskh* or abrogation.

> Naskh is based on the fact that the Qur'an was revealed to Muhammad at different times over a period of about twenty-two years. Some parts of the Qur'an came later and some parts came earlier. To solve a contradiction, they decided that new revelations would override (*nasikh*) previous revelations (Gabriel, 30).

Muhammad's revelations released him from the burden of keeping his teaching straight. He evidently lacked the ability to remember specific phrases or the details of religious histories he was narrating. So, if what he said on a Monday differed minutely or even majorly from what he said on the subject two years ago, stick with what he said on Monday.

> If We pleased We could take away what We have revealed to you (Surah 17:86).

> When we cancel a message (sent to an earlier prophet) or to throw it into oblivion, We replace it with one better or one similar. Do you not know that God has power over all things? (Surah 2:106).

The Qur'an, itself, demonstrates that Muhammad's contemporary critics (especially Medinan Jews knowledgeable of the Old Testament) criticized this shifty and convenient doctrine.

> When we replace a message with another – and God knows best what He reveals – they say: 'You have made it up;' yet most of them do not know (Surah 16:101).

The Jews of Medina never accepted his revelations as divine because Muhammad's revisions of the Old Testament simply demonstrated his ignorance on the matter. Finally, Muhammad militantly removed any detractors from the town. Dr. Farah commented on Islam's prophet, "Although his knowledge of the scriptures was not as deep as that of the experts, it enabled him, at least to his own satisfaction, to meet the criticism of his Jewish adversaries in Medina; criticism which lapsed so strongly into derision that he could eliminate it only by uprooting the Jews from the city and its environs" (Farah, 85).

---

[6] Examples of inconsistent doctrine have already been cited. But there were changes in practices such as worship forms as well. When Muhammad initially instated the *salat* (5 daily prayers), he taught Muslims to bow toward Jerusalem. After his fallout with the Jews at Medina, he taught his followers to pray facing Mecca (Surah 2:142-147).

The doctrine of Abrogation authorized Muhammad to "cut-and-paste" the Bible! However, when Muhammad began his prophetic career in A.D. 610, the Old Testament canon had been closed for a millennium (the New Testament completed for five centuries). The audacity to *correct* the Scriptures was just too much for "the People of the Book" to accept. It still is.

Now, fast-forward 1400 years to the present and consider the conflicting messages the world gets about the *real* Islam. Is it inherently peaceful and tolerant (just like twenty-first century post-moderns love their religion) or is it tyrannical and violent? Is it inclusive or exclusive? Are the *jihadists* hijacking the Qur'an or are they simply obedient to its precepts? Because of Abrogation, Muslim scholars argue over which direction was actually Muhammad's last word. The Qur'an really does teach it both ways! However, when the Qur'an is interpreted through the lens of the *hadith*, the war verses tend to stand unquestioned and un-abrogated.

The standard of Scripture, set forth in the Bible, is Truth (2 Tim. 3:16-17; John 17:17). Truth does not contradict itself. Furthermore, Jesus argued that the Scripture cannot be broken (John 10:35) and His detractors did not disagree. Jesus did not come to *nasikh* the Old Testament but to fulfill it (Matt. 5:17-18; Luke 24:44-49). Genuine scripture is not forgotten, corrupted, or overridden – it is fulfilled (Isa. 55:10-11; Matt. 24:35).

Muhammad Was A Self-Appointed Prophet

Modern Christians do know how to answer proponents of a latter-day revelation and they have contended with groups that follow self-appointed prophets, as well. Muhammad belongs on the same list with Joseph Smith, Brigham Young, Charles Taze Russell, Ellen G. White, and Herbert W. Armstrong. Sure these other "prophets" were not as influential as Muhammad, but they are of the same ilk. Turn fear to faith. There is nothing supernatural about self-serving prophecies. Christians are better prepared to take the gospel to Muslims than they realize.

Despite the Apostle Paul's warning in Galatians 1:6-9, Muhammad claimed that the angel Gabriel confronted him in the mountains outside of Mecca and gave him the message to preach: Islam. While claiming to be the progression (or rather, correction) of Christianity, Muhammad's message breaks so completely from New Testament Christianity that it constitutes another religion.

For a time, Muhammad wanted to be viewed as a prophet in the Biblical tradition – an Abraham or a Moses – for Arabians. But the content of his teachings and the character of his life quickly exposed him as a fraud to people with a Biblical background.

Anyone can claim to be a prophet, but if God has not chosen him then he is a false prophet (2 Pet. 2:1). How does one determine who is a real prophet? God gave two tests for the Israelites to use and discern genuine prophet-hood.

1. A sign or wonder would accompany the prophet's message (Deut. 13:1-2). This test continued into the New Testament, in that, miracles and signs confirmed the identity of Jesus Christ and the preaching of His apostles (John 20:30-31; Mark 16:20).

2. The prophet's message must be consistent with all previously confirmed revelation and scripture (Deut. 13:2-5). God does not contradict Himself. Jesus Christ was not contradicting the Old Testament; His gospel fulfilled it (Matt. 5:17-18; Gal. 3:19-25).

Muhammad did not pass these tests. According to the Qur'an, he worked no miracles, signs, or wonders.[7] The Qur'an, itself, was supposed to be the sign that convinced people of his prophetic credentials.[8] As to the second test, Muhammad made little pretense that there would be consistency between his teachings and the Bible. Instead, he attacked the Bible and asserted it was a corruption of Allah's word. Furthermore, he endowed himself with the power of Abrogation.

Islam's prophet failed both tests of genuine prophet-hood and was unwilling to personally abide by the message he preached to others. A casual reading of Surah 33 demonstrates that Muhammad was a law unto himself.

Let's start with polygamy. Muslim men are limited in their polygamy to four wives (Surah 4:3). But Muhammad could marry as many women as he wanted.

We have made lawful for you, O Prophet, wives to whom you have given

---

[7] According to Surah 6:37 and Surah 29:48-50. Here we emphasize that the Qur'an says he worked no signs or miracles. The Qur'an is what Muslims accept as the inspired word of Allah, free from any fault. In the *hadith*, Muhammad is said to have worked miracles. For instance it is reported that he cut the moon in half one night with his finger. On another occasion Allah made water shoot out of Muhammad's fingers to provide for his thirsty soldiers and livestock.

[8] Consider Surah 10:37 and Surah 17:88.

their dower, and God-given maids and captives you have married, and the daughters of your father's brothers and daughters of your father's sisters, and daughters of your mother's brothers and sisters, who migrated with you; and a believing woman who offers herself to the Prophet if the Prophet desires to marry her. This is a privilege only for you and not the other believers. We know what we have ordained for them about their wives and maids they possess, so that you may be free of blame, for God is forgiving and kind (Surah 33:50).

History tells us that Muhammad had between thirteen and sixteen wives following the death of his first wife, Khadijah. His youngest bride was Aisha and she was only nine years old when they wed.

Now, when Muslim men choose to marry multiple wives, the Qur'an directs them to do so "only if they can love them all with equity" (Surah 4:3). Islamic scholars have interpreted this passage to mean that a man has a set rotation of relations with his wives and he is not at liberty to ignore the rotation. However, Muhammad got a revelation that allowed him to be with any wife he desired, whenever he desired.

You may defer the turn of any of your wives you like, and may take any other you desire. There is no harm if you take any of those (whose turn) you had deferred. This would be better as it would gladden their hearts and they will not grieve, and each will be happy with what you have given her. God knows what is in your heart, for He is all-wise and benign (Surah 33:51).

The Qur'an directs a proper etiquette for visiting Muhammad. Apparently he tired of Muslims dropping by unannounced or staying too long or asking too many questions or even looking at his wives. So, Allah intervened.

O you who believe, do not enter the house of the Prophet for a meal without awaiting the proper time, unless asked, and enter when you are invited, and depart when you have eaten, and do not stay on talking. This puts the Prophet to inconvenience, and he feels embarrassed before you; but God is not embarrassed in (saying) the truth. And when you ask his wife for some thing of utility, ask for it from behind the screen. This is for the purity of your hearts and theirs. It does not behoove you to annoy the prophet of God, or to ever marry his wives after him. This would indeed be serious in the sight of God (Surah 33:53).

Notice at the end of Surah 33:53 that Muhammad's widows could not marry another Muslim man. However, Muhammad could (and did) marry the widows of some of his *jihad* raiders (Surah 33:50).

A final example of self-serving prophecy is requiring Muslims to bless their prophet. His name is too special to be spoken or written by Muslims without the accompanying phrase, "peace be upon him." Fourteen hundred years or so later, Muslims still revere their prophet in this way. Supposedly, Allah commanded Muslims to address Muhammad in this fashion.

> God and His angels shower their blessings on the Prophet. O believers, you should also send your blessings on him, and salute him with a worthy greeting (Surah 33:56).

The Qur'anic evidence of self-serving prophecies goes beyond these examples. Sadly, one out of six people on Earth believes this Surah to be the eternal, uncreated, uncorrupted word of Allah. Such selfish prescriptions are believed to be divine.

Muslim apologists try to defend Muhammad's violent raids, biblical ignorance, fiery rhetoric, and lechery[9] by contextualizing him in sixth century Arabia. They argue that, if modern religious students would just remember the kind of chaotic, might-makes-right society that Muhammad was raised in and eventually conquered, they would appreciate that he was no worse than the next Arab and better than most. But consider that Christians have no cause to rationalize any of the statements or actions of Jesus Christ. There is no reason for Jesus' disciples to be ashamed or make excuses for His words or behavior to other cultures or times. His message and manner are transcendent and timeless. That's a message that Christians need to share with others.

Why Do Muslims Fight?
Fearful Christians can allay some concerns by learning more about Islam. It is not so different from common experiences with other man-made religions. What is to be done about the fear of violence? Understanding why some Muslims commit acts of terror inspires the greater urgency among disciples of Jesus Christ to take the gospel to their neighbors.

> Whatever I tell you in the dark, speak in the light; and what you hear in the ear, preach on the housetops. And do not fear those who kill the body but cannot kill the soul. But rather fear Him who is able to destroy both soul and body in hell (Matt. 10:27-28).

---

[9] Besides the child-bride Aisha, Muhammad took his son's wife, Zaynab, for himself. Again, special revelations from Allah commanded Muhammad to perform what the Apostle Paul describes as an "unheard of" sexual immorality (1 Cor. 5:1). Read about it in the Qur'an, Surah 33:36-38.

The threat of physical persecution is in no way supposed to quiet the voice of the faithful. In fact, raise your voice on the housetops.

What gain is there for the Muslims who kill others or die themselves in suicide missions hoping to kill unbelievers? The Qur'an teaches that death in *jihad* (the holy struggle in the cause of Allah) is the only way a Muslim is assured Paradise. Otherwise Muslims have to live out their lives trying to do more good deeds than bad deeds in order to go to Paradise.

There is no savior in Islam. Each person tries to save himself. Muhammad's teaching on the Final Judgment is that a Muslim will have all the deeds of his life placed before him on a giant scale – good deeds on one side and evil deeds on the other. If one has done more good in life then he goes to Paradise – more evil and he goes to Hell. Which will weigh more? Here's the catch, the Qur'an does not reveal how much any deed weighs. How good is good enough? How many times will a young boy have to help a little old lady across the street to make up for cheating on his grammar test at school? No one knows.

Islam is truly a salvation by works religion. The Qur'an states, "Remember that good deeds nullify the bad" (Surah 11:114).

> When one converts to Islam, they are converting to a lifestyle of meritorious works. They perform good deeds which hopefully outweigh their bad deeds. . . .No substitutionary death is necessary in Islam. Humans transgress against Allah, and humans can make it right by performing good deeds, Surah 9:53-63; 11:114. This is a true religion of works. There is no grace, and there is no savior. It is the Muslim against himself. Will he do more good or more evil in his lifetime? (Roberts, 111- 112).

The glory of the gospel of grace shines brightly against the bleak background of works righteousness. The words some Christians may take for granted would be truly amazing to some Muslims' ears.

> For by grace you have been saved through faith, and that not of yourselves; it is the gift of God, not of works, lest anyone should boast. For we are His workmanship, created in Christ Jesus for good works, which God prepared beforehand that we should walk in them (Eph. 2:8-10).

Five particular works are required of every Muslim to be devout and stand a chance on Allah's scales. They are known as the Five Pillars of Islam.

1. *Shahada* (Surah 2:112) – Confessing faith in Islam. Reciting this simple mantra is all that is involved with a person submitting and becoming

Muslim: "There is no God except Allah. Muhammad is the prophet of Allah." This confession is the first pillar of Islam. When a person says that, he is a Muslim.

2. *Salat* (Surah 4:103) – This is the ritual prayer recited five times a day: dawn, noon, mid-afternoon, sunset, and nightfall. There are prescribed bows and ablutions to be done, and all while facing Mecca.

3. *Zakat* (Surah 2:110) – This is Muslim almsgiving. Zakat is a compulsory annual contribution of at least 2.5% of income for the poor and needy of the Muslim community.

4. *Sawm* (fasting) during Ramadan (Surah 2:183) – the holy month of Ramadan is observed by a complete fast from food, drink, and sexual relations from sun up to sun down. Then when the sun goes down there is great celebration in the evenings. The infirm are excused from fasting, if that would harm them, however.

5. *Hajj* (Surah 2:196) – A Muslim is required to make one pilgrimage to Mecca once in his life to perform special rites and rituals at the *Ka'bah*. This trip is called the *Hajj*. Islam retains holy sites while Jesus Christ taught His followers that God is worshipped in spirit and in truth (John 4:20-24).

A system of salvation by works is exhausting and discouraging. Put yourself in the Muslim's shoes for a moment. Could you do enough good deeds in the remainder of your life to outweigh every careless word, every impure thought, every wicked transgression? Are you that smart, that strong, that noble, and that good? Who is up to that task? Honest, devoted Muslims turn to the Qur'an and find there is only one sure way to eternal reward.

> So, when you clash with the unbelievers, smite their necks until you overpower them, then hold them in bondage. Then either free them graciously or after taking a ransom, until war shall have come to end. If God had pleased He could have punished them (Himself), but He wills to test some of you through some others. He will not allow the deeds of those who are killed in the cause of God to go to waste. He will show them the way, and better their state, And will admit them into gardens with which he has acquainted them (Surah 47:4-6).
>
> If you are killed in the cause of God or you die, the forgiveness and mercy of God are better than all that you amass. And if you die or are killed, even so it is to God that you will return (Surah 3:157-158).
>
> And those who were deprived of their homes or banished in My cause,

and who fought and were killed, I shall blot out their sins and admit them indeed into gardens with rippling streams (Surah 3:195).

That is the end of a man-made religion – a religion without a savior. Their hope lies in *suicide*. In fact, the eternal reward for fallen *jihadists* has prompted some Muslims to call *jihad* the sixth pillar of Islam.

Socio-political pundits think that Muslim terrorists are all poor, disenfranchised youths.[10] They reason that few jobs and little education pushes Muslims to such extreme measures. The theory is that by improving economic conditions in Muslim countries militant recruiting can be curtailed. But blue jeans, cheeseburgers, and automobiles aren't going to rewrite the Qur'an. Basically the pitch is Materialism – if the West could just give Muslims reasons to love this life a little bit more, perhaps they will be less concerned about how their soul will fare eternally. It is really insulting when you think about it.

Christianity provides what Islam, as well as Materialism, cannot – the Savior. Jesus Christ provides the living hope for all mankind that tomorrow can be better than today (1 Pet. 1:3-5). (I will show how Islam undermines the doctrine of Christ later in this lecture.) Each day brings Christians one day closer to an eternity with the redeemed.

The reality of Islam challenges Christians to turn fear to faith and care more for their fellow man's soul –a Muslim's soul – than their own creature comfort.

The Trouble of Double-Minded Disciples

Christianity can survive the threat of Islam but there is danger if disciples are double-minded. Are saints in the United States responding to the challenge of Islam as Americans first, or as Christians? Patriotism and Christian devotion do not have to be opposed to one another, but they certainly are not synonymous. The threat of Islam forces American Christians to settle the first-love in their hearts: Is it God or Country?

The Christian's response to the challenge of Islam should not be the same as the U.S. State Department's response. The challenge is different and the appropriate response is different. While the U.S. State Department is concerned with battling the terrorist activities of some Muslims – it completely

---

[10] In 2007, the London Airport bombing was planned and executed by Muslim architects and doctors. They did not lack in education, wealth, or a Western societal influence. Neither did they lack in devotion to the Qur'anic teaching of *Jihad*.

lacks the equipment, strategy, ability, or will to confront the real enemy: the false religion of Islam. Brethren do have the weapons to engage and win spiritual warfare – not in the name of Liberty or America, but in the name of Jesus Christ (2 Cor. 10:3-5; Eph. 6:10-18).

Well-meaning brethren can get consumed with the danger Islam poses to the United States. They must not forget the eternal threat Islam poses to souls. U.S. citizens want to know what their leaders are doing to safeguard airlines, defend borders, and protect national security. But what are saints doing to secure a soul from the influence of Islam or even rescue a soul from the clutches of this false religion? The goal of the gospel is not the preservation of any national state but the redemption of souls. In Christ's kingdom, all Christians are citizen-soldiers.

God's eternal plan for the ages never included a corporal messianic kingdom. Bible believers rightly correct Premillennialists, Postmillennialists, Dispensationalists, and Zionists for their tireless "prophetic" expectation and endeavors toward a Theocratic State. The true New Testament contention is that Jesus' kingdom is His church – the body of the redeemed. Perhaps some saints need to be reminded also that Christ's kingdom is not of this world (John 18:36). Thus, it is neither the Israel of 1948 nor the United States of America. His kingdom supersedes any physical territory for the citizenship is composed of precious souls from every tribe, tongue, people, and nation. All scripture is inspired; the U.S. Constitution is not.

There is no biblical authority for a Christian State. God has neither authorized nor legislated it in the pages of the New Testament. Not surprisingly then, historical examples of "Christian Nations" are cautionary tales for future civilizations. They have been and will continue to be the unholy hybrid of politics and apostasy. The true church has always suffered under such conditions.

Some brethren today may have a greater interest in the preservation of their nation or culture than the proclamation of the gospel. They worry plenty about corporal threats and mayhem or the potential of persecution – where is the worry for lost souls? For example, there was an occasion some time ago, when I was preaching on the differences between Islam and Christianity. As the service dismissed that evening, a brother led the closing prayer and said, "Lord, help all them Muslims to see what a bunch of idiots they are." He concluded with stirring words to the effect, "May the United States of

America stand forever." When he was done praying, I wasn't sure if I was supposed to say, "Amen," or recite the Pledge of Allegiance.

Muslims are not idiots, they are deceived. The U.S. State Department defines the enemy as particular terrorists. Christians understand the real enemy is the false religion of Islam, and he who is behind *all* false religions. While terrorists should be brought to justice for their crimes, Muslims must be brought to Jesus for their salvation. He died to redeem their souls as well (1 John 2:2).

Answer the Threat of False Religion

False religion is one of Satan's oldest and most effective weapons. Jesus Christ explained that the devil is a murderer, a liar, and the father of it (John 8:44). In Satan's arsenal of wiles and "fiery missiles," errant faith systems surely bring the greatest return for his effort (Eph. 6:11-12, 16). The devil plants the seed for every apostasy and false gospel that attack the Lord's church from within (Matt. 13:24-30; 2 Cor. 11:13-15). Likewise, his evil genius should be credited for the myriad of man-made world religions and philosophical alternatives to Christianity. These darken men's eyes to the truth and rob God of His rightful glory (Rom. 1:20-25).

False religion is insidious. Under the guise of truth, enlightenment, and eternal reward, millions of souls through the ages have committed themselves to darkness and the bondage of sin. Adherents have a misplaced confidence and false hope. They raise their children into the same errant systems. In this way, the devil keeps generation after generation deceived and lost.

Yet the danger of most false religions is imperceptible due to the veneer of altruism. Religions seem to help mankind. They appear genuine and re-demptive. Western culture – including U.S. society – has largely accepted that all religions are basically the same. Whether it be called post-modern thought, multi-culturalism, or religious pluralism, the prevailing societal attitude toward religion is that all faith systems are equally good and le-gitimate. This attitude says, "Sure the names and number of deities differ, there are different holy books, and every religion has its own name for an afterlife; but, basically every religion teaches people to respect each other, do no harm, help the less fortunate, and try your best. So pick the one that works for you." While that sounds so inclusive and tolerant, such a men-tality actually manifests disrespect toward every religion. Robert Morey challenged people to do better.

In the field of comparative religions, it is understood that each of the major religions of mankind has its own peculiar concept of deity. In other words, all religions do not worship the same God, only under different names. The sloppy thinking that would ignore the essential differences which divide world religions is an insult to the uniqueness of world religions (Morey, 53).

The exclusive claims of Christ make it impossible for Bible believers to accept religious pluralism (John 14:6). There is the truth of the gospel recorded in the Bible (Col. 1:5), and then there is every competing religion and philosophy that is antagonistic to the faith (2 Cor. 10:4-5; 1 Tim. 6:20-21). Thus, the adherents of Islam are lost and their influence only entices (in some cases coerces) people away from the true and living God, to damn them as well. "Blind leaders of the blind" personifies every errant religion, including Islam (Matt. 15:13-14).

The freedom of religion that the U.S. guarantees for her citizens is a precious grace that has allowed Christians to assemble, worship, and evangelize without fear of persecution. We are thankful for this. But the fate of Christianity is not tied to the fate of America or Western Civilization. Nations rise and nations fall. Could Christianity survive the persecution of an antagonistic Theocratic State? It was born into such circumstances!

What Christians must realize and embrace is that the clash with Islam is not won by nations, armies, or policies. Victory can only be achieved mind by mind, heart by heart, and soul by soul as individuals learn and obey the gospel of Jesus Christ. If a Christian gets resolved and dedicates himself to be more active and devoted in *the Lord's work*, he can win a soul to Christ. One renewed mind can help America. But does it follow the other way? What if a Christian gets resolved to be a more active *American*? The country gets his best energy and effort. Are souls the priority or is legislation, candidates, and policy the priority? Can you legislate conversions to Christ?

It is time for Christians to get resolved: The answer to Islam is not "God and Country." It is God. As long as double-mindedness lingers on this point, brethren are hindered in making the real difference: answering false religion and leading a lost soul to the savior Jesus Christ.

The Trouble of Apathetic Disciples

Christianity can survive the threat of Islam but there is danger if disciples are apathetic. Lukewarm Christians have long sickened the Lord (Rev. 3:14-19). When local churches decline it means that brethren are not teaching the gospel to non-Christians. There might be any number of reasons for this situation, but this is the reality of the situation. Apathy is likely a major cause. Many brethren today are too busy and distracted by vocation, entertainment, hobbies, and the like, to invest the effort to teach the gospel to another person. Many struggle with getting their own children to worship assemblies regularly, let alone instilling the faith in them.

Some people cannot comprehend the devotion militant Muslims manifest when they orchestrate a terrorist attack that is inevitably a suicide mission. They kill and die for their religion. They understand the Qur'an to instruct such behavior against unbelievers and there is the assurance of Paradise if they do die in the *jihad*. If anyone in the world should understand such complete surrender to the will of a higher power, it should be New Testament Christians. The Bible calls them, "a living sacrifice" (Rom. 12:1-2). Early Christians like Stephen and the apostle James showed that following Jesus Christ meant making sacrifices up to, and including, their lives. However, the message of the Bible is radically different from the Qur'an.

> Were the Bible to command Christians to take life for God's glory, rather than lay it down, Christians would be militant also, if they were genuinely committed to the truth, Psalm 119:151; John 17:17; Colossians 1:5-6; 1 Timothy 3:15. Muslims find themselves in this very predicament and are wholly devoted to an evil deception they believe to be the truth (Roberts, 16).

There is so much Muslims do to propagate their religion beyond *jihad*, though. In the West, terrorist bombings will not spread and increase the influence of Islam as effectively as an articulate presentation of their beliefs coupled with the general moral uprightness of their families. Any culture will work to resist a perceived military invasion. But Islam's clear moral and religious absolutes dynamically fill the religious void left in Western culture by the effects of secularism, religious pluralism, and Christian denominationalism. If more of "Christendom" cared to follow Jesus, the picture would be different. But that would mean conviction and work. Sadly, many believers are too distracted, lazy, or apathetic to do more than occasionally assemble in the name of Jesus.

Conversely, Muslims are working hard at spreading their religion. William Wagner's research chronicled three population centers that Muslims are actively proselytizing in the U.S.

1.   Muslims are targeting academic institutions with Islam. "Islam has

taken advantage of American openness and has made great progress in *Da'wah*[11] in our schools that are closed to Christianity. The educational institutions of the West will be a major battleground for Islam in the future" (Wagner, 49). Colleges and Universities that are struggling financially accept large donations from wealthy Muslim nations, and in turn build Islamic Study Centers or Institutes of Religion. These are taught by Muslim professors trained in the sponsoring nations. Even elementary and secondary schools in the U.S. are exposed to Islamic doctrine under the titles of "Multicultural Studies" but Christianity is not given equal time.

2. Muslims are targeting prisons with Islam. "It is estimated that more than 300,000 prisoners are converts to Islam, and that the rate of conversion may be more than 30,000 each year" (Wagner, 50). Some prisons have significant Muslim populations and retain a Muslim chaplain to minister to them.

3. Muslims are targeting minority populations with Islam. "Islam is focusing on people groups in America and the West and is creating strategies to meet the needs of these target peoples. As of now the numbers are not large, but as Christians have learned, people who feel displaced or alienated are more open to conversion than those who have deep roots. The minorities in America fit into this category" (Wagner, 57).

Are Christians getting outworked by Muslims?

Is it apathy that is keeping Christian parents from raising their children in the nurture and admonition of the Lord? When it is observable that our children will have greater exposure to Islam at school than previous generations could have imagined, how important do home devotions, good Bible classes, and participation in the local church become? What else should brethren be learning about and teaching their children about to equip them to discern God's truth from errant religions in their "Multi-cultural Studies" course? Christianity is, after all, words of truth and reason (Acts 26:25). This requires work, but the work will answer the challenge of Islam!

Is it pride that is keeping Christians from preaching to criminals? Ney

---

[11] *Da'wah* means invitation. It loosely equates to the Christian concept of evangelism. When Muslims work to teach their faith to non-Muslims, restore backsliding Muslims to the faith, or just set a proper example of living the Muslim lifestyle before others, this is *Da'wah*.

Rieber's *A Resource for the Study of Islam* came about as a result of his working in prisons to spread the gospel. In his preface, he relates how encountering Muslims in that setting forced him to learn about the religion. Perhaps more brethren need to follow his example. Muslims are having great success in correctional facilities.

Is selfishness or racism keeping Christians from reaching out with God's word to minorities? If you do not care about the soul of your neighbor, proponents of false religions will. It is ungodly to look down on a person for his race or poverty (Col. 3:11; Jas. 2:1-4, 8-9).

Well-funded Muslim communities are moving out of their storefronts and engaging in building campaigns across the country. Headlines and public controversy have accompanied planned mosques everywhere from Manhattan, NY to Murfreesboro, TN. Clearly Muslims are working to propagate their faith. The distinct architecture of mosques, amidst the established church buildings and business offices of the "nice section of town," sends a message of legitimacy and permanency to the community. Islam is here to stay.

The neighbors and children of New Testament Christians could be inoculated against the false religion of Islam, but only if they have received the Truth. May it not be the apathy of saints that enables a false religion to steal away hearts and minds that might otherwise be influenced for Christ.

It is time to move from apathy to zeal.

Christianity: Survival or Revival?
Christianity cannot be overthrown because it is of God (Acts 5:38-39). Controversy and persecution have purifying effects as they purge pretenders from the church (1 Pet. 4:12-13). Both hypocrites and aberrant versions of Christianity wane in the face of hardships. Christianity is not going anywhere, of course it will survive.

But in our moment – this society, at this time – survival should not be the goal. Survival sets the bar far too low for Christians blessed with the freedom of religion, personal liberty, education, affluence, and the latest communication technologies.

> For everyone to whom much is given, from him much will be required; and to whom much has been committed, of him they will ask the more (Luke 12:48).

On top of all that, New Testament Christianity has a 200 year head-start on this continent over the Muslims. This is not the time for survival, but revival – the goal is revival!

The challenge of teaching Muslims the gospel seems daunting. Is it even possible? Is there any hope for people who have denied Jesus Christ? Let's ask Peter (John 18:15-18, 25-27; 21:15-19). Could people who have violently opposed the Truth be won over by it? How would Paul answer (Gal. 1:22-24)?

Talking Points with Muslim Contacts

Peter and Paul would encourage Christians today to make every effort to preach the gospel of Jesus Christ to people of other religions – especially Muslims. Besides their personal experiences, their life's work was to take the Word to a world where nearly everyone was of another religion – Jewish sects, Greek philosophies, polytheists, and pantheists (Mark 16:15; Col. 1:5-6, 23). But even Christians who want to see the church thrive and revive wonder where to begin talking to a Muslim about Christ.

There is some common ground to be found between Muslims and Christians. Some of the moral values that most Muslims espouse are shared by Bible believers. For instance, Muslims typically oppose alcohol consumption, theft, fornication, adultery, homosexuality, and murder. Many work to shield their families from immodest dress, rock'n'roll music, and secular philosophy. Most are pro-marriage (though Christians reject the polygamy permissible in Islamic states), pro-family, pro-community, and industrious.

Always remember when talking to a Muslim, you are speaking to that individual. He may or may not be open to discussing religion. Find out what he believes. There is a wide spectrum of interpretation and practice of the Qur'an among Muslims – particularly in the West. The Muslim you meet may or may not interpret the Qur'an via a straightforward reading of its teachings. Do not assume or attribute any belief to a Muslim that he does not personally affirm. Get to know that person as much as you can. Some Muslims will refuse any kind of interaction with brethren because the Qur'an specifically forbids it.

O believers, do not hold Jews and Christians as your allies. They are allies of one another; and anyone who makes them his friends is surely one of them; and God does not guide the unjust (Surah 5:51).

O believers, do not make friends with those who mock and make a sport

of your faith, who were given the Book before you, and with unbelievers;
and fear God if you truly believe (Surah 5:57).

Yet, other Muslims will be quite approachable.

For instance, a few years ago I had lunch with the president of the Islamic
Center of Columbia (TN). It was a great experience. A local civic organization had invited him to speak and explain the tenets of Islam to their club.
A luncheon preceded the presentation. Surprisingly, the menu was sausage
and kraut! I observed that the president quietly sat at the head-table sipping
a glass of water while everyone else around him ate. I'm sure it was an
unintentional mistake and that few in the room realized there is an Islamic
prohibition on pork. But how unfortunate. After his speech (and answering
individuals' questions privately for an additional 45 minutes), I asked him
if I could buy him lunch. He accepted.

At a local restaurant, we began with small talk and get-to-know-you
conversation. He grew up in Jerusalem. He was raised in a Muslim family,
living in a Jewish neighborhood, attending a private Catholic school. Upon
graduation, he traveled to the U.S. to attend medical school and stayed to
go into medical practice. Over the course of our lunch, the conversation
turned to religion. We talked about Jesus mostly.

He was genuinely misinformed about the biblical revelation of Jesus.
He was convinced that the most common Bible title for Jesus was, "son
of Mary." I kindly corrected him, explaining that while it is the most common title for Jesus in the Qur'an, He was only called "son of Mary" on one
occasion in the Bible, and that by his detractors (Mark 6:3). At issue here
was the identity of Jesus; is He truly the Son of God or a mere mortal? The
president did admit he could be mistaken on what the Bible said.

Islam denies that Jesus Christ is the Son of God. What Christians term,
"the good confession," Muslims label, *shirk*, the unforgivable sin (Surah
4:48; 5:72-73). *Shirk* means association and speaks to associating anything
created with the creator, Allah. *Shirk* is idolatry. Muslims hold that Jesus is
a created being and to them, being a Christian is being an unbeliever and
an idolater.

> The Christians say: "Christ is the son of God." That is what they say with
> their tongues following assertions made by unbelievers before them. May
> they be damned by God: How perverse are they! (Surah 9:30).

The Jesus that most Muslims know is the one revised and re-written by the teachings of the Qur'an. The Qur'an's Jesus was created in the same manner as Adam (Surah 19:35-36; 3:59), was a prophet who taught Islam to the Jews, worked miracles (Surah 5:110), and was miraculously translated to Paradise without tasting death. He did not accept worship, He would not be called the son of God (Surah 5:72; 9:30; 17:111), He did not die upon the cross (Surah 4:156-158), and there was no resurrection. The Quran's Jesus is an Islamic prophet.

The other main discussion we had at lunch that day was about the cross of Christ. The president explained that it makes no sense for Jesus to die on behalf of others. If people do wrong before Allah, then people can do right before Allah. Allah can choose to forgive whoever He wants; why should forgiveness be predicated on the death of an innocent? He was convicted by the clear teaching of the Qur'an.

Remember that good deeds nullify the bad (Surah 11:114).

The challenge is that we were following two distinct books. The Bible gives no such economy of works. The wages of sin is death, not community service (Rom. 6:23). Therefore Jesus died as the propitiation for sins to redeem and justify sinners (Rom. 3:23-26; 1 John 2:2). No sinner has the ability to save himself; salvation is by grace through faith in Jesus Christ (Eph. 2:8-10). Redemption is accomplished by the blood of Jesus (Eph. 1:7; 1 Pet. 1:18-19). While the gospel calls men to "be saved from this perverse generation" (Acts 2:40), they cannot save themselves. Sinners merely respond, avail themselves, of salvation offered in Jesus Christ. The obedient and faithful response to the gospel message is repentance, confession, and baptism into Christ for the remission of sins (Mark 16:15-16; Acts 2:38-41; 8:36-39; Gal. 3:26-27; Heb. 5:8-9).

Our lunch ended amicably though neither one of us persuaded the other. Here are some lessons I took away from my talk with the president of the Islamic Center. Perhaps they will be helpful to other brethren in the future.

Be mindful of the religious tenets of Islam when trying to build a bridge and influence a Muslim neighbor or coworker for Christ. Without compromising the convictions or doctrine of Christ, try to honor the conscience and sentiments of the Muslim with whom you are talking (1 Cor. 9:19-22).

Try to be hospitable and invite him out to eat or even to your home, but not on a Friday (or Friday evening) when Muslims attend Mosque.

Do not repeat the civic club's blunder and serve foods that the Old Testament identified as "unclean." Muhammad enjoined the Jewish dietary regulations on Muslims.

Be prepared to talk about Jesus, God, Adam, Noah, Abraham and a host of others that Muslims think they know from the Bible – but they do not. Many Muslims assume more overlap of detail and doctrine between the Bible and the Qur'an than actually exists. You might be the first person to share the biblical identities and accounts of these well-known names with a Muslim contact.

Here are some additional considerations when trying to share the good news with Muslim contacts.

Avoid any perceived familiarity with Muslim members of the opposite sex. As much as possible, Christian women talk to Muslim women and Christian men talk to Muslim men. A member of the Lord's church in Montgomery, AL told me of his effort to befriend a Muslim coworker. The coworker had recently immigrated to the U.S. and his family was still in Iran. The Christian was talking about family to the man and sharing several photographs of his wife and children. He asked the Muslim, "Do you have a picture of your wife?" "I do."

"Oh great, can I see it?"

"No, you may not."

My brother in Christ was surprised and offended at his coworker's curt reply. What my brother in Christ failed to realize was (in all likelihood) their Iranian next-door neighbor had never seen the uncovered face of this man's wife, so he certainly wasn't going to show her face to some American infidel! Ironically, he had insulted his Muslim coworker's sense of modesty and propriety while trying to befriend him.

Another consideration is how you will handle your Bible in the presence of Muslims. The Qur'an is the holiest object in a Muslim's home. It is supposed to reside in the highest place in the house. It is never to touch the ground. That is how Muslims are taught to handle a holy book. So, if Christians set Bibles under their chairs or toss them into the backseat of the car or slap them around on a podium, it says to Muslims that the Bible is less than holy. They already believe it is a suspect volume, Christians must be careful to avoid nonverbally discrediting the Bible further in Muslim eyes by reckless handling.

Remember that the gospel converts one soul at a time. The world's 1 billion Muslims present an enormous mission field for Christians to work . . . and so we must go to the work. It is time for Christians to turn fear to faith, embrace singleness of purpose, replace apathy with zeal, and so meet the challenge of Islam with the light of gospel truth.

Bibliography

Ali, Orooj Ahmed. *Al-Qur'an: A Contemporary Translation*. Princeton, NJ: Princeton University Press, 1993.

Dashti, Ali. *Twenty Three Years: A Study of the Prophetic Career of Mohammad*. Translated by F. R. C. Bagley. Costa Messa, CA: Mazda Publishers, 1994.

Farah, Caesar E. *Islam* 6th Edition. New York, NY: Barron's, 2000.

Gabriel, Mark A. *Islam and Terrorism*. Lake Mary, FL: Charisma House, 2002.

Morey, Robert. *The Islamic Invasion*. Las Vegas, NV: Christian Scholars Press, 1992.

Rieber, Ney. *A Resource for the Study of Islam*. Ft. Worth, TX: Star Bible Publications, 1993.

Roberts, Andrew. *Night and Day: A Comparative Study of Christianity and Islam*. Summitville, IN: Spiritbuilding Publishing, 2005.

Wagner, William. *How Islam Plans To Change The World*. Grand Rapids, MI: Kregel Publications, 2004.

The Threat of the Breakdown of the Home

Phillip Owens

Cultural changes often come so incrementally that they are imperceptible to many, especially younger people. However, to the unbiased casual

---

Phillip Owens was born in Birmingham, AL in 1960, and grew up in that city. He attended the Ensley and later Midfield congregations. His father baptized him about the time he graduated high school.

Phillip attended Georgia Tech (1978-1980). During this time in Atlanta he began filling in as preaching and teaching opportunities presented themselves. The first person he baptized was a schoolmate at Georgia Tech. In 1981, he moved to Athens, AL where he finished his Bachelor's degree in Secondary Education in the fields of English and Social Sciences. There he worked in a two-preacher arrangement with Lynn Headrick and the Jackson Drive congregation. From 1983-85 he preached with the Holland's Gin congregation north of Athens and also taught Bible with the Athens Bible School. During that time he met Leigh Ratliff from Hanceville, whom he married in 1986.

Phillip moved to Dallas, TX for a year's work with the Easton Rd. congregation (1985-1986). Phillip and Leigh moved from Dallas to Waycross, GA for four years of work with the church on Tebeau Street (1986-1990). Their son Wesley was born there in '89. During the time in Waycross, Phillip also drove to Brunswick, GA to help with the work there. They moved to work with the West End church in Richmond, VA (1990-1993), then to Hobart, IN for five years (1993-1998). Moving back to Athens in 1998, Phillip worked with the Jackson Drive congregation until 2005, followed by a five year period of work with the Elgin Hills congregation in Rogersville, Alabama. During eleven of twelve years in Athens, he taught Bible each day with the Bible School. Phillip and his family moved to Birmingham in June, 2010, and he has worked from then to the present with the Flint Hill congregation in Bessemer.

Music has been a hobby for Phillip all his life, and he has taught song worship leading everywhere he has worked. He has also done much radio work, as well as written pamphlets and articles for bulletins and newspapers. He is currently working on Bible class material which takes students through the whole of the Bible.

observer who is at least middle aged and can make comparisons to earlier years, the *typical* American home is in shambles. Simply finding a home in which there is a husband and wife who are also the biological parents of their children is often difficult. Evidence abounds that this is true.

We understand that every generation has its problems with immorality and other sins, but generally speaking, there is a vast difference between most American homes now and homes during the 1950s and 1960s. Many scoff at the idea of going back to the television days of *Leave it to Beaver, Lassie,* and *Father Knows Best.* Now on television, not only does a father never know best, he is usually portrayed as a goon. And if television shows only slightly reflect American culture, *Desperate Housewives, Modern Family,* and *King of Queens* paint a dismal picture of typical families.

The purpose of this study is to show how and why the home has broken down, how it has affected other areas, and what Christians can do to counter it. Providing such should give Christians hope for an intact family for themselves and ammunition against a culture whose hedonistic philosophies are destroying them.

Christians who are aware of why most families in America are in disarray, and who know what the Bible teaches on the home, are in a grand position. Knowing and practicing God's will helps us keep our own families together here, and enjoy heaven in the hereafter. Additionally, God can use us as a "channel of blessings" for others. Not only can we help them see how God's wisdom and superior guidance provide the glue to keep families together, but we can also most importantly help them see what they need to do to be saved. Such a study can help us be "lights in the world" of "a crooked and perverse generation" (Phil. 2:15).

Past American Homes Generally Reflected
Respect for Bible Principles

In 1998, journalist Tom Brokaw wrote *The Greatest Generation,* a book about people who were children during the 1920s, came of age during the depression of the 1930s, fought overseas in the Second World War during the 1940s, and returned to build families, careers, and communities. These men and women are in their eighties and nineties now. The book chronicles their struggles and heroic efforts as they successfully made life overall better for everyone than what they earlier experienced. Brokaw even has a section of chapters entitled, "Love, Marriage, and Commitment," three ideas the Bible connects, but sadly which most in our country now do not (Mal. 2:14; Matt. 19:6).

More recently Brokaw commented on that "generation" in *The Wall Street Journal* and said, "As I began to write the wartime accounts of that generation, I realized how much they were formed by the deprivations and lessons of the Great Depression. During that period life was about common sacrifice and going without the most ordinary items, such as enough food or new clothes. . . .So many veterans told me they got their first new pairs of shoes and boots when they enlisted" (June 6, 2009).

My own father was among those. He told me that when he enlisted, not only was that the first time he had new shoes, but that boot camp was also the first time he remembered having three meals a day. He gained thirty pounds in six weeks, and thought that military service life was a breeze compared to how things had been at home. Black and white photographs of young men being inducted during those years indicate that obesity was not a problem. For most Americans, life during the 1930s and 1940s was tough. Living with little food and few material possessions doesn't make one righteous, but it helps keep most from a sense of entitlement and selfishness, and usually helps produce more thankfulness when conditions improve.

Furthermore, with no government subsidies, families were more interdependent. During the years between the 1920s and 1940s, the United States was still primarily an agrarian society. Children were expected to help more with manual labor jobs around the house or farm. All needed to "pull their weight" for the very survival of each other.

Most American families were intact as the Bible teaches (Eph. 5:22-6:4). Quite unlike today, fathers were usually husbands, mothers were their wives, and they lived together with their children. Fathers brought in the "dough" and mothers made the bread. Mothers were more homemakers than breadwinners.

Discipline in the home and school was more common than not. Obedience on the part of children was expected, and corporal punishment was meted out for rebellion without those in authority being fearful of recrimination.

Structure, consistency, supervision, and general teaching on morality in the family – basic Bible principles – made schools different fifty years ago from now. Most have seen a list of "top problems" teachers encountered in the 1940s versus the 1990s. Talking out of turn, chewing gum, making noise, running in halls, cutting in line, and dress code infractions had top billing for 1940s problems. Fifty years later, drug and alcohol abuse, pregnancy, suicide, rape, robbery, and assault show rottenness in the very core of society, which in its basic unit is the family. While not wanting to paint all families and society in general as a utopia, at the same time there was more respect for God's will and ways in family life than at present.

Language that is commonly spoken by parents and children or allowed to be heard (such as on television, radio, or in songs, etc.) has tremendously regressed the last two generations, but it only mirrors the decline of our overall culture. One's speech is an index to his heart (Matt. 15:18). Public speech is an index to the collective heart of a community. Therefore, the speech we commonly hear indexes a profane and careless society with an obsession for things sexual. Forty years ago, the kind of language heard now in families was "locked" to locker rooms. Men knew to "clean up" their language in public. This does not mean that profanity, vulgarity, and coarse remarks about sexual matters were justified in private, but deep down people understood that such was not "healthy" for anyone and they were only "getting away" with it for the time. Such was called "foul" speech and was generally abhorred.

When families allow God's name to be used carelessly in profanity and euphemisms, and speak so openly and loosely about sexual matters that are dealt with in Scripture with delicacy (see 1 Cor. 7:1-5), such evidences a spiritual pathology. While cursing and profanity are as old as man, for at least the first seventy years of the twentieth century, respect for God and His word kept it out of most public discourse. The firestorm that *Gone with the Wind* set off in 1939 with the use of one phrase attests to this. While America has never been a "Christian nation" insofar as the Bible describes it, there was obviously more respect for and belief in God and the Bible as His word then than there is now.

These Biblically based elements which tied families together affected not only home life, but also entertainment, schools, the work place, and local churches. In general, these virtues affected all of American society. Again, we certainly would not paint those years as a utopian, but among the population *generally speaking,* there was a higher sense of duty, morality, commitment, devotion, and respect for things related to God than there is today. While it is easy for people of one generation to overstate the virtues of their own and deprecate those among succeeding generations, casual observations reveal that what we are saying is true. Additionally, statistics paint the same dismal picture.

Statistical Shifts in Families during the 1960s and after Indicate a Breakdown of the Home

Fifty years after those black and white photographs of malnourished young inductees were taken, our country had not only defeated the Axis Powers of the Second World War, but we had also witnessed the collapse of the Soviet empire. Our country was viewed by the rest of the world as being economically prosperous and militarily supreme. However, despite greatness in those areas, we were then and continue to be in a decades-long cultural decline.

In 1993, Bill Bennett and The Heritage Foundation published *The Index of Leading Cultural Indicators.* Six years later, he updated and expanded it adding a subtitle: *"American Society at the End of the 20th Century."* To my knowledge, it is the most statistically detailed assessment of changes in our culture for an approximate forty year period, 1960-1998. Mostly from census and other government records, Bennett quantified areas in "crime, the family, youth behavior, education, popular culture and religion, and civic participation" (Bennett, 2). Among his findings are these depressing statistics:

*   A 511% increase of out-of-wedlock births from 1960-1997 (47).

*   In 1994, for the first time in American history, more than half of all firstborn children were conceived or born out of wedlock (53).

*   Between 1960 and 1998, the percentage of single-parent families more than tripled (57).

*   In 1960, married couples made up almost three-quarters of all households. By 1998, only one-half (64).

*   Number of cohabiting couples increased from 439,000 in 1960 to 4.24 million in 1998, a tenfold increase (64).

*   16 out of every 100 marriages ended in divorce in 1960; 40 out of every 100 in 1998 (69).

*   Odds that a child would witness the divorce of his parents in 1960 – 1 in 4; in 1998 – 1 in 2 (71).

*   Between 1973 and 1996, the abortion ratio increased 35% (81).

- Approximately 60% of children under six years of age *living in families with only a mother* had an income below the poverty level, over five times as many children under six *in married-couple families* (74).

- The United States has the highest divorce rate among Western nations (69).

- The United States has the highest incidence of single-parent families of any industrialized nation (3).

- Among men and women between their mid-20s and mid-30s, living together before marriage is more common than not (3).

Bennett summarizes:

> The nation we live in today is more violent and vulgar, coarse and cynical, rude and remorseless, deviant and depressed, than the one we once inhabited. A popular culture that is often brutal, gruesome, and enamored with death robs many children of their innocence. People kill other people, and themselves, more easily. Men and women abandon each other, and their children, more readily. Marriage and the American family are weaker, more unstable, less normative (5).

Even among politically liberal organizations whose members have little or no respect for the Bible, their statistics indicate that more incidents of child abuse, greater poverty, and less achievement in school come from homes of single parents or co-habiting couples, than from homes of married couples. In a May, 2003 article written by Mary Parke, published by the *Center for Law and Social Policy* and entitled, "Are Married Parents Really Better for Children? What Research Says About the Effects of Family Structure on Child Well-Being," she summarizes:

> Research indicates that, on average, children who grow up in families with both their biological parents in a low-conflict marriage *are better off in a number of ways than children who grow up in single-, step- or cohabiting-parent households* (italics mine, p.a.o.). Compared to children who are raised by their married parents, children in other family types are more likely to achieve lower levels of education, to become teen parents, and to experience health, behavior, and mental health problems. And children in single- and cohabiting-parent families are more likely to be poor. . . .

> In individual situations, marriage may or may not make children better off, depending on whether the marriage is "healthy" and stable. Marriage may also be a proxy for other parental characteristics that are associated with relationship stability and positive child outcomes. The legal basis

and public support involved in the institution of marriage helps to create the most likely conditions for the development of factors that children need most to thrive – consistent, stable, loving attention from two parents who cooperate and who have sufficient resources and support from two extended families, two sets of friends, and society. Marriage is not a guarantee of these conditions, however, and these conditions exist in other family circumstances, but they are less likely to.

Sin costs in many ways. Teenage pregnancies, lower levels of education, behavioral and mental health problems, and higher suicide and crime rates all cost taxpayers billions of dollars. In addition, rather than helping the problem, it is exacerbated by most in high office as they refuse to acknowledge where the real problems lie, and think that by the government's throwing more money into already failed social programs that somehow conditions will improve. As many have said, doing the same thing over and over again and expecting different results is insanity. Yet this is where we find our federal government in relation to the decline of the family. The reason government fails in these areas is because the root problems are *spiritual* in nature. Social ills which many in government think can be eradicated with more money, are only *symptoms* of deeper problems. Social programs attempting to treat truly spiritual problems is tantamount to putting a band aid over a splinter.

Why Is the American Family in Disarray?

While there are many secondary reasons for the breakdown of the home, the primary reason is *a lack of respect for God and His Word.* It is fascinating to note *how* the practice of God's word in any human relationship always improves that relationship. Whether the relationship is between employer and employee, husband and wife, parent and child, citizen and civil government, or members of the church toward elders, deacons, and preachers, there is an efficiency, energy, and prosperity when God's word is followed by all. Since God has spoken in very detailed ways concerning marriage, the family, including specific responsibilities of husbands, wives, parents toward children, and children toward parents, it follows that when God's Word is disregarded in this basic unit, problems will occur.

We do not live in a vacuum. Many influences affect family life. I have chosen three areas which I believe have brought a disregard for God resulting in the dissolution of the family. These include: (1) the writings of a few influential men whose common denominator is disbelief in the inspiration of the Bible; (2) economic prosperity and materialism brought about by political and economic freedoms; and (3) mothers leaving the home. *Keep in mind that the primary reason is a rejection of God.*

1. Writings of influential men have fostered disrespect for God's Word.

All behavior is caused. These causes are based on beliefs. In schools, students are much more likely to misbehave when a teacher is out of the room than when in the room. Why? Students believe that some punishment will be handed down if the teacher *sees* their misbehavior, versus belief that no punishment will come if he doesn't see it. This is basic human nature.

Paul argued that *the historical fact of Christ's resurrection* affected his behavior and should affect the Corinthians. "And why do we stand in jeopardy every hour? I affirm, by the boasting in you which I have in Christ Jesus our Lord, I die daily. If, in the manner of men, I have fought with beasts at Ephesus, what advantage is it to me? If the dead do not rise, 'Let us eat and drink, for tomorrow we die'" (1 Cor. 15:30-32). If Christ had not been raised, Paul and the Corinthians wasted their time and were persecuted for nothing! Such would mean that hedonism is the philosophy to follow. This is the basic philosophy of our day, and what often causes divorce after a brief marriage. A mate doesn't completely "satisfy" the other in every way, and since one's pleasure in life is the chief goal, divorce is the way to opt out.

On the other hand, belief in Christ's resurrection and its implications (eternal reward in heaven and eternal punishment in hell) empower Christians to undergo all manner of persecutions and remain faithful and committed in less than ideal situations (Eph. 1:18-21; Phil. 3:9-10; Rom. 8:18). Commitment to remain in a less than great, but scriptural, marriage when some would bail out, being honest when dishonesty might lead to financial improvement, and in general doing the right thing when the wrong thing is more appealing and less demanding are all behaviors that come from a deep belief – a belief in God, the resurrection of Christ, and the inspiration of His Word.

But what if intelligent men deny the Bible is from God and are able to influence the masses not to believe? Would that not affect behavior? If there is no God, the Bible is obviously not His Word, it carries no weight as a moral standard, and there is no logical reason to be concerned about either heaven or hell. And if we can not be sure about that, why be concerned about commitments in marriage? If there is no heaven or hell, the only discomfort we may endure for marital "indiscretions" or failures with children would be in the court of public opinion, and if enough people can be convinced that there is no God or final judgment, even public scorn may be turned into approval. This is what is happening now relative to homosexuals and their attempt to redefine marriage.

General acceptance of false ideas takes time. But when given enough time and advancement by those considered as "intellectuals," damage is inevitable. During the 1800s and through the mid-1900s, there was a general belief in God and the Bible as His inspired word. Speeches and writings of Lincoln and other renown leaders reflect this deep respect. However, during those same years at least *five* influential men were at work whose writings would undermine respect for God and His Word. I believe their influence is largely responsible for the breakdown of the American family.

First, Charles Darwin (1809-1882) wrote The Origin of Species *in 1859, and later* The Descent of Man, *both of which counter Bible teaching as to our origin as well as our relation to the lower creation.* If we are nothing more than a higher link in an evolutionary chain, our uniqueness and relation to God are gone. Furthermore, if God's Word is not true concerning our origin, is any of it to be trusted?

Darwin was an atheist. His work was a *naturalistic* explanation of our origin; God was left out. *But God has spoken concerning our origin, and it counters Darwin's inferences.* Whom are we to believe? Darwin was a "scientist," so his "findings" (or better, guesses) were taken seriously. Perhaps Genesis 1 needed to be "reinterpreted," at least in such a way as to accommodate Darwin's theories, many thought. His works have affected the fields of biology, sociology, psychology, and provided the basis for anthropology.

Darwin's widely accepted works have done incalculable damage to a world view that places God as the Originator of all things. When God is left out, mankind loses his high and unique position over the rest of the universe. Rather than believing that one is special since he was made in God's image and special to God, giving one a true sense of self worth and self respect, he is left to believe that he is nothing more than a later link in an evolutionary chain of events, and consequently worth less! This also affects the respect we should have for others – they were made in God's image also! Though evolutionists would deny this, I believe there is a "link" between Darwinian thinking / teaching and crimes, including murder (see Gen. 9:6). Abortion could also be tied to consequences of this false teaching. Life is not special.

Which idea fosters more respect for self and others: the idea that we were made with certain likenesses to our Divine Creator who loves and wants the best for us, and wants us to grow to be like Him in character; or that we are simply a link in a long chain of evolutionary events, and are in one sense of no more value than a dog? Speaking of dogs, while the Bible teaches humane treatment of animals, emphasis these days concerning "animal rights" is another consequence of Darwinian thinking. Jesus Himself declared that a man "is of more value than a sheep" (Matt. 12:12). Having little self-respect, as well as lack of respect for others, are logical by-products of Darwinianism. Statistics show that one reason teenage girls allow themselves to be sexually "used" is due to a lack of self-respect.

Another consequence of Darwinian thinking is the abolition of distinct roles between the sexes. In marriage, God assigned headship to belong to the husband and a role of submission for the wife corresponding to the relation existing between Christ and His church (Eph. 5:22-33). However, such teaching has become "sexist" and chauvinistic in our culture. Furthermore, God made distinct differences between the sexes as to spiritual leadership roles. These differences were not based on custom, culture, or education, but rather on things done at creation and shortly thereafter (see 1 Tim. 2:11-15; 1 Cor. 14:34). Confusion and chaos in families as well as "women preachers" in denominations have been consequences of Darwin's influence. Beliefs do have consequences!

Second, the writings of Karl Marx (1818-1883) have undermined the work ethic and personal responsibility in the family. Marx was an atheist and hostile toward all religions. He wrote the *Communist Manifesto* in 1848, and in it he pits the bourgeoisie, those who owned means of production, against the proletariat, those whose only commodity was their labor. He believed that arts, culture, and religion were only diversions imposed by the producers to keep the minds of the workers off their revolutionary and rightful destiny. In essence, communism, which he envisioned as a "classless society," is the answer to social problems caused by capitalism and a free market. Marxism, or communism, is in reality totalitarianism, big government with few in authoritarian positions and all others in peasantry.

Communism's weaker sister is socialism. While it allows some private ownership of goods and services, it seeks to manage them through collective social control. However, both communism and socialism are based on the principle that goods and services produced are controlled and redistributed by a centralized organization. Furthermore, the heart of both socialism and communism is a belief in government as the answer and provider for the good of society. You might ask, "How does this affect the family?"

There are at least two major spiritual problems that grow out of and are associated with these systems of government and economics. *First, both socialism and communism deny what the work ethic promises.* The "work ethic" describes the moral and financial benefit that should come from diligent, hard work. This is a theme throughout Ecclesiastes (see chs. 2:24-26; 5:18), is mentioned often throughout the Bible (beginning with Gen. 2:15), and is basic common sense. If a good or service is provided by an individual, he should be rewarded for it. This is obviously God's view. However, Marx's theory is summarized in the phrase, "From each according to his ability, to each according to his needs." Government takes from producers (those with "ability"), then redistributes to non-producers, the slothful, and everyone else including producers according to what the government says are their "needs." Such collectivism destroys incentives which fuel a free market and encourage hard work. If one who works hard receives the same pay as those who are slothful, incentives to continue to work hard are destroyed. While Marxism sounds benevolent, it is not practical as evidenced by the masses of peasants where it is the form of government.

A second major spiritual problem growing out of Marxism is that it denies personal responsibility in the family. Until the last half century, most in our country believed what the Bible teaches, that *the welfare of our own family is the family's responsibility (1 Tim. 5:8).* If a man is slothful and will not work, he should not eat (2 Thess. 3:10). Benevolent needs for families are to be met by families first, then by the church if families are unable (1 Tim. 5:16). However, regardless of how diligent or slothful a person is, government is the "provider" in a Marxist society. Whether one works diligently or slothfully, government still provides what it believes one "needs." In that sense, a person doesn't "make" money; government "gives" what it thinks one "needs." Therefore, Marxism makes people dependent on government and not themselves for their financial upkeep.

Our great country has incorporated many elements of socialism for years. For example, if a man fathers one or several children and is not married to the mother, government provides housing, and WIC (Women, Infants and Children, a division of the Department of Agriculture) provides milk and other necessities. In the name of doing good and being a benevolent government, it actually exacerbates the problem. When those who bring children into the world are not held responsible for their upkeep or welfare, the practice continues on and on. Children who grow up in such environments without fathers and in unstructured homes are statistically more likely to follow their fathers' example. The family continues to disintegrate. Marx's influence is seen in most schools and university social science departments. What sounds a benevolent tone on the surface is actually anti-God, anti-freedom, and destructive to the family.

Third, Julius Wellhausen (1844-1918) was an influential German Bible scholar whose writings have led to disbelief in the Scripture. He wrote *The Composition of the Hexateuch* in 1877 in which he attempted to prove that Moses did not write the Pentateuch, but that it is a compilation of likely four documents that were derived from independent sources that predated its compilation by centuries. Eventually they were combined into its present form by several "redactors" or editors. This was called the documentary hypothesis or the Wellhausen hypothesis. A year later, he wrote *Prolegomena to the History of Israel,* which was an attempt to trace Israel's development as a nation and religion not to God and inspiration, but rather to non-supernatural origins. As one has said,

> The revolution wrought by these newer constructions, however, is not adequately realized till regard is had to their effects on the picture given in the OT itself of Israel's history, religion and literature. It is not too much to say that this picture is nearly completely subverted. By the leaders of the school, . . . the supernatural element in the history and religion is totally eliminated, . . . little is left standing. The history of the Pentateuch, . . . is largely given up. Genesis is legend, Exodus hardly more trustworthy, Joshua a romance. . . . None of the laws – even the Decalogue – are allowed to be certainly Mosaic. . . . The treatment accorded to the Pentateuch necessarily reacts on the other historical books; the prophetic literature suffers in an almost equal degree through disintegration and mutilation (ISBE, II: 752).

Rather than take what the Scripture says at face value, *Wellhausen and other liberal scholars began from the presupposition that nothing miraculous was ever done.* Such rationalistic assumptions excluded prophecy, since by its very nature it can only be explained as coming from God. Therefore, prophetic statements were explained away as being made after the events they described. But if this were true, prophetic statements are actually lies; they state things will happen in the future when the writer knew they had already occurred! The creation, flood, parting of the Red Sea, and any other miracle are dismissed. The Bible becomes nothing more than legend and myth.

If Wellhausen was correct, the whole of the Bible cannot be trusted since New Testament writers vouched for the authenticity of Old Testament events. Paul declared that Adam was the first man (Acts 17:26; 1 Cor. 15:45); Jesus verified stories concerning the creation (Matt. 19:3-6), flood (Matt. 24:37-39), destruction of Sodom and Gomorrah (Matt. 10:15; 11:23-24), Jonah (Matt. 12:40), and stated that Moses gave the Law (John 7:19). But if those events never occurred, then Jesus was not God's Son because God could not lie and be God (Tit. 1:2)!

Jesus Christ was a historical person who discussed historical events in a historical document (the Bible). If the history on which all of it is based never occurred, the Bible has no value whatsoever. With no confidence in the Bible as being true, nothing it teaches relative to morals is worthy of consideration. Of course, this has severe consequences in the family relationship.

Wellhausen's writings have dominated seminaries for most of the twentieth century. As a result, for the last forty or so years, many denominations that once embraced the Bible as the inspired word of God have only given it lip service. People are not brainless. When they hear supposed preachers deny what the Bible plainly affirms, if they don't study for themselves, and most do not, they lose confidence in the Bible. This explains why some denominations allow homosexuals to be prominent leaders! They have no confidence in the Bible as being from God. Beliefs have consequences.

Fourth, Sigmund Freud (1856-1939) applied Darwin's biological evolutionary theories to psychology resulting in sexual permissiveness, which has led to daily public conversations obsessed with their intimate details. Like Darwin and Marx, Freud was an atheist. Freud's interest in philosophy turned him to study Darwin's theories of evolution, which in turn led him to study medicine. Continuing his interest in philosophy, Freud took a special interest in the writings of Ludwig Feuerbach (1804-1872), who in his *Essence of Christiainty* wrote that God and things spiritual are simply projected creations of men to hold out something that would fulfill their own wishes. Rather than man being created in the image and likeness of God, man created God in an image he liked! Freud expressed contempt for all religions. Whenever atheists begin to explain the causes of human behavior from a worldview in which God is not only rejected, but where there is also hostility toward Him and His Word, the theories are flawed.

A Freudian foundational theory was that sexual urges are the driving force behind all human behavior. Freud believed that our actions and mental problems come from repressed sexual desires. Therefore, those urges need to be discussed openly, and when properly analyzed and controlled, greater social progress results. Consequences of his influence have led to the "sexual revolution" and "free love" of the 1960s and 1970s, which have exacerbated the breakdown of the family. Rather than practicing self control as the Bible teaches, "expressing oneself sexually," "coming out of the closet" for homosexuals, and the "if it feels good do it" mentality all have roots in Freudian thinking.

Furthermore, by-products of his theories result in a hostility toward anyone or organization which would "judge" such behavior as wrong. The rapid move of many in government and society to accept homosexual marriages on the same basis as a heterosexual marriage stems from Freud's influence.

Fifth, John Dewey (1859-1952) is considered the founder of the "progressive education movement," which in many ways has undermined teaching of absolute "values" in schools. Dewey was another atheist, a board member of the American Humanist Association when it created *Humanist Manifesto I,* and was one of its signers. Similar to Freud, Dewey rejected all fixed or rigid, moral behavior. Truth was relative and absolutes were not to be considered.

Dewey believed that as evolving biological organisms are molded by their constantly changing environments and those environments constantly change, man also constantly changes. The logical conclusion is that there are no moral absolutes. Man must look within himself for direction, an obvious denial of Jeremiah 10:23. Further, since the environment is constantly changing, it is useless to teach fixed, moral absolutes in schools. He did not believe in revealed truth, but that anything thought to be truth had to be determined experimentally.

During the 1920s, Dewey introduced his "progressive" theory that children were better taught by "experiencing" or "feeling" all things. Whereas education had emphasized two "domains," the "cognitive" dealing with intellect, and "psychomotor" dealing with vocational skills, during the 1920s Dewey introduced the "affective" domain. Emphasis shifted to feelings, attitudes, values, and beliefs. This gained ground during the 1960s. Progressive education reduces the role of the individual and stresses collectivism or groups, whereas traditional education stressed individualism as the final product of education. Progressive education seeks to adjust a curriculum to the interests of special "groups," whereas traditional education sought to adjust the individual pupil to the curriculum which provided him skills to deal with life in a competitive market.

Beginning with the presupposition that there are no moral absolutes, many educators have used atheistic indoctrination techniques which have undermined moral restraints and absolutes which the Bible and many good parents teach. "Values clarification," "behavior modification," "psychotherapy," "group therapy," "role playing," and "inquiry" are headings describing these techniques (Maddoux, 50-73).

Except for Wellhausen who is best described as a deist, the other four men were atheists. Practically every area of education, including seminaries, has been influenced by these men. While others have obviously influenced culture and families in a deleterious way, the writings of these men have certainly been largely responsible. As earlier mentioned, changes in the family have come incrementally. But the collective beliefs of our society have obviously caused these changes. We have regressed from most having Bible-based intact families to the point where even homosexual marriages are being debated. These anti-God philosophies have created beliefs that are anti-family!

2. Affluence and materialism have caused many to forget God, causing a breakdown in the family.

God (and Moses) warned that when Israel entered the Promised Land and were given cities they did not build, houses full of all good things which they had not filled, hewn-out wells which they did not dig, vineyards and olive trees which they had not planted, "then beware, lest you forget the Lord who brought you out of the land of Egypt, from the house of bondage" (Deut. 6:10-12). While the United States is not Israel of old, human nature is such that when groups of people are continually given things for which they did not work, they cease to be thankful and rather cultivate a thinking of entitlement. Material prosperity, political freedom, and all kinds of electronic devices have given many in our generation a sense of self-sufficiency. Pride is its twin sister. God has not been thanked. If a society has been taught that there is no God, then there is no reason to be thankful, which is similar to the Gentile world during the first century (Rom. 1:21).

Even a century before this downward spiral accelerated, Abraham Lincoln recognized that the successes our young nation had experienced brought a forgetfulness of God. During the midst of the Civil War, Lincoln signed a "Proclamation appointing a National Fast Day" to be observed April 30, 1863. In that eloquent proclamation, laced with awe and respect for God, He stated that "it is the duty of nations as well as of men, to own their dependence upon the overruling power of God, . . . and to recognize the sublime truth, announced in the Holy Scriptures and proven by all history, that those nations only are blessed whose God is the Lord," a reference to Psalm 33:12. He believed that the Civil War "may be but a punishment, inflicted upon us, for our presumptuous sins, to the needful end of our national reformation as a whole People."

As to how he believed prosperity had adversely affected our young country by 1863, he said,

> We have been the recipients of the choicest bounties of Heaven. We have been preserved, these many years, in peace and prosperity. We have grown in numbers, wealth and power, as no other nation has ever grown. But we have forgotten God. We have forgotten the gracious hand which preserved us in peace, and multiplied and enriched and strengthened us; and we have vainly imagined, in the deceitfulness of our hearts, that all these blessings were produced by some superior wisdom and virtue of our own. Intoxicated with unbroken success, we have become too self-sufficient to feel the necessity of redeeming and preserving grace, too proud to pray to the God that made us!

> It behooves us then, to humble ourselves before the offended Power, to confess our national sins, and to pray for clemency and forgiveness.

We have known many who have been blessed with this world's goods and used them for righteous purposes as the Scripture teaches (1 Tim. 6:17-19). But Jesus mentioned "the deceitfulness of riches" (Matt. 13:22), and warnings abound concerning affluence (Mark 10:24; 1 Tim. 6:9-10). The most common among us is blessed materially and physically far above what any king would dare to dream only a century ago. It would seem that given "the Greatest Generation's" work ethic and dedication to better our country materially, plus the economic freedoms politically granted, they were successful in bringing prosperity to many. However, with multiplied economic prosperity, a new set of problems has arisen, and most seem to look everywhere but to God for the answers. "Give me neither poverty nor riches – Feed me with the food allotted to me; Lest I be full and deny You,

And say, 'Who is the Lord?' Or lest I be poor and steal, And profane the name of my God" (Prov. 30:8-9).

Material prosperity and advanced technology have given us so many "fun" things, but most of them actually "clutter" our lives and rob us of time spent reading God's Word, praying, attending gospel meetings and Bible classes, and engaging in other spiritual activities that we used to have more time to do. Christians have mentioned how they will check their email, go on the internet for something that should take only a minute, then come to realize two hours later how they had been "distracted," and actually "got nothing done."

Several hours a day spent on our jobs is necessary. But when we add hours a day in entertainment by television, movies, Facebook, sports, music, "surfing the web," and other activities characteristic of a life of luxury, many even among Christians forget God. There are so many more "things" now that distract our attention, all resulting from our advances and material prosperity. Even among people who have been taught fundamental truths concerning God, prosperous times have caused material things to replace Him in their thinking. A lack of hearing the Word leads to a lack of faith (Rom. 10:17). A lack of faith leads to a lack of commitment even in marriages and responsibilities toward children. Hence a breakdown of homes can be linked to our prosperity and materialistic culture.

3. Mothers leaving children has led to the breakdown of the home.

Related to the above, during World War II, many young women and wives of servicemen overseas joined the war effort by entering the work force. They performed all kinds of jobs from clerical help to factory work. In fact, posters such as "Rosie the Riveter" were made celebrating their work.

After the war ended in 1945, the G.I. Bill helped veterans go to colleges and technical schools and to buy homes with no down payment. Larger houses and automobiles were being built. Wheels of the American economy were spinning. Inflation was low and jobs were plentiful. Further, many women who had entered the work force during the war remained in it after the war. Extra money was helpful, and the appreciation for a job well done from those other than family was gratifying. Those larger houses and automobiles of the 1950s were available, but two incomes certainly made them more affordable than one. This brought a dilemma. How could women balance a career on one hand with a husband and children on the other?

For many wives and mothers, a decision was made to leave their children with relatives or others during the day. But mothers were often tired at night and behind on housework. Husbands and children more often than not saw the wives and mothers when they were not at their best and did not look their best. Other husbands in the workplace saw them just the opposite. Not only did office "romances" grow in number, but also for the first time children were being reared by those other than their mothers and fathers. Divorces began to rise. What had *generally* been accepted as best for families – that younger wives and mothers be "discreet, chaste, homemakers, good, obedient to their own husbands" (Tit. 2:4-5) – was being replaced by the "career" woman. After all, they were making life for children "much better than we had it during the depression days," we were told.

This continued to the point that during the 1980s, a term describing children coming home from school to an empty house was coined – "latchkey kids." Children wore a key to the house around their necks or somewhere else on their person. However, while prosperity and material possessions accrued, children had no supervision, instruction, or companionship from mothers. What may have been viewed by mothers as only a few hours of unsupervised time became opportunity for young teens to experiment with drugs and sex. "Values clarification," no God taught in schools, and no supervision at home led to many pregnancies. Many dysfunctional families have come as a consequence of absentee mothers, and the cycle continues.

Reasons for the Breakdown of the Home Are the Same
That Have Affected Conversions

Insofar as the growth of the Lord's church is concerned, the 1940s and 1950s saw congregation after congregation spring up all over the country. Conversions increased with increased populations. Gospel preaching was more respected, and baptisms were more common occurrences then than now. Many already believed in God and the Bible as His Word; it was a matter of teaching the truth and battling over false teaching concerning what to do to be saved, and how to worship God properly. To a much larger degree than now, a great deal of what the Bible taught in moral matters was already practiced.

I am very aware of the growth the Lord's church experienced in my home town of Birmingham, Alabama during those years. In the western part of the city, a building for one congregation of two hundred plus Christians would be no farther removed than a long walk from another with the same number. Older Christians who lived through those years have described them as "exciting times." Numerous Bible classes, two-week gospel meetings with morning and evening services, debates, tent meetings, radio preaching, and baptisms were a common part of life. Things have changed.

While new congregations have begun in some places since the 1960s, not only has the number of Christians not kept up with the population as far as percentages is concerned, there has also been an overall decline in the sheer number of Christians in this city. Why?

I have heard preachers accuse Christians of a lack of zeal in teaching others, a lack of personal evangelism. This may be true to a degree. But some older preachers I have known who baptized twenty to thirty during tent and gospel meetings during the 1950s, still preached the same message in the same way thirty to forty years later with vastly different results. I don't believe preachers and Christians in general are all to blame. The gospel Paul preached had much more success in some cities like Philippi, Thessalonica, and Corinth, than it did in Athens. The hearts of the hearers have to be taken into consideration. It would seem that during those earlier years gospel preaching was "in season," and now it is "out of season" (2 Tim. 4:2).

Again, why is this so? I believe that many of the same reasons that have caused a decline in number of Christians in this city are the same reasons that make it more difficult to convert people to the Lord everywhere in the country. And these reasons are the same that are causing the dissolution of the family as mentioned before! *It all relates to our culture which has been saturated with disrespect for God and His Word!*

Can America Survive the Breakdown of the Home?
If the Bible and secular history are believable, it doesn't look good. Lincoln wanted all "to recognize the sublime truth, announced in the Holy Scriptures and proven by all history, that those nations only are blessed whose God is the Lord." Solomon said, "Righteousness exalts a nation, But sin is a reproach to any people" (Prov. 14:34). Certainly God will judge us individually for eternity, but unrighteousness in a collective sense brings problems even in this life.

For example, our stock market is basically built on trust – confidence in people and their corporations. Money is invested with confidence that it will be used properly for expanding corporations, etc. Money is loaned by financial institutions trusting that it will be repaid. We have witnessed what happens when people default on their loans in a collective way, when many are untrustworthy. Lending institutions bankrupt. Printing money to bail out certain institutions costs everyone else in inflation! The point is that morality matters! Honesty counts! It has physical repercussions. Just as virtues, such as honesty, help keep a society "glued" together, sexual virtues do the same.

It is faith-building and eye-opening to see how a society prospers in various ways when people generally respect God's Word, and how it degenerates into social chaos when it refuses to acknowledge God.

British anthropologist J. D. Unwin wrote *Sex and Culture* in 1934. He had no convictions as we might, and he applied no moral judgments on his findings. However, after studying through eighty-six different cultures, including Roman, Greek, Sumerian, Moorish, Babylonian, and Anglo-Saxon civilizations through several hundred years, he concluded, "In human records there is no instance of a society retaining its energy after a complete new generation has inherited a tradition which does not insist on prenuptial and postnuptial continence" (Sheldon). In other words, societies come apart when a majority believes fornication either before or after marriage is acceptable!

In Bill Bennett's book, *The Broken Hearth,* he says:

> My concern is that we are now embarked upon an experiment that violates a universal social law: In attempting to raise children without two parents, we are seeing, on a massive scale, the voluntary breakup of the minimal family unit. This is historically unprecedented, an authentic cultural revolution – and, I believe, socially calamitous. We may be under the illusion that we can cheerfully deconstruct marriage and then one day decide to pull back from the brink. But as a friend of mine puts it, once you shoot out the lights, can you shoot them back on again? As the long record of human experimentation attests, civilizations, even great civilizations, are more fragile and perishable than we think (69-70).

Homosexual Marriages Can Lead to Social Chaos
Not only have we spiraled downward with the dissolution of marriages between men and women, now our country has taken another hit with attempts to legalize homosexual marriages. In an article entitled "The Destruction of Marriage Precedes the Death of a Culture," Louis Sheldon quotes Dr. Stanley Kurtz, a fellow with the Hoover Institution who has written extensively on the impact of homosexuality. He states that same-sex marriages will lead inevitably not only to the destruction of marriage completely, but it will also create all kinds of "other bizarre sexual arrange-

ments including polygamy and polyamory (groupings of males and females into a 'married' unit)" (Traditional Values Coalition Education and Legal Institute). Dr. Kurtz believes this will bring social chaos and litigation nightmares over custody of children. The reasons are obvious. Two of the same sex cannot produce children. A third party of the opposite sex has to be involved! Who has custody?

This is depressing, but factual. We have no way of knowing what these social "experiments" will eventually bring, what will be the nature of our country or government fifty years from now, or anything else. The Lord may come before then.

But it is difficult to believe that the United States we presently know can survive as a world power with our economic and material prosperity in our present moral decline. It simply has never occurred before. God has providentially used all kinds of nations, events, and groups of people to accomplish His larger purposes in times past, whether by punishing a nation that generally rejected Him or blessing another that honored Him. Our present recession, overall national debt, costs associated with illegal immigrants, and the free ride our politically correct culture gives Islam may answer this question.

Can Christianity Survive the Breakdown of the Home?

Yes! Christianity begins with an individual's belief in and obedience to Jesus Christ, and a determination to follow Him faithfully. If one's family members before him are Christians, if he has a faithful wife and children who follow Jesus, his own practice of the Lord's will is obviously encouraged tremendously.

However, if the wife of that same Christian has left him, if children have allowed the world to take precedence over the Lord, and he has no physical family who comes to his aid, he can still follow Jesus and be saved eternally. He is still a Christian! Regardless of the breakdown of his *physical* family, he has a much larger *spiritual* family that will not break down. "There is no one who has left house or brothers or sisters or father or mother or wife or children or lands, for My sake and the gospel's, who shall not receive a hundredfold now in this time – houses and brothers and sisters and mothers and children and lands, with persecutions – and in the age to come, eternal life" (Mark. 10:29-30).

If the kind of "hate crime" legislation is passed that homosexuals are demanding, religious freedom as we know it may be a thing of the past.

Persecution in the form of being jailed for simply speaking against homosexual behavior may not be far removed. Therefore, the complexion of local churches could change. Tax free status, freely assembling in large public auditoriums, ability to preach freely in public places and on radio and television without recrimination may be limited or denied completely. Can we still practice Christianity? Yes. But our circumstances and freedoms to do so may change.

What Can Christians Do to Counter This Breakdown in their Own Homes?

I am by nature an optimistic person, and our study thus far has been pessimistic and depressing. But there is hope! God spared that ungodly city of Nineveh from being overthrown when they repented at the preaching of Jonah (Jon. 3:5-10). With only six more righteous people, God would have spared as wicked a city as Sodom (Gen. 18:32). In an idolatrous city like Lystra, a religiously divided home could produce a Timothy, about whom Paul said he had "no man like-minded, who will care truly for your state" (Phil. 2:20). We have good reasons to be optimistic; the Bible assures us that we "can do all things in him" who strengthens us (Phil. 4:13). We can do what is right, and we can avoid what is wrong. Following are some things we can do to counter these ungodly influences that tear at our own homes:

1. "Bone up on" evidences concerning the resurrection of Christ and the Bible's inspiration. Religious discussions with people in the world these days center more on whether or not God exists and if the Bible is reliable. Four of the five men mentioned earlier whose writings have spawned disbelief were all atheists. We need to meet them on their own turf. Furthermore, knowing evidences for the resurrection of Christ and the Bible's inspiration helps us in other areas as well (such as with Islam). If Christ was raised from the dead, God is! It is all a "package deal." Inspired apostles preached to atheists along these lines (Acts 14:15-18; 17:22-31). In addition to the Bible's unity, fulfilled prophecies, brevity, and other internal evidences, there is a wealth of good material in books and on the internet relative to this subject. We should keep ideas concerning evidences always before our children. Faith must be fed continually for it to grow. Children quickly understand simple illustrations. Be thinking of them so you can use them effectively.

2. Know the enemy (1 Pet. 5:8). Paul said concerning Satan that "we are not ignorant of his devices" (2 Cor. 2:11). Politically correct language disguises Satan's purposes. Those who are morally bankrupt often portray themselves as intellectuals and those who strive to be moral as "back woodsy," ignorant, judgmental, and closed minded.

3. Be aware of redefined words. Ahab accused Elijah of being a "troubler of Israel" (1 Kings 18:17). However, the reverse was actually the case. Young people have grown up in a culture that has redefined certain words and phrases that make immorality seem right. Rather than "tolerance" meaning to allow something but at the same time disagree and believe it is wrong, young people often think this means to accept another's beliefs and lifestyles as *equal* to your own. "Freedom" has meant the opportunity to do what we know we *ought* to do, whereas many young people believe this means the ability to do anything we *want* to do. "Truth" has meant an absolute standard of right and wrong. To many young people, truth is whatever is right for you. These are huge differences, and they are all related to morals. We need to be able to articulate these differences to our families so they will not be deceived.

4. Don't be desensitized to how terrible sexual sins are, especially homosexuality. *Flee* **from them and teach your family to do the same (1 Cor. 6:18).** While our culture seeks to justify all manner of immorality and make it seem normal, even joking about it and belittling those who speak against it, God calls adultery "a heinous crime" (Job 31:11). Homosexuality brought God's wrath in the destruction of cities (Gen. 19), was an "abomination" (Lev. 18:22) deserving the death penalty in the Law (Lev. 20:13), is "against nature" in the New Testament (Rom. 1:26-27), and though it will keep people from heaven if unrepented of, it is actually an activity that can be stopped, evidencing the fact that people are not "born that way" (1 Cor. 6:9-11). Sexual sins often precede other sins in Bible listings (Rom. 1; 1 Cor. 5; 6:9-11; Gal. 5:19-21; Eph. 5:3; Col. 3:5-9; 1 Tim. 1:10-11). Perhaps this is due to their attractive nature and far-reaching consequences in this life, and especially to families. If we are not watchful, we will follow the path in our families that Alexander Pope warned against in his *Essays on Man:*

> Vice is a monster of so frightful mien,
> As to be hated needs but to be seen;
> Yet seen too oft, familiar with her face,
> We first endure, then pity, then embrace.

5. Be aware of how young people are tempted and try to help them. This is sometimes difficult. As parents, I believe we should talk with them about popular "stars," entertainment they listen to, what is going on among their friends, etc. Talk with them openly about how Christians are to be different and why. If we can show the background or history behind sources of their temptations, and explain the spiritual side of them, reasonable young people will listen. It also gives them ammunition to fight their own "demons."

6. Be faithful to one's own wife, husband, and children. It is difficult to find something sadder than the breakdown of a marriage of two Christians. Someone or both failed in their faithfulness to their vows. The terrible influence is inestimable. We are aware of marriages in which one became unfaithful to his spouse, and then their teenage children who had been morally pure went wild! Be alert to one's own weaknesses. Love your spouse and let him or her know it. Children are a heritage of the Lord (Ps. 127:3), and they deserve our time, attention, instruction, discipline, and good examples. Our family constitutes the closest companions we have on earth. They know when we are hypocritical. A good and faithful example in parents brings confidence and optimism for children to do the same. If Mom and Dad can have a good marriage, why can't I?

7. Don't flirt with disaster. The openness with which our culture discusses sexual matters can excite the senses and invite the very thing Jesus condemned – fantasizing about fornication (Matt. 5:27-30) which can lead to fornication and cause divorce (Matt. 5:31-32). Sexual urges are so strong that Paul said, "Flee fornication" (1 Cor. 6:18). Run from it and everything that leads to it. Keep a safe distance from anyone of the opposite sex who is not your spouse anywhere, including local churches. Don't put yourself in situations where you are tempted or you tempt someone else to commit fornication. Teach your children the same. Moral purity is absolutely necessary for the stability of the home.

8. Look for opportunities to talk with others about how following the Scriptures will prevent the breakdown of the home. Due to the prevalence of divorce, it is easy to converse about this. Most people have this problem somewhere in their family. The greatest need is to be saved from all sins, which includes sins dealing with the breakdown of the family. We can use these opportunities to evangelize. The first order of business is to show people that God is, the Bible is His Word, and Jesus Christ was a historical character who lived, died for our sins, and was physically raised. Heaven and hell hang in the balance as to whether or not we follow Him. While problems come, following Jesus will eliminate many unnecessary ones. Since God created us and knows us best, His instructions are always for our good here and in the hereafter (Deut. 6:24; 1 Pet. 3:10).

Conclusion

Christians understand that by following God's word, the *bulk* of blessings He promises is reserved in heaven (1 Pet. 1:3-5). However, God favors us in many ways now. For our "good," God instituted marriage from creation (Gen. 2:18). He instructs us concerning our behavior in it, and planned that by it children would be brought into the world (1 Tim. 2:15; 5:14). When our behavior in every relationship is patterned after the example and teaching of Jesus Christ, many unnecessary problems that the world commonly experiences and which are brought on by their rejection of God are avoided. This obviously includes the breakdown of the home.

God's kingdom, His people will always exist until the end of time (Dan. 2:44). While our American culture has reshaped what for years was more in line with God's view of the home, God's people can remain faithful regardless of our culture and future of our country. God will help us if we seek His will in all things. "Trust in Jehovah with all thy heart, And lean not upon thine own understanding: In all thy ways acknowledge him, And he will direct thy paths" (Prov. 3:5-6).

Bibliography

Bennett, William J. *The Broken Hearth.* New York: Doubleday, 2001.

_____. *The Index of Leading Cultural Indicators: American Society at the end of the 20th Century.* New York: Broadway Books, 1999.

Breese, Dave. *Seven Men Who Rule the World from the Grave.* Chicago: Moody Press, 1990.

Brokaw, Tom. "Sacrifice and the Greatest Generation." *The Wall Street Journal,* June 6, 2009, p. A11.

_____. *The Greatest Generation.* New York: Random House, Inc., 1998.

D'Souza, Dinesh. *What's So Great about Christianity.* Carol Stream, IL: Tyndale House Publishers, Inc., 2007.

Federer, William J. *America's God and Country.* Copell, TX: Fame Publishing, Inc., 1996.

Maddoux, Marlin. *America Betrayed!* Shreveport: Huntington House, Inc., 1984.

McDowell, Josh. *The Last Christian Generation*. Holiday, FL: Green Key Books, 2006.

Orr, James. "Criticism of the Bible." *The International Standard Bible Encyclopaedia*. 1939.

Parke, Mary. "Are Married Parents really better for Children? What Research says about the effects of family structure on child well-being." *Center for Law and Social Policy*, May, 2003.

Sheldon, Louis P. "The Destruction of Marriage Precedes the Death of a Culture." Traditional Values Coalition Education and Legal Institute. Dec. 6, 2010, *http://www.traditionalvalues.org/pdf_files/deathofmarriage.pdf.*

Christianity Can Survive . . .

The Threat of Apathy
Aaron Veyon

Apathy is defined as "an absence of emotion or enthusiasm" (*WordWeb Online Dictionary*), or a "lack of interest or feeling; indifference" (*Reader's Digest Oxford Complete Wordfinder*). In a society that has become more and more self-centered and self-absorbed, and in a day and time in which blatant immorality has become the norm, a discussion of the threat of apathetic attitudes in America is greatly needed.

I believe there are a number of factors that have contributed to the rise of religious indifference in America over the years. One factor is the desensitization to sin. I recall, as a young boy, when my grandfather would talk about all the sweeping changes in America that had occurred since the time he was a young boy. While he seemed generally grateful for the vast improvements in technology and medical science, he was often bothered by what he called "the plague on the American soul" (which was his reference to the only two forms of transmittable media available at the time: the television and radio). He enjoyed watching his TV, but he observed over time that something sinister was gaining more airtime with each passing

Aaron Veyon was born January 7, 1968 (the fourth of five boys) to John and JoEllen Veyon. He grew up in the small town of Paden City, West Virginia. After graduating from Paden City High School in 1986 he attended the West Virginia Northern Community College in New Martinsville, WV, while holding various jobs. In 1989 he moved to Cambridge, Ohio where he took a job working for the 84 Lumber Company as a manager trainee, and later he became a contractor sales representative. Aaron did a lot of appointment preaching during those years. In 1996 he became the full time evangelist with the Old Bates Hill church of Christ, located outside of Summerfield, Ohio. In early 1998 he began working with the Elk Fork church of Christ (near Middlebourne, WV) where he labored for nearly eight years. In 2005 Aaron and his family moved to Fredericktown, Ohio to labor with the Fredericktown church of Christ (a work that continues to the present). Aaron is married to Rebecca (Conrad) and has five children (Kyle, Megan, Silas, Maddie, and Luke).

year. He noticed that more skin was being shown and that indecent, suggestive bodily movements were not as shocking to the American public as they once were. Sex was now talked about with more openness, and was acted out with more blatancy on television and in movies. He noticed that the younger generation was growing restless with the older generation, and that there was a growing rebellion against higher authority and, to some degree, against religion. As the years went by, all of these things became more and more prevalent. He grew appalled and would occasionally make a comparison to Lot's experience in Sodom: "for that righteous man, dwelling among them, tormented his righteous soul from day to day by seeing and hearing their lawless deeds" (2 Pet. 2:8). That was almost forty years ago! I wonder what he would think now.

I think Grandpa was correct in his observations. The moral integrity of America has in many ways changed, not for the better but for the worse. It seems that the rebellious, free-loving generation of the late sixties has set the tone for every generation to come after them. It reminds me of what God said to Judah through Jeremiah the prophet: "And you have done worse than your fathers, for behold, each one follows the dictates of his own evil heart, so that no one listens to Me" (Jer. 16:12).

Another factor that plays into apathetic attitudes (at least in our society) stems from over abundant blessings. I heard a preacher say one time that he felt that America has been cursed with the blight of abundance. We are a spoiled people. We have everything at our fingertips. Anything we could possibly want and more is at our disposal. If we want something (even if we can't afford it), we'll just slap the credit card on the counter and add that toy's purchase to the already growing debt we've accumulated over the years. We have lost the sense of contentment and accountability. We want to blanket our lives in comfort, because our comfort is the most important thing. We want it and we're going to have it! We justify. We have developed the attitude that you only live once, and life's too short, so go for the gusto. From one generation to the next, we have departed from God-centered living and have gravitated toward self-centered living. We have been deceived into thinking that we alone are the masters of our souls. We slowly bought into the same lie that Eve bought into: "You will be like God" (Gen. 3:5).

This society has become so opposed to the acceptance of God that He is no longer allowed in most public schools. His words are no longer tolerated on the walls of many of our courthouses. Any semblance of Christianity comes under immediate attack by the watchdogs of humanism. More and more we are becoming a godless (that's God-less) nation. David once said, "The wicked shall be turned into hell, and all the nations that forget God" (Ps. 9:17). Scary thought, isn't it?

Naturally, since God has become a lesser part of our culture, we have forgotten from whom all blessings flow. "The earth is the Lord's, and all its fullness" (1 Cor. 10:26). We have forgotten that. We have failed to heed the divine warning with regard to material blessings: "Beware that you do not forget the Lord your God. . ." (Deut. 8:11). Beware lest "you say in your heart, 'My power and the might of my hand have gained me this wealth'" (v. 17). This generation has in many ways brought to fruition the sobering words spoken by Paul in Romans 1:21-22: ". . . because, although they knew God, they did not glorify Him as God, nor were thankful, but became futile in their thoughts, and their foolish hearts were darkened. Professing to be wise, they became fools." These are just some of the factors that have eventually led to the spirit of apathy toward religion in America, as it exists today.

Apathy Threatens the Survival of Christianity

There are a number of reasons why apathy is a direct threat to Christianity. For one thing, it has become so prevalent that in many places it has become increasingly difficult to interest people in the gospel; "to open their eyes, in order to turn them from darkness to light, and from the power of Satan to God, that they may receive forgiveness of sins and an inheritance among those who are sanctified by faith" in Christ (Acts 26:18). Unlike my grandfather's generation (and those who preceded him), the majority of my countrymen today just don't seem to be interested in spiritual things.

I think that the events of September 11, 2001 (and the days and weeks that followed) are a fair example of just how much of a threat that apathy is to Christianity. That day got everyone's attention. Most Americans were sent reeling by the unexpected attacks on our country. As I recall, that same evening, several of our senators and members of congress stood on the steps of our nation's capital and sang "God Bless America." Finally, it seemed that God was back in the minds and collective consciences of our governing leaders. (I remember thinking that it was such a shame that it took such a tragedy to get their attention.) Similar sentiment was shared by Americans all across the land. For a while people seemed to be church going again. But, as the days turned to weeks and the weeks to months, things drifted back to where they were before. The spiritual revival that so many of us hoped for this country was just a small blip on the radar screen of morality. In fact, many sinful agendas have gained in popularity since that day. For example, homosexuality has gained a greater foothold. Same-sex marriage has spent more time in national spotlight. We now have, passed into law in the years following 9-11-01, a "hate crime" law designed to protect homosexuality.[1] There seems to be far more interest today in things that are contrary to the will of God than there is in coming to know God and to please Him.

It's at times like this that I think of the mediation of David in Psalm 36:1-4. He said, "An oracle within my heart concerning the transgression of the wicked: There is no fear of God before his eyes. For he flatters himself in his own eyes, when he finds out his iniquity and when he hates. The words of his mouth are wickedness and deceit; he has ceased to be wise and to do good. He devises wickedness on his bed; he sets himself in a way that is not good; he does not abhor evil."

The spirit of apathy creates some obvious concerns for the Lord's people in our culture and time. One thing that is of great concern among many sound congregations is that they are only getting older. Many of the stalwarts of the gospel from my own youth have been making a steady departure from this life. In many places, congregations that were once youthful are now middle-aged or elderly. When I was a boy, it seemed like many of the congregations had as many children as adults. But now, in many of these same locations, the children are few, the attendance is far down from what it once was, and it is far more challenging to share the gospel with neighbors and friends. I realize that this is not the case everywhere. Many of us are quite aware of congregations that are growing and thriving very nicely. But unfortunately, that is not the case in many of the places where the gospel used to thrive. Recently, while attending a worship service with another congregation, I noticed that their membership was far down from where it used to be. Upon asking one of the brethren about it, he said, "People either move away, fall away, or pass away, and there's not many new souls taking their place in the pews." But why is that? For the most part people are just not that interested. If this trend continues, some of those congregations will become non-existent in the next generation or two.

---

[1] For documentation of this see: FoxNews.com: *http://www.foxnews.com/politics/2009/10/28/obama-signs-defense-policy-includes-hate-crime-legislation/*; CNN.com: *http://www.cnn.com/2009/POLITICS/10/28/hate.crimes/index.html?iref=allsearch*; Newsmax.com: *http://www.newsmax.com/US/Obama-Muslim-Hate-Crime/2009/10/28/id/335834*

Apathy's Influence in the Church

As if it weren't bad enough that there seems to be a prevailing lack of interest in godliness in our society, the church has also fallen under attack in recent years. Too many of our brethren have befriended the world and have been drawn to the things of this world, and they have become indifferent to right living. Worst of all, they bring that influence into the church. John said, "Do not love the world or the things in the world. If anyone loves the world, the love of the Father is not in him. For all that is in the world — the lust of the flesh, the lust of the eyes, and the pride of life — is not of the Father but is of the world. And the world is passing away, and the lust of it; but he who does the will of God abides forever" (1 John 2:15-17).

Now there are various reasons why and how this happens. One reason that this happens is because we have slowly become desensitized to sin. When I was a boy living at home, we weren't allowed to watch anything that involved swearing, indecency, crude, derogatory humor, etc. I can't tell you how many times my brothers and I had to turn the channel or turn the TV off because of some offense to our Christian eyes and ears. But these kinds of things are greatly tolerated by many Christians in this generation. I had a young brother in Christ tell me recently that he hears swearing at school, so he didn't see the big deal in hearing it in a movie. I told him that there is a big difference between school and home. He has no control over what his classmates do around him at school, but he has full control over whether or not he allows that moral filth to come into his house. Think about it. Surely you wouldn't let some woman walk into your house and undress in front of your family; and surely you wouldn't let her start swearing like a sailor in front of your kids without showing her the door. But as long as it's on that magical box we call "the TV," that makes it alright. Listen, brethren, the concept of 1 Corinthians 15:33 is not limited to just friendships.

Another factor that has played into this is that we have allowed our children to get into so many extra-curricular functions, events, and habits of leisure that it has successfully driven a wedge between our spiritual life and our secular life. And guess which one wins out most of the time. In many Christian homes, children spend an inordinate amount of time (hours and hours) playing the Wii, Xbox, PlayStation, etc., to the exclusion of any real spiritual training. In fact, they are just not that interested in spiritual things. Bible study is boring to them. It's not exciting like those video games. And many Christian mom's and dad's don't seem to find that trend alarming at all. We are teaching our children that life is all about them. God is only a small part in our lives. I fear that many of our children will never come to have God-centered lives. They will grow into adulthood having been trained toward self-centered living – and *we* have allowed it to happen! Brethren and friends, these children are the next generation. Who among them is going to be future elders and deacons in the church? Who among them is going to become sound gospel preachers? Who among them is going to be women professing godliness?

There is nothing wrong with children playing games, engaging in sports or participating in school plays (and things of that nature), but there is a problem when those things conflict with our spiritual lives. Sometimes when brethren miss a worship service, and I ask them about it, they say something like, "Well, little Johnny had football practice on Sunday afternoon and so we couldn't make services in the evening," or, "Sally had a play rehearsal after school and it ran into the evening, so that's why we weren't able to make it Wednesday night." I marvel that brethren see a greater need to be committed to these temporal things than to be committed to the Lord and His people. What's worse is that this is teaching those very children that it's acceptable to God to compromise spiritual things if there's something that you want to do more. Solomon said, "Train up a child in the way he should go, and when he is old he will not depart from it" (Prov. 22:6). Did you know that the opposite is also true?

Another problem that has crept into the church is a spirit of laziness. For example, it seems that brethren just don't study the Bible like they used to. There does not seem to be as much interest in it as there was a generation ago. Some time ago, in a gospel meeting, I was conducting the adult Bible class on a Sunday morning, and I asked the brethren what the shortest verse in the Bible was. One of them, a Christian of many years, proceeded to quote Genesis 1:1. (Actually, it is John 11:35, "Jesus wept." That's something that even small children know.) On another occasion, at another time and place, I commented that God always answers the prayers of the righteous (albeit, His answers are either "yes," "no," or "wait awhile," as one brother put it). After my comment, one of the sisters spoke up (a Christian of about 15-20 years) and said, "That's not true! Haven't you ever heard the country song, 'Thank God For Unanswered Prayers'?" I was flabbergasted.

About a generation or two ago, we had so many walking Bibles among our brethren (brothers and sisters who knew the Bible like the back of their hand; who could quote book, chapter, and verse to anyone at any time). While I know that there are brethren who can still do that today, they seem to be far fewer than in previous generations. After dealing with brethren here, there, and yonder over the recent years, I have concluded that (with many of them) they want to be spoon-fed the gospel. They don't want to have to work for the knowledge of God's will. Once a brother in Christ actually said to me, "Just tell me what I'm supposed to believe, and I'll believe it." That is a far cry from what the Lord expects of each of us. Paul said, "Therefore do not be unwise, but understand what the will of the Lord is" (Eph. 5:17). Brethren, you cannot understand the will of God if you don't study it (cf. 2 Tim. 2:15). But, some are just not interested enough in the will of God to put the effort into study.

The spirit of apathy is alive and well in many congregations across this land. That is a tragedy. Satan has successfully seduced and deceived many from among us, and they, like Demas, have left us, having loved this present world (2 Tim. 4:10). Some of them have literally left, and others are sitting in the pew right next to us, but it is evident by the conduct of their lives that their heart is a million miles away from fellowship with God. John said, "If we say that we have fellowship with Him, and walk in darkness, we lie and do not practice the truth" (1 John 1:6).

What Can We Do to Overcome Apathy?

Religious indifference is a problem everywhere. The evidence of this is seen in the efforts that many churches make in order to get people interested in "coming to church." This is not just something that denominations do, even some churches of Christ engage in these efforts. Some brethren don't seem to have the confidence that the old Jerusalem gospel will have much of an effect on people today, so they try to liven things up, to make Christianity "fun." To be sure, Christians should enjoy their life in Christ, but that joy is to be based on our deep love for God and His church, not on how much fun we have while attending worship services. The moment we have shifted our focus from what is pleasing to God to what is pleasing to us, that is the moment when we have gone from God-centered living to self-centered living. This is counter-productive to our fight against apathy in the church.

To accommodate indifferent attitudes, in some places, preaching is far less Bible-based and is far more entertaining. The social gospel has become very popular among brethren in this generation. More emphasis seems to be placed on the social aspect of our lives together than on the spiritual, and so there is more emphasis placed on pot lucks, games, get-togethers (etc.) and far less on home Bible studies, singings, and personal work. While there is certainly nothing wrong with eating together and playing games together, to do those things to the exclusion of, or to the reduction of, spiritual things is out of kilter with the will of God. It focuses more on the temporal and less on the spiritual/eternal. This is not the answer to our problems. This only creates bigger problems.

Overcoming apathy in the church is a difficult task, because we have no control over the hearts of those who are spiritually indifferent. We know that Paul said (for example), "Brethren, if a man is overtaken in any trespass, you who are spiritual restore such a one in a spirit of gentleness, considering yourself lest you also be tempted" (Gal. 6:1), but this will not work if the weak or fallen brother refuses to be restored. Therefore, our best hope of purging the church of apathy is to first make sure our *own* lives are God-centered. Get used to this idea and say it to yourself: "A better church begins with *me*."

What are some things we can do personally in an effort to overcome apathy?

1. "Get yourselves a new heart and a new spirit" (Ezek. 18:31). It all begins in your heart (cf. Matt. 15:18-19; Luke 6:45; Rom. 10:10). Many of our brethren are aware that we have to desire to walk our walk of faith, but their heart is just not in it. They wish they had the desire. Ezra "prepared his heart to seek the law of the Lord, and to do it" (Ezra 7:10). That's what we have to do. We have to develop the attitude that God comes first, not us. Ecclesiastes 12:13 reveals to us that God didn't create us to serve ourselves; He created us to serve Him. We have to train our hearts to realize that we don't obey God simply because we *have* to, we obey God because we *want* to (John 4:23-24).

2. "And you shall love the Lord your God with all your heart, with all your soul, with all your mind, and with all your strength" (Mark 12:30). Love is a learned thing (cf. Tit. 2:4). We need to learn to fall in love with God all over again. (Applying step one above makes this step possible.) When Jesus quoted the greatest commandment in Mark 12:30, He appealed to every aspect of the human experience. The heart, soul, mind, and strength are a reference to the emotional, spiritual, intellectual, and physical makeup of man. In other words, you shall love the Lord your God with every fiber of your being. When you have completely and lovingly surrendered your life to Christ, then finally the clay will be ready for the Potter's hand (Isa. 64:8).

3. ". . . and when you have returned to Me, strengthen your brethren"

(Luke 22:32). These are the words that Jesus said to Peter in His anticipation of Peter's denials of Him. Jesus foretold that Peter would fall, but He also knew Peter would be restored. Jesus charged Peter "strengthen your brethren" after he was restored. I would like to draw from this an idea pertinent to our discussion on apathy. No one knows the dangers of apathy better than one who had previously experienced it (just as no one would know what it means to deny and disappoint the Lord better than one who had previously done so). Such a person could give valuable assistance to brethren who are currently suffering from the same dilemma (cf. Gal. 6:1-2).

4. "Brethren, pray for us" (1 Thess. 5:25). There is power in prayer (Jas. 5:16). Christians are always in need of prayers. Satan already has the world. His task now is to get back those souls he lost to Christ. His attacks on the church are continual and they are ferocious. One of the most effective weapons he has employed to destroy congregations and the spiritual lives of many of God's children is apathy. If he can find a way to get you disinterested in godliness, he knows you will cease to be godly – and then he has you. It is no wonder that Paul commands us to "pray without ceasing" (1 Thess. 5:17), "continuing steadfastly in prayer" (Rom. 12:12).

Brethren, I pray that you will find this study to be useful and that it will result in much and everlasting good in your lives. May the Lord ever be longsuffering with us in our weaknesses, strengthening us and establishing us by His word. May we always find favor in His sight.

Christianity Can Survive . . .

The Threat of an Anti-Christian Government

Heath Aaron Robertson

Abraham Lincoln, whose life greatly impacted the nature, growth, and strength of our nation, said this about the Bible:

> In regard to this Great Book, I have only to say that it is the best gift which God has given to man. All the good from the Saviour of the world is communicated to us through this Book. But for this Book we could not know right from wrong (Owen, 169-170).

It is quite remarkable, in light of what is now considered to be politically correct, that the source of this statement is a politician and not just any politician, but the President. However, Lincoln was not alone in his

---

Heath Aaron Robertson was born on October 16, 1985 in Memphis, TN and raised in Bartlett, TN. After meeting at Florida College, he married Renee Bunting on December 15th, 2007. Their first child, Hanna, was born on December 3rd, 2009.

Heath became a Christian at the age of fourteen and preached itinerantly until he was eighteen. During that period, he sat at the feet of several capable preachers. He attended the Preacher Training Program of the Ellettsville, IN Church of Christ. At age eighteen, he began his first full-time work in Sparta, TN. He spent the summer of 2005 working with the Pine City, MN congregation. He attended Florida College (2005-2007) and graduated with an A.A. degree. For his first year and a half at Florida College, Heath preached and taught often as a member of the Riverview congregation. During his final semester, he worked with the South Livingston congregation in a training situation. In the summer of 2006, he had the privilege to encourage and work with Christians in Colombia, South America. He has preached itinerantly in many States.

On September 5th, 2008, Heath and Renee moved to Bergen, Norway where Renee was born and raised while her father and grandfather preached the gospel there. Their work there was short-lived because of a change in immigration laws. They returned to the States on May 24th, 2010. They currently live in Cullman, Alabama where Heath works with the Highway 157 congregation.

opinion of Scripture. The majority of America's founders and early leaders had similar respect for God and His Word.

For many who had long prayed for the opportunity to serve and worship God freely, America was a dream come true. It is no stretch to say that America was founded upon biblical principles. Indeed, in our very *Constitution* one can easily see that its writers were men who, for the most part, considered the Bible to be timeless. They recognized that the Word of God was not intended just for the use of individuals or families. History tells us they understood that, if a nation is built upon and anchored to the Scriptures, its potential would be unmatchable. In this writer's opinion, their theory has been proven in American history.

A great many things have changed since those early days. Not only has America, in many areas, forsaken its biblical foundation, but religious freedom is quickly fading. Especially against Christianity does the future look dark. Interestingly enough, it is in the name of "freedom" that freedom to practice New Testament Christianity is being threatened. The biblical views on homosexuality and child rearing are two examples of areas being attacked. The majority of homosexuals and their defenders are seeking to make illegal any verbalization of or actions which suggest that homosexuality is an improper or immoral lifestyle. Any type of corporal discipline of children is already illegal in some European countries and the same is being passionately advocated by many in the United States. While the First Amendment of the Constitution demands that no laws be made "prohibiting the free exercise" of religion, activist groups and other interested parties consider the preaching of the truth to be *unconstitutional*. Granted, it is unconstitutional and an abomination to God what some do in the name of Christ. But to preach and practice the pure truth and to humbly and lovingly try to convince the world of the corruption of sin and its need to repent and obey God are completely within the boundaries of the Constitution.

While we solemnly await our government to begin its war against Christ, Christians in other nations are already being persecuted for their faith. Yet, they are not the first. Corrupt and proud nations have tried time and again throughout history to rebel against the will of God. We must look to those who fought this battle before to find assurance that Christianity can survive the threat of an anti-Christian government.

Historical Examples of Governments That
Opposed God and His People

The Captivity of Judah

While the story of Judah in captivity is obviously not about anti-*Christian* governments, it is about governments who were against God and His people. It would help to remember that all this began with the sin of God's people themselves. From the beginning, God was clear as to what would happen to His people if they forsook Him (Deut. 28:32-45). The prophets foretold that God Himself would hand them over to captivity and destruction (Jer. 20:4-5; Isa. 39:5-7). The prophecy began its fulfillment through Babylon in 605 B.C.

> In the third year of the reign of Jehoiakim king of Judah, Nebuchadnezzar king of Babylon came to Jerusalem and besieged it. The Lord gave Jehoiakim king of Judah into his hand, along with some of the vessels of the house of God; and he brought them to the land of Shinar, to the house of his god, and he brought the vessels into the treasury of his god (Dan. 1:1-2).

While sin brought this on, in the next few verses of Daniel, we find out that there were faithful servants of God who suffered along with the rest (Dan. 1:3-8). To make matters worse, the nations that God used to punish Judah went too far in their treatment of them and did not recognize that it was only because of God that they had the power that they did (Zech. 1:12-15). Because of this, God's people underwent extreme tests of their faith at the hands of proud men wishing to control the world.

- They were indoctrinated with Babylonian literature and philosophy (Dan. 1:4).
- They were forced to eat food that would "defile" them (Dan. 1:8).
- They were commanded to worship idols (Dan. 3:1-6).
- They were renamed after the false gods of their captors (Dan. 4:8).
- They were despised, mocked, and ridiculed for their faith (Dan. 6:3-5; Ps. 137:3).
- They were commanded not to pray and were punished for doing so (Dan. 6:6-24).

Most likely, many Jews forsook the Lord or were killed because of persecution. Many were probably wondering whether the Lord really was in control or if He even existed! However, seventy years later, the Jews were being released by Cyrus, king of Persia, to return to their land (Ezra 1:1-3)! If the people had been listening to the prophets in faith, they would have known that God promised deliverance and restoration.

> But you, O mountains of Israel, you will put forth your branches and bear your fruit for My people Israel; *for they will soon come.* For, behold, I am for you, and I will turn to you, and you will be cultivated and sown. I will multiply men on you, all the house of Israel, all of it; and the cities will be inhabited and the waste places will be rebuilt (Ezek. 36:8).

He even foretold the length of the captivity and that one named Cyrus would release them (Jer. 25:11-12; Isa. 44:28-45:13). God was always in control. For this reason, a remnant was brought safely through to continue carrying out God's purposes despite the efforts of those anti-God governments.

Persecution by the Jews

The Jews had tried their best to stop Jesus from preaching His message, even stooping to lying and murder. Naturally, when Jesus' disciples began preaching the gospel, the Jews sought to end their work quickly, sparing nothing and no one. Although the church grew at an unbelievable pace in its early days, the leaders of the Jews were not going to take the time to consider whether it was actually the power of God behind these Christians.

> The word of God kept on spreading; and the number of the disciples continued to increase greatly in Jerusalem, and a great many of the priests were becoming obedient to the faith. And Stephen, full of grace and power, was performing great wonders and signs among the people. But some men from what was called the Synagogue of the Freedmen, including both Cyrenians and Alexandrians, and some from Cilicia and Asia, rose up and argued with Stephen. But they were unable to cope with the wisdom and the Spirit with which he was speaking. Then they secretly induced men to say, "We have heard him speak blasphemous words against Moses and against God." And they stirred up the people, the elders and the scribes, and they came up to him and dragged him away and brought him before the Council. They put forward false witnesses who said, "This man incessantly speaks against this holy place and the Law; for we have heard him say that this Nazarene, Jesus, will destroy this place and alter the customs which Moses handed down to us" (Acts 6:7-14).

It is interesting to note that Stephen made no effort to defend himself but rather utilized this opportunity to preach the truth to his accusers (Acts 7:2ff). However, their response was less than noble (7:51-60). Stephen was stoned to death for simply teaching what he believed was right and true. It is the attitude of the Jews here that is the very thing we fear is slowly becoming the prevailing mentality in America. If this is true, the events following Stephen's death are predictions of dark times ahead. Stephen's death marked the beginning of what was called "a great persecution . . .

against the church" (8:1). Their champion persecutor was a young, up-and-coming Pharisee named Saul. He seemed to have been a leader of the mob that killed Stephen (7:58; 8:1). After this, the Bible describes Saul's work as "ravaging the church" (8:3).

If the situation in America does develop to parallel this account of the early church, we are not left without hope. In fact, we are not just given a hope of what might be, but rather of what assuredly will be, if we follow their footsteps. The persecution of the Jews caused the Jerusalem church to scatter (Acts 8:1). One might think this would be the beginning of the end for the church of Christ. However, rather than disband, "those who had been scattered went about preaching the Word" (8:4). As a result, the church began to expand very quickly into the outer regions of Judea and into Samaria (8:4-13). The Jews meant to discourage and destroy the church but instead their persecution became the catalyst for the worldwide spread of the gospel! Christianity not only survived this anti-Christian government but also flourished because of it!

Rome: Babylon Arises Again
Without doubt, the preachers and teachers of the early church spent much time teaching the Old Testament writings. Paul wrote numerous statements about the importance of learning from the Old Testament and that it would help one to more perfectly understand Christ and the New Covenant (Rom. 15:4; 1 Cor. 10:11; Gal. 3:24; 2 Tim. 3:14-17). The early Christians would have been very familiar with the Babylonian captivity that we looked at earlier. So, in the mind of a Christian, one could not suggest anything worse than that the current world power was like the Babylonian Empire that was so wicked toward God's people of the past. However, we find that very thing being proclaimed about Rome in the book of Revelation (18:1-3).

Daniel prophesied that Rome would not only be like Babylon but actually much worse!

> Then I desired to know the exact meaning of the fourth beast, which was different from all the others, exceedingly dreadful, with its teeth of iron and its claws of bronze, and which devoured, crushed and trampled down the remainder with its feet, and the meaning of the ten horns that were on its head and the other horn which came up, and before which three of them fell, namely, that horn which had eyes and a mouth uttering great boasts and which was larger in appearance than its associates. I kept looking, and that horn was waging war with the saints and overpowering them (Dan. 7:19-21).

Under the reign of the same world-power in which the Christ would come and His kingdom would be established (Dan. 2:36-45), Daniel prophesied that His "saints" would be at war with that world-power and it would even begin to overpower them!

As Rome rose to power, loyalty to the Empire and Emperor was demanded. "This loyalty found expression in offering or burning incense to the image of the emperor" (Hailey, 60). Some of the emperors were not quickly comfortable being worshipped. However, Domitian, who reigned from circa A.D. 91-96, actually sought worship and demanded to be called "Lord God" Caesar (Hailey, 70). A brief study of the nations that formed the Roman Empire reveals ruler worship occurring in their past causing emperor worship to be "easily adopted" (Jenkins, 5). Pride for and loyalty to the Empire combined with the religion of emperor worship made a clash with Christianity inevitable.

Emperor worship soon became mandatory. That is, it was mandatory if they wanted to be able to work, buy, or sell. As the Christians became known for their refusal to burn the incense and recognize the emperor as "Lord God Caesar," they were accused of treason and even atheism. Then, anything they considered persecution before this time became a light punishment compared to what was beginning to occur.

> The Penalties, inflicted upon the Christians, were in accord with well and long established Roman laws. The large claims of Christianity brought it within the clutches of these laws. The empire was not so tolerant or so easy going as it has sometimes been made to appear. The Roman magistrates could inflict a great variety of punishments, all according to law and the view which they desired to take of Christianity. "It might be treated as an unlicensed religion, or as high treason, or as sacrilege, or as magic; perhaps also as incest. Introducers of new religions, if of good birth, were to be banished to an island; otherwise they were to be put to death. Those guilty of high treason, if of good birth, were to be beheaded; if not, to be exposed to the beasts or burned alive. In either case they might be tortured. Sacrilege was similarly punished, with the additional alternative of crucifixion, but with the exclusion of torture in the case of citizens. Magic was punishable with exposure to wild beasts, burning or crucifixion; incest with banishment. Such a combination of crimes—which were wrongfully ascribed to the Christians—in one and the same set of men made the Roman officials intolerant." The penalties were often inflicted with the utmost cruelty without regard to age or sex. In the great Coliseum at Rome,

the sufferings of the Christians were made to serve as amusements for the Roman populace (Sell).

Persecution continued, although not constant, for circa 250 years. Revelation 6:9-11 tells us that the Christians who were already "slain" at this point were still in a state of unrest and were asking, "How long, O Lord, holy and true, will you refrain from judging and avenging our blood on those who dwell on the earth?" If these were the feelings of those who were already dead, one could imagine what the Christians, still living through the persecution, were asking!

But again, as we look into the words of the prophets, God always knew the end from the beginning and was in complete control. God prophesied of His victory over Rome and that those who would stand with Him would also be victorious (Dan. 7:21-27). Consider the following promise God made to the first century Christians:

> Then another angel, a third one, followed them, saying with a loud voice, "If anyone worships the beast and his image, and receives a mark on his forehead or on his hand, he also will drink of the wine of the wrath of God, which is mixed in full strength in the cup of His anger; and he will be tormented with fire and brimstone in the presence of the holy angels and in the presence of the Lamb. And the smoke of their torment goes up forever and ever; they have no rest day and night, those who worship the beast and his image, and whoever receives the mark of his name." Here is the perseverance of the saints who keep the commandments of God and their faith in Jesus. And I heard a voice from heaven, saying, "Write, 'Blessed are the dead who die in the Lord from now on!'" "Yes," says the Spirit, "so that they may rest from their labors, for their deeds follow with them" (Rev. 14:9-13).

God promised that justice would be rendered upon all who worshipped "the beast and his image." He also told them that, if they were to die before judgment was rendered, they could welcome death as a blessing! We should note that this proclamation was not only to comfort but also to warn. God's people had to refuse to take part in Rome's sin. For even if their betrayal of Christ would allow them to survive a bit longer, their eventual death would bring them face to face with God and a punishment far worse than what Rome could ever inflict.

Rome, like all the other nations of the past who have persecuted God's people, eventually crumbled while the kingdom of God still stands today. Hindsight is such a powerful thing. Christians on this side of history, as

God prophesied in Revelation 19:1-6, look back on these things and cry out, "Hallelujah! Salvation and glory and power belong to our God!" And so, if we too must face the beast of the pride of men, they may seem in control and we may die "because of the Word of God" (Rev. 6:9), but in the end the faithful will shout victoriously, "Hallelujah! For the Lord our God, the Almighty, reigns" (Rev. 19:6)!

What Must Christians in America Do in Order That Christianity May Survive the Attacks Against Us?

In times of trial or suffering it is not only important that we understand we *can* overcome our problems but also *how* we are to overcome them. However, it is crucial that we understand we are discussing the survival of Christianity, the Way, and *not* of individual Christians. One cannot help but notice that, in all three examples we examined, some of God's people were killed during the course of each period in history. As God made clear in Revelation 14:9-13, we might be required to die to fulfill our purpose. And our purpose is not about us but rather it is to promote the Way, be the light, and glorify God at all costs. If fulfilling those things brings about our death, we too may welcome death as a blessing.

So, how can we fulfill our purpose in time of persecution?

We Must Always Remember That God Is in Control. God told the captive Jews that He had "plans" for them (Jer. 29:11). God was always in control; He was carrying out *His* plans! It is often difficult to acknowledge this during troubled times. In fact, many often turn away from God to seek what they hope will be an easier path. Some, because their *perception* of God conflicts with what His Word says, develop their own theories about what God wants or what His plans are and begin to put words in His mouth. The people began to do this in Jeremiah's day. God plainly said to the people, "Do not let your prophets who are in your midst and your diviners deceive you . . . they prophesy falsely in My name" (Jer. 29:8-9). Teachers and preachers must continually stress that God's thoughts and ways are often very different from our own and they are always "higher" (Isa. 55:8-9). Whether it is politically correct or offensive to anyone, if it is truly God's Word, it is the truth and we must not accept anything else.

> And we know that God causes all things to work together for good to those who love God, to those who are called according to His purpose (Rom. 8:28).

Don't misread this verse! "Good" is not describing the lives of "those who love God" but rather the *result* of those lives. God's purposes are always for good. So, the result of a life that has been spent loving God, thus doing His will, will naturally be "good." That might require discipline "so that we may share His holiness" (Heb. 12:10). It may require a life immersed in suffering and pain because our commitment to Christ demands a life that conflicts greatly with the way the world lives (1 Pet. 1:6-7; 2 Tim. 3:12). We must never forget that God rules. If we love God and are faithful, we can and will, one way or another, overcome whatever we face in this life (1 Cor. 10:13).

We Must Carry On. God told those in Babylon that the captivity would last for seventy years (Jer. 29:10). So, it was needful that they accept that and carry on with their lives. He gave them three particular commands in Jeremiah 29:4-6. First, they were to "*build houses*" (v. 5). Many probably thought they should be ready for deliverance at a moment's notice. But God's command to use their time and resources to set up house in Babylon crushed any hope of escaping the seventy-year length. Also, they were to "*plant gardens*" (v. 5). If they must build a house and grow their food then they would need an income. They would have to interact and seek employment among the very people who dragged them to this foreign land! Finally, they were to *continue building and raising their families* (v. 6). Could you even imagine raising a family in a land of such wickedness and worldliness? I bet you can. Many places in America are not all that different. Nevertheless, they were to carry on in this land and situation without neglecting to represent themselves as the holy people of God.

Peter had similar thoughts for the Christians dispersed throughout the Roman Empire (1 Pet. 1:1, 13-19). "Reading this, we can easily see the emphasis Peter placed upon the 'work' and 'conduct' of these 'sojourners,' calling upon them to out-think, out-live, and out-die the pagans among whom they lived as resident aliens" (Turner, 161). If we are to undergo persecution of any kind, it is not a time to mope around, wish things were different, and neglect our commitment to Christ, brethren, and our families. "The hope of future generations depends not on great things, but on faithfully doing simple things–build, plant, multiply, seek the peace of the enemy" (Ward, 177).

We Must Obey Civil Authority. "Submit yourselves for the Lord's sake to every human institution" (1 Pet. 2:13). This may be the most difficult thing on this list for Christians in America to accomplish. This does not so much have to do with the difficulty of the task itself but rather because of the American attitude that even many of God's people have adopted. We have taken freedom to mean that laws are subject to individual interpretation and, if those in authority don't keep them or just bend them a little, then I can do the same. Do we "use our freedom as a covering for evil" (1 Pet. 2:16)? Many Christians I know can't even drive their car half-a-mile without speeding. Brethren, if we will not submit when there is no widespread persecution, why would we ever think we would do so during such a time? We have much preparation to do in this area.

If our government is against our God and His ways, then why should we submit to them? "For such is the will of God that by doing right you may silence the ignorance of foolish men" (1 Pet. 2:15). Christ's example of enduring ridicule, shame, suffering, and even death is powerful (1 Pet. 2:20-23). He was able to accept wrong and refrain from lashing back because He "kept entrusting Himself to Him who judges righteously" (1 Pet. 2:23). The only instance in which God is pleased with our disobedience of human authorities is when they demand things contrary to His will (Acts 5:29). Otherwise, "whoever resists authority has opposed the ordinance of God and . . . will receive condemnation upon themselves" (Rom. 13:2).

We Must Seek Peace. The Lord told the captives to "seek the welfare of the city where I have sent you into exile" (Jer. 29:7). Again, the Lord was clear that the captivity would last seventy years and they needed to accept it. However, rebellion was on their minds instead. Jehoiakim led a revolt in a time he thought he could catch Nebuchadnezzar off guard (2 Kings 24:1). The only problem was that it was not just Nebuchadnezzar who wanted Judah to remain in captivity but the Lord as well. So, the Lord caused armies to go up against them and their uprising was snuffed out (2 Kings 24:2). God's plan was for them to do the very opposite–seek peace during their stay.

We, too, are in exile. Whether the government of our nation exalts the ways of Christianity or punishes those who exercise them, we should never be totally comfortable in this world (Heb. 11:13-16). However, can we accomplish our purpose during our stay if we are always causing tension between ourselves and those of this world? No, "the challenge for elders and gospel preachers today is to create that same remnant attitude in the church" (Ward, 178) that was demanded of the Jews in captivity.

Why is this attitude so necessary? Having lived in the prosperous nation of Norway, I came into contact with many immigrants who came for work. They often came without family or friends and would stay for very long periods of time. I often wondered what kept them going. It was hope. They hoped they could make enough money to return home and start up some business there or bring their family to Norway and make their home there. They knew they were going to have to stay awhile so they settled down and tried to live peaceably among a people who were very different from them.

The Lord said, if the place in which we live enjoys welfare, we "will have welfare" (Jer. 29:7). So, we should promote peace and morality wherever we are. It makes a great deal of sense.

> First of all, then, I urge that entreaties and prayers, petitions and thanksgivings, be made on behalf of all men, for kings and all who are in authority, so that we may lead a tranquil and quiet life in all godliness and dignity. This is good and acceptable in the sight of God our Savior, who desires all men to be saved and to come to the knowledge of the truth (1 Tim. 2:1-4).

We Must Continue to Be Salt and Light. Jesus said that His disciples are to be "salt" and "light" on the earth (Matt. 5:13-14). We are to flavor and brighten the world with righteousness and holiness. The more tasteless and dark the world becomes, the greater the need for us to fulfill this aspect of Christianity. Consider Mathetes' description in *The Letter to Diognetus* of second century Christians who were living under an anti-Christian government:

> For the Christians are distinguished from other men neither by country, nor language, nor the customs which they observe. For they neither inhabit cities of their own, nor employ a peculiar form of speech, nor lead a life which is marked out by any singularity. The course of conduct which they follow has not been devised by any speculation or deliberation of inquisitive men; nor do they, like some, proclaim themselves the advocates of any merely human doctrines. But, inhabiting Greek as well as barbarian cities, according as the lot of each of them has determined, and following the customs of the natives in respect to clothing, food, and the rest of their ordinary conduct, they display to us their wonderful and confessedly striking method of life. They dwell in their own countries, but simply as sojourners. As citizens, they share in all things with others, and yet endure all things as foreigners. Every foreign land is to them as their native country, and every land of their birth as a land of strangers. They marry, as do all [others]; they beget children; but they do not destroy their offspring. They have a common table, but not a common

bed. They are in the flesh, but do not live after the flesh. They pass their days on earth, but they are citizens of heaven. They obey the prescribed laws, and at the same time surpass the laws by their lives. They love all men, and are persecuted by all. They are unknown and condemned; they are put to death, and restored to life. They are poor, yet make many rich; they are in lack of all things, and yet abound in all; they are dishonored, and yet in their very dishonor are glorified. They are evil spoken of, and yet are justified; they are reviled, and bless; they are insulted, and repay the insult with honor; they do good, yet are punished as evil-doers. When punished, they rejoice as if quickened into life; they are assailed by the Jews as foreigners, and are persecuted by the Greeks; yet those who hate them are unable to assign any reason for their hatred.

To sum up all in one word–what the soul is in the body, that Christians are in the world. The soul is dispersed through all the members of the body, and Christians are scattered through all the cities of the world. The soul dwells in the body, yet is not of the body; and Christians dwell in the world, yet are not of the world (Turner, 171-172).

They made an impact. They added flavor and light to the hopeless and misguided world in which they lived.

One way in which we could impact our world in the same way is through good works. God said that we should be a people of good works (Tit. 2:11-14; Eph. 2:10). What could we do to have a greater impact on those outside of Christ, especially those who persecute us, than to do something good for them (Rom. 12:20-21)? It is sad that we seldom seek out and use opportunities to do good to others.

We must also continue to preach the gospel, even when that is the very thing that causes the world to hate us. There is no better way to brighten the world than with the light of God's Word (Ps. 119:105). I, however, have buried the Word deep within me at times when it was burning to come out. Why? I didn't want to deal with the immediate consequences. It would have been so easy for the Christians who were scattered from Jerusalem to tuck their tails and never speak out about Christ again (Acts 8:1). However, their faith caused them to keep preaching as they went their way (Acts 8:4)! It would even be easier and more justifiable (in our minds at least) to preach only the things that would not bring any problem or controversy. Paul makes it very clear that neglect to preach the truth in its entirety would make one guilty of the blood of those who fall because of it (Acts 20:26-27). We must preach "in season and out of season" but especially "out of season" (2 Tim. 4:2).

There is one thing I must suggest concerning preaching "out of season." If the government were to decide that preaching the truth on homosexuality or any other subject was illegal, that does not mean we need to preach about it all the time. In other words, we shouldn't be looking for a fight. Our preaching should be guided by what is *needful* and nothing else.

Last, but certainly not least, we must continue to build up one another and worship (Heb. 10:24-25). How will we flavor and brighten the world if we are becoming tasteless and our light is flickering? One of the best ways we can ensure the survival of Christianity is to build a strong church now. Let us never forsake God or our brethren by choosing something else instead of worshipping or spending time with our spiritual family! If you do, when those dark days arise, you'll wish you hadn't.

Conclusion

If the American government chooses to wage war on the saints, who will stand in the end? As during the Roman persecution of the church, the answer may not lie in the immediate future but in looking toward the Day of Judgment (Rev. 7:12-17). Some of God's people will most likely die before it is over (Rev. 2:10), but they who "have washed their robes and made them white in the blood of the Lamb" will be victorious. So, I leave you with the exhortation of the Hebrew writer:

> But remember the former days, when, after being enlightened, you endured a great conflict of sufferings, partly by being made a public spectacle through reproaches and tribulations, and partly by becoming sharers with those who were so treated. For you showed sympathy to the prisoners and accepted joyfully the seizure of your property, knowing that you have for yourselves a better possession and a lasting one. Therefore, do not throw away your confidence, which has a great reward. For you have need of endurance, so that when you have done the will of God, you may receive what was promised. FOR YET IN A VERY LITTLE WHILE, HE WHO IS COMING WILL COME, AND WILL NOT DELAY. BUT MY RIGHTEOUS ONE SHALL LIVE BY FAITH; AND IF HE SHRINKS BACK, MY SOUL HAS NO PLEASURE IN HIM. But we are not of those who shrink back to destruction, but of those who have faith to the preserving of the soul (Heb. 10:32-39).

Bibliography

Hailey, Homer. *Revelation: An Introduction and Commentary*. Grand Rapids: Baker Book House, 1979.

Jenkins, Ferrell. *Studies in the Book of Revelation*. Temple Terrace: Florida College Bookstore, 1993.

New American Standard Bible: 1995 Update. LaHabra: Lockman Foundation, 1995.

Owen, G. Frederick. *Abraham Lincoln: The Man and His Faith*. Wheaton: Tyndale House Publishers, 1976.

Sell, Henry Thorne. "Study 9: The Church In Persecution." *Studies in Early Church History*. Willow Grove: Woodlawn Electronic Publishing, 1998.

Turner, Allan. "Submit to the King of Babylon," *Living in Captivity: God's People in a Time of Crisis*. Ed. Daniel W. Petty. Temple Terrace: Florida College Press, 2010. 159-172.

Ward, Keith. "Seeking the Welfare of the City," *Living in Captivity: God's People in a Time of Crisis*. Ed. Daniel W. Petty. Temple Terrace: Florida College Press, 2010. 173-185.

Christianity Can Survive . . .

The Threat of Political Correctness
Bobby Leon Graham

For thirty to thirty-five years Western society has heard much about Political Correctness. Just what has been happening and what are the dangers of this movement? Is it possible that what is called "Political Correctness" has an objective besides politics? Because of its spiritual

---

Bobby Leon Graham was born August 30, 1946 to Mary and Leon Graham, Florence, Alabama. He spent most of his years growing up under the preaching of Curtis Flatt and Franklin T. Puckett. His father served as an elder at College View for thirty years. His father is now at the Helton Drive congregation (last twenty years) and his mother is deceased

Bobby graduated from Coffee High School in 1964; attended Florida College two and one-half years; graduated from Athens College and finished his Master's Degree in Education. Bobby did schoolwork at Athens Bible School for thirty-three years, serving as teacher, assistant principal, and principal; he still teaches Bible and conducts elementary chapel.

Bobby began preaching in 1962 while still in high school, preaching once per Sunday and increased to twice per Sunday after a few months; he preached through college in Florida and Alabama.

Bobby married Karen Ruth Hodge from Akron, Ohio, in November 1967; they have three children: Richard; Mary Katherine, who is married to Darren Winland (preaches in Limestone County, AL) and has two children; and Laura Ruth married to Jeremy Paschall (preaches in Cullman, AL); all three are faithful Christians. He has preached at Somerville Road in Decatur with Granville Tyler, three churches in Limestone County; Richmond, VA (West End); Trinity, AL; Huntsville, AL (Chapman Acres). Bobby has written for *Gospel Guide*, edited by Billy Norris, for forty-one years; he has helped train several young preachers from the North Alabama area and Canada for many years. He has served as an elder in two congregations; has stressed in his own work "mission meetings" in destitute fields, making many trips to New England states and also such work in the mountains of VA and KY and twelve preaching trips to Belize. Bobby currently writes the Question and Answer column in *Truth Magazine*.

implications, this campaign poses dangers in the spiritual realm. *Political Correctness* poses another—but not the most formidable—hindrance to the work of the gospel of Jesus Christ in our present generation. "For still our ancient foe doth seek to work us woe; His craft and power are great, and armed with cruel hate; on earth is not his equal." This is but another attempt of Satan to undo the Lord's work and defeat the Lord's people. People committed to the Lord Jesus Christ and devoted to His cause should not and shall not allow this most recent effort to succeed. Earlier generations enlisted in the army of Lord Sabaoth have been thus challenged to fight, to speak out, to oppose, to advance, to pray, and to be strong like men (1 Cor. 16:13).

> A mighty fortress is our God,
> A bulwark never failing;
> Our helper He, amid the flood
> Of mortal ills prevailing:
> For still our ancient foe
> Doth seek to work us woe;
> His craft and power are great,
> And, armed with cruel hate,
> On earth is not his equal.
>
> Did we in our own strength confide,
> Our striving would be losing;
> Were not the right Man on our side,
> The Man of God's own choosing:
> Dost ask who that may be?
> Christ Jesus, it is He;
> Lord Sabaoth, His Name,
> From age to age the same,
> And He must win the battle.
>
> And though this world, with evil filled,
> Should threaten to undo us,
> We will not fear, for God hath willed
> His truth to triumph through us:
> Let goods and kindred go,
> This mortal life also;
> The body they may kill:
> God's truth abideth still,
> His kingdom is forever.

Whether godless attempts, modern or ancient, be our focus, our enemy remains the same (1 Pet. 5:8-9); and those implements of spiritual warfare which have always worked in crushing Satan under our feet will still succeed (Rom. 16:20; Eph. 6:10-20). Our part is to make sure that our faith in God and confidence in the Scriptures do not waver, lest the fight be lost.

Our purpose in this lesson shall be to demonstrate how Political Correctness affects Biblical doctrine, thus threatening Christianity, and to identify the means available to the Christian in countering this force of evil. It shall also be our purpose to motivate God's people to rise to the challenge and "fight the good fight of the faith, lay hold on eternal life, unto which you were called and did confess the good confession in the sight of many witnesses" (1 Tim. 6:12). Could there be any more worthy Commander, any more worthwhile effort, any more needed battle, and any more enduring reward? Rise up, O man of God! Let us prepare to fight!

What Is Political Correctness?

Someone said, "Political Correctness is having to say you're sorry." It finds offense in the most unlikely places and even seeks it in innocent and harmless conversation. Just what is political correctness?

> Political Correctness (PC) is the communal tyranny that erupted in the 1980s. It was a spontaneous declaration that particular ideas, expressions, and behavior, which were then legal, should be forbidden by law, and people who transgressed should be punished. It started with a few voices but grew in popularity until it became unwritten and written law within the community. With those who were publicly declared as being not politically correct becoming the object of persecution by the mob, if not prosecution by the state (Philip Atkinson, "The Origin and Nature of Political Correctness," *www.ourcivilisation.com/pc.htm*).

The terminology is somewhat misleading because it suggests that this ideology relates to political matters; while this is so, it certainly is not limited to this area. In fact, all areas comprising the arena of American life are affected by Political Correctness, with hardly any area being exempted. The thinking, actions, ideas, and direction of the world are touched by Political Correctness; and this includes almost all aspects of our culture — government, education, civic matters, art, business/industrial, language, literature, athletics, and others. This all-encompassing philosophy is ostensibly designed to prevent behavior, practices, language, policies, and ideas which are offensive to the socially disadvantaged or people discriminated against through insult, exclusion, or marginalization by any sector of society. Both social and institutional offense are targeted. This practice is often taken to extremes by its adherents and practitioners, so that absurd situations are created. The list of areas affected by this philosophy is a long one: occupational, gender, racial, cultural, sexual orientation, disability, and age-related matters. In other words, no one is supposed to say or do anything that would negatively affect anybody in these compartments of American life by distasteful, contemptuous, or other pejorative means. One weakness of this approach becomes immediately apparent: Who shall judge what is offensive and enforce the mandates? Another fallacy of the current approach also comes to the forefront: What basis or standard shall we employ in such judgments?

The ideas associated with Political Correctness are not simply left-wing political thinking of a group attempting to conform to society's mold. While conformity is a part of their identity, their objective is broader and deeper than conforming; they are trying to reshape society from the ground level up! The destruction of spiritual principles and long-standing moral principles is the more dangerous result that will follow if this movement succeeds. Make no mistake: Compromise on every front is the design of this godless approach!

Perhaps this is a good time to stress that this lecture is not a defense of partiality, rudeness, discourtesy, or unkindness. We do not defend inconsiderate treatment of individuals or groups in either word or deed (Matt. 7:12; 22:39; 1 Pet. 3:8). For instance, ethnic slurs do often convey ideas which God's people should avoid, lest they disparage the worth of any person or lessen the appeal of the gospel to the lost (1 Cor. 9:19-23). The Christian should remember the statement of Paul: "And this I do for the gospel's sake, that I may be partaker of it with you." As we continue, it shall become clear that Christians can treat people right, because of their devotion to Christ and His work, but oppose the lurking evil pushing this movement.

What Is the Origin of Political Correctness?
What is the source of such thinking as this? What explanation is there for its origin? What might have begun as an innocent and even well-intended effort by some has become, I believe, a tool in the hands of people bent on our national destruction by a radical re-structuring of our civilization.

Marxism, long an economic ideology, is designed to level society, removing the advantage held by any group except the one in control. When Political Correctness attempts to level all groups in society by fiat, it becomes "cultural Marxism." One has to travel only to the nearest college/university campus to witness a bastion of Political Correctness. There every "victim" group—the homosexual-rights group, the feminists, and whatever minority group wants such defense—finds its defenders in the proponents of Political Correctness. Women's Studies, Black Studies, Environmental Studies, and Homosexual Studies have been departmentalized to elevate the standing of the groups whom they represent and the "victim" cause they plead. Campus political liberals persecute and prosecute any speaking, writing, or acting out of accord with their designs and desires. They work to intimidate all who oppose them, through their labeling of the opposition as homophobic, racist, insensitive, discriminatory, or sexist. Their ultimate design is to narrow the options of what is politically/socially acceptable. If you do not understand that they are working overtime to transform our country (and all countries built on the western model) into a model of their liking, you have been asleep and need to wake up! All dissent is forbidden, in spite of Constitutional guarantees to the contrary. Our freedom is at stake, even the freedom to preach the gospel of Christ. It is not just a "phase through which our nation is passing." If you have tended to pass it off as merely amusing or half-serious, I hope to shake you all the way to your roots. What will you then do about it?

Examples of Political Correctness

A survey of modern American/Western culture provides a sampling of how Political Correctness has impacted life:

1. In the field of language, such historic terms like "homosexual," "handi-capped," "Negro" or "black," "fireman," "He" or "Father" in reference to God, "bums," "mankind," and "stewardess" or "mailman" are often avoided by the politically correct crowd. Bedtime stories have become politically correct. Even the Bible and denominational hymnals have been affected by this movement, as gender-neutral versions heralded by liberals are the result.

2. In matters of morality, there has been a determined effort to galvanize sodomy with normalcy and respectability, thereby branding its op-ponents as homophobes. Every kind of filth has reached the level of acceptance with large constituencies. Various religious groups have done the once-thought-impossible by accepting homosexuals into both the membership and the "clergy." Anybody daring to speak out against such is branded as bigoted, narrow-minded.

3. In the field of education, Women's Studies and Ethnic Studies—replace-ments for Western Civilization and American History—have become the

base for attacking and re-shaping much politically incorrect thinking. American heroes have become villains; all victims of American aggression have become heroes; abortion has worked its way into acceptance; an egalitarian family structure has become the model; the husband has become an unnecessary appendage in the home; absolute and objective truth has become verboten; and personal, existential truth has become the norm. In many respects college and university campuses have become the most bigoted environment in the country, as demonstrated in the Ben Stein movie *Expelled* in recent years. Schools on lower levels have stopped using the "Honor Roll," and teachers have changed from red pens to purple ones for marking papers.

4.   In the area of government, tolerance is limited to other religions than "Christianity," while "Christianity" has been ridden out of town under the guise of separation of church and state. Multiculturalism is the excuse introduced to take its place. References to God and Christ in school graduation ceremonies, prayers to the "Christian" God, and Christmas celebrations in schools and displays on public property have been victims. Islamic rights have become the focus of much government action, and the ACLU has become the legal arm of the Liberal Movement to accomplish these ends. Capital punishment is now viewed by the PC crowd as a tool to subjugate and punish minorities.

5.   In the arena of religion-science, evolution has become the darling of many and its acceptance has become a test of admission to many university faculties. Creationists are castigated as uneducated buffoons.

A Brief Analysis of Political Correctness

Would it awaken you if I tell you that the bias of these proponents is anti-God and anti-spiritual? I shall demonstrate during the balance of our study that this is true. I make no idle charge. Humanistic philosophers could not be more enamored with this movement. Enemies of Christianity find delight in this movement's success. Just as economic Marxism seeks to remove all economic differences through compulsion, so cultural Marxism seek to obliterate all religious and cultural differences as advantages or impediments through social pressure, coercion, and ridicule. Hardly ever will you hear reasoned defenses of the behavior being advocated, but name-calling and disparagement of the objectors abound. *Multiculturalism* is the watchword of the movement, as it attempts to make all beliefs equally acceptable and valid (*pluralism*). Here lies the root of the spiritual dangers of Political

Correctness, and New Testament Christians know that all beliefs, doctrines, and practices are not equal. One Lord is not as good as another Lord, nor is one faith as good as another faith (Eph. 4:4-6).

Analysis of the entire ideology indicates the following aspects, all of which demonstrate that it is a *competing spiritual ideology* making an unspiritual attempt to alter society's spiritual moorings:

1. The *Basis* upon which Political Correctness operates is the corrupt, decadent religious system already existing. The abuses of this system operating in opposition to true New Testament religion abound, so much that they have become the system of denominational "Christianity." The system is the consequence of the many abuses of true Biblical religion. Except for the tolerance allowed in this decadent "Christianity," there could be no such attack as that of Political Correctness. It seems to be easier for many to roll over and play dead than to fight for what is right!

2. The *Hypocrisy* of Political Correctness exists because this ideology commends and encourages the same crumbling system which makes it possible, giving it support and encouragement in preference to genuine New Testament Christianity. Yes, a mutual support system operates between this movement and so-called Christianity. At the same time, the Political Correctness movement launches criticism after criticism at "Christianity."

3. The *Thrust* of Political Correctness is the satisfaction of all cultures by a leveling of all manifestations of superiority or advantage except those favored by the enforcers. Ensuring this result is the *permissive attitude encouraged* toward all beliefs, teachings, and practices. Political Correctness, which is the Ecumenical Movement transferred from the smaller stage of Protestantism to the world stage occupied by World Religions, does in our age what Freemasonry taught and encouraged on a more limited basis by its acceptance of all religions believing in God. The *"one faith is as good as another"* and *"one church is as good as another"* approach of Protestant denominationalism for many decades has prepared fertile soil for sowing this iniquitous seed of Political Correctness.

4. The *Modus Operandi* of this movement is first to ignore and then to attack the idea of God, an objective standard of authority, the restrictions and principles of revealed religion, the reality of a divine Savior (Jesus

Christ), and the superior morality of the Bible. All such doctrines are subject to frequent attack because of the exclusive nature of all such doctrines. It is simply impossible to believe in the God of the Bible, or in Jesus Christ the Son of God, and to follow the religious tenets of Political Correctness.

5. The *Effect* of the movement is seen in its fostering of a diluted morality, a passive zeal, and a timid discipleship in "Christians," thereby weakening "Christianity." By its various means of attacking and conquering, the movement seeks a minimizing of "Christianity," or at least its diminished influence.

What Are the Spiritual Mistakes of Political Correctness?

1. The first mistake is *pretending to know more about God's work and will than God knows.* Whenever religious people speak for God without divine authority, you can mark it down that they think they know as much as God knows, possibly more than He knows. Anytime we speak or act without divine authority from the Bible, we err in the same way. The attitude encouraged is one of *not worrying about what the Bible says.* How many of us have encountered someone saying, "I can't believe in a God who judges and punishes!" The Bible is filled with incidents recorded to warn us about disobedience and urge our obedience. Life has taught us the truthfulness of such claims as Deuteronomy 6:24, but the principle was true long before we tested it.

2. The second mistake made by advocates of this ideology is *substituting the counterfeit for the genuine.* God always teaches and encourages the genuine; men often invent the counterfeit. Human history is dotted with the inventions of men who had no regard for God and the wisdom of His way, and so it continues until this day. The genuine always surpasses the counterfeit, the fake. The system of Political Correctness is so filled with counterfeits that it becomes a fake system, and those who advocate it perpetrate a fraud upon humanity. The *sham of modern Christianity* enjoys the commendation of this movement, while the *true religion of the New Testament*— conceived by God before the foundation of the world, promised by God and later prophesied by Old Testament worthies, previewed in the types and shadows of the Old Testament systems, heralded by John the Baptist, prepared for and initially introduced by Jesus Christ, and finally fulfilled by the teaching of the apostles and prophets of the New Testament period—remains God's choice but a reject by man. So it was with Jesus the chief cornerstone—chosen by God, but rejected by men (1 Pet. 2:4).

3. Another spiritual mistake of Political Correctness is its *tolerance of other saviors*, even to the rejecting of the world's only Savior. Hare Krishna, Buddha, Zeus, and especially Allah often receive better press than the One who was virgin-born, miracle-attested, and resurrection-proved; but we know which One will be on the throne in the final judgment (2 Cor. 5:10).

4. The *pick-and choose approach to the Bible* over true discipleship stands as a fourth mistake. The usual handling of the Bible by the proponents of Political Correctness involves an acceptance of those teachings meeting human standards (personal preference, test of tradition, majority support, existential experience, Jesus-Group acceptance, etc.), but repudiation of those failing such tests. Whenever humans decide the test or construct the filter through which valid and relevant ideas must pass, the result will always be human, not divine (Matt. 4:4). Only Deity is qualified to direct our steps (Jer. 10:23; Isa. 55:8-9).

5. The idea that *disagreeing with others' beliefs or showing them what the Bible teaches is unkind and intolerant* is another spiritual mistake which prevails in this movement. The two are not equal! If such were the case, then it would require that these proponents accept those areas in which they disagree with me; but they refuse to do so, because they wish to be in the driver's seat. Not even Jesus, often heralded as kind, non-judgmental, and passive enough to accept whatever you want to throw at Him, tolerated error and remained kind and sweet when people refused to accept His frequent appeals for repentance (Matt. 23). It is not extremist to disagree with a false teacher or to refute error; but if it is, I plead guilty to being an extremist! I refuse to be silent about matters I consider mandates from God.

6. The *fundamental and undergirding mistake* of the entire Political Correctness movement is the attempt to humanize God and deify man. When man becomes the source of wisdom, information, and knowledge but God is relegated to the back shelf of the library of antiquity, the first and basic error has been committed. The root of all sin is the *replacement of God with man*. When man becomes the rebel, all of his acts constitute rebellion (Rom. 1:18-32)! Ancient Judah followed this course, according to Jeremiah 2:9-13, prompting God's lawsuit against His own people. The situation was so unparalleled that the Lord called the heavens to witness it and declared that not even the pagan nations had thus forsaken their own gods. Judah had changed their glory for something unprofitable. Her evils were twofold: forsaking God and inventing others to take His place.

Additional Proof of the Spiritual Mistakes of Political Correctness

Proponents often castigate the Bible and those who adhere to it as bigots. Their often-heard cry is, "Why Worry about What the Bible Says?" Those concerned about the Bible are also viewed as extremists. If one believes that Jesus is the only Savior of the world, this is marked as "proof number one" of his extremism. Likewise, any willing to be so extreme as to offer their judgment that the non-Christian is lost is consigned to the trash-heap as judgmental. Have you noticed that all such statements made and positions held point in one direction? Have you noticed that all extremists and bigots are in the group having a close affinity with the Bible? People willing to moderate their beliefs and positions to agree somewhat with the proponents of Political Correctness somehow escape their label and judgments. Do you think it is remotely possible that they are just as extremist and judgmental as those they thus label? The truth is that the "labelers" and the "labeled" are poles apart and which one is which depends on who does the labeling. It just happens that those controlling the media and speaking the loudest are the ones who had an agenda and first pushed that agenda. Don't forget that they are as extremist and judgmental as anybody else in the world! Ours is not the first time that humanistic philosophy, godless ideology, and the secularist mind set have formed a combine to maintain their place in the driver's seat of society.

How Can the Religion of Jesus Christ Survive/Overcome Political Correctness?

In order for the Lord's people to survive this attack and to conquer Political Correctness, they must *recognize the enemy for what he is*. He often includes those claiming to be proponents of "Christianity," though they view it as a body of human beliefs and practices, handed down by tradition from earlier generations, which often altered and modified them to fit their own times. In fact, the suggestion of those with this view of matters is to modify, conform, syncretize, and compromise. Such has been the perpetual approach that has brought modern Christianity to its present state. It seems reasonable that this approach must continue, if the kind of "Christianity" our world has inherited is to have what it takes to survive. Current thinking advises:

> In our preaching we must not attack denominationalism or false teaching. Tolerate it in silence, and pray that a passive utterance of the gospel will correct the condition. The result: A nonaggression pact with the devil. Are we to think that by not attacking Satan he will not attack us? (M. Kurfees Pullias, "No Nonaggression Pact with the Devil").

On the other hand, true Christianity, that which originated with Jesus and His apostles and first streamed from the fountain of divine truth in the First Century, stands as the pure stream of water before it reaches the contaminations and pollutions of lower regions. How can it survive in its unpolluted condition? We must understand and view the teaching and practice which Jesus sanctioned as the way of salvation and life as He did, nothing more and nothing less. We must *adopt the attitude of Jesus* toward it! Away with the suggestions of some that "Christianity" can survive without the Bible and the God of its past, and that we should modify and compromise to survive.

The cultural context in which Jesus and His apostles worked to generate this divine teaching and the movement which it produced must also be acknowledged as antithetical to the means and goals of the Lord and His people. Paganism among the nations was certainly not friendly to Christians; the view toward this new movement was that it was founded upon atheism, because it failed to espouse belief in any of the current deities of the heathen. Likewise, the mysticism of the ancient cults, the Judaism that had developed along human lines in recent centuries, and the rising threat of Gnosticism near the end of the First Century—none was friendly to what the God of heaven and earth had in mind from times eternal! We must recognize that nothing worldly has ever viewed the Lord's work favorably at any time in history. Our world has never been "a friend to grace." *All that is of the world is God's enemy (Jas. 4:4)!*

Christianity can survive, even as it has ever survived through the ages, if its adherents will *commit themselves to more than its survival*. No New Testament Christian will be satisfied with anything less than the advancement of the kingdom of Jesus Christ. From the time of the Lord's inauguration at God's right hand in heaven, it was never the will of the King or the design of the gospel of the kingdom that the kingdom merely continue to exist (Matt. 28:19-20; Mark 16:15-16; Luke 24:46-47). Spiritual progress demands that the message be declared by adherents fully persuaded of its truthfulness and relevance!

The *orders of the King* demand that foes must be slain, enemies must be opposed, arguments must be answered, and every high thing that exalts itself against the knowledge of God must be cast down (2 Cor. 10:3-6). "Upon the side of Christ no change in orders or battle tactics has been issued for nearly two thousand years. Jesus has no living ambassadors. Those he appointed long since are dead, but the messages presented unto them to convey have been indelibly preserved. There can be no doubt as to the wishes and commands of Christ" (Pullias). The accomplishments here stipulated are readily *realized through spiritual weaponry, not carnal*. Those weapons deriving their might from the Almighty God are not selfish ambition, lies, misrepresentation, gossip, envy, suspicion, slander, cruel reproaches, reviling, biting and devouring each other, or intrigue to promote a human cause. Truth, only truth, has the endorsement of the One who is truth and can be nothing else, for use in advancing His cause and slaying any foe. Both the positive and the negative work of the kingdom of God call for truth and only truth, and disciples of the Author of truth will devote themselves to His work and His ways of doing that work (John 18:36-37). The use of such carnal means and weapons fits into the same category as the use of food, fun, and other carnal lures as enticements to spiritual ends. To employ men's carnal means or standards and to aspire to their carnal goals is to denigrate the cause that we plead, disparage the message of truth which we proclaim, and dishonor the King whom we serve. As the truth goes forth on its mission, there also goes with it the assurance of God that it will accomplish its task (Heb. 4:12-13; Isa. 55:9-11).

The *fervor and enthusiasm* generated by the gospel and the spirit of gratitude for what God has done must then work together to fuel our efforts to spread the glad tidings of Christ as the duly appointed Ruler in the kingdom of God. The gloom and pessimism associated with defeat must give way to the optimism and positive thinking associated with success and confidence. God's work is one of victory, the gospel is the advance declaration of the victory, and disciples of the Lord are the victors (Rom. 8:28-39; 1 Cor. 15:53-58; 1 John 5:4-5; Rev. 12:10-12). "We can't do it" will then become "I can do all things through Christ, who strengthens me" (Phil. 4:13). Christ knocks the "t" out of "can't."

Why should the Christian be optimistic in this battle? There are godlessness, ungodliness, faithlessness, worldliness, carnality, materialism, and much more abounding in our time—all of which can dismay us. What is there to keep us forward-looking and positive-thinking? God has given us the information and motivation needed to carry through in this struggle. May I suggest some "fuel for our fire":

•   Gospel is still powerful (Rom. 1:16).
•   God still has a remnant (Rom. 11:5).
•   See the big picture—eternity (Eph. 1).
•   God will not desert you (Heb. 13:5f; Eph. 1:18).

- Temporary difficulty can help (Phil. 4:11).
- God hasn't failed in a promise (Tit. 1:2).
- Jesus Christ is still in control (Rev. 1).

If you find this fuel lacking in power, you are definitely driving the wrong vehicle and heading in the wrong direction. No child of the Lord should remain idle or indolent. With the gospel as our guide, the lost as our opportunity, Satan as our challenge, the church as our family, and heaven as our eternal abode, what could keep us from the task of surviving, overcoming, and conquering?

> Christ, in His personal ministry, waged an aggressive battle against Satan and his agents. The apostles did likewise. The leaders of the Restoration Movement in America waxed bold in the fray. Every true gospel preacher since the apostles has followed their example. Brethren, the life of the church of Christ is at stake; therefore "watch ye, stand fast in the faith, quit you like men, be strong" (1 Cor. 16:13).

> Sign no nonaggression pact with the devil (Pullias).

What we have learned in this section of our study is that we must respond with faith and courage to overcome the foe (1 John 5:4), but God has already spoken to keep us engaged in the battle. Victory is ours if we keep ourselves in the love of God by loving Him with all our heart, soul, mind, and strength and loving our neighbor as ourselves (Matt. 22:37-40).

Bibliography

Atkinson, Philip. Political Correctness. Website: *http://www.ourcivilisation. com/pc.htm.*

Katz, Jonathan I. What is Political Correctness? Website: *http://wuphys. wustl.edu/~katz/ pc.html.*

Pullias, M. Kurfees. *No Nonaggression Pact with the Devil.* No Source Information.

Christianity Can Survive . . .

The Threat of a Diluted Message

Bob Waldron

Introduction

When I first thought of this topic, it unleashed a flood of thoughts that are particularly pertinent in the face of an increasing paganizing of the world, and in view of the threat of global Islam. All one has to do to see this pertinence is to reflect on the areas that were first evangelized, the eastern Mediterranean seaboard, north Africa, and modern Turkey. Today, a church after the New Testament order can hardly be found in those areas. The church also spread throughout most of Europe and the countries all around the Mediterranean, and beyond. The fact is that churches after the

Bob Waldron was born September 19, 1941, son of Randel and Carrie Dasher Waldron. He grew up in Waycross, GA and attended Florida College (1959-1961). Bob finished his Bachelor's degree at Florence State College (now University of North Alabama) in 1963. He married Sandra Lee (daughter of Irven Lee) in 1963 and to this union two children were born: Ryan Waldron and Laura Waldron Black. Bob and Sandra have four grandchildren. Bob preached his first sermon in 1959 and began preaching every Sunday at Newburg, AL (1961-1963). Since then, he has preached at York, AL (1963-1966); Butler, AL (1966-1968); Sumiton, AL (1968-77); Westview in Hartselle (1977-1981); Hanceville, AL (1981-1988); Clay (1988-1993); Eastside in Athens, AL (1993-2007). For many years Bob has preached 10-12 meetings per year, plus multiple trips to Brazil and to the Czech Republic. Bob and Sandra, his wife, have collaborated in writing 12 full sized books, including *History and Geography of the Bible Story*, nine books covering the whole Bible, a book on Bible teaching called *A Generation That Knows Not God*, and a book exploring our relationship with God called *Christ In You the Hope of Glory*, plus a number of tracts and booklets. Bob wrote the commentaries on Nahum in the *Truth Commentary* series on the Minor Prophets and on *1 and 2 Samuel* (2011). He is currently working on commentaries for that series covering 1 Kings - 2 Chronicles. In May of 2007 Bob cut back on his local preaching to devote more time to his writing. However, in April of 2008, after forty-seven years in Alabama, he moved to Florida to work with the church at Trilacoochee, a few miles north of Dade City, FL. He is now busy writing the commentary on 1 and 2 Kings.

New Testament order are exceedingly scarce in those parts of the world as well as in the world at large.

One is tempted to blame Islam with the scarcity of churches, particularly in countries around the eastern half of the Mediterranean and in north Africa. The fact is that churches in these areas, as well as in Europe and north Africa, were lost before Islam ever arose. They were lost to a perversion, to a dilution, of the gospel message.

By the time Islam showed up, many of the people invaded by Islamic forces basically considered religion a matter of six of one or a half dozen of the other, and the general population found it possible to make the switch. Because pluralism is the official policy of our government, because of the increasing paganizing of our society, and because nominal Christianity possesses only the husk of Christianity wherever it is found, our society is ripe for the taking. I am afraid that many of our citizens would be glad to make the switch to Islam as long as they could keep their guns.

Paul told the elders of the church at Ephesus: "I know that after my departing grievous wolves shall enter in among you, not sparing the flock; and from among your own selves shall men arise, speaking perverse things, to draw away the disciples after them" (Acts 20:29-30). He also predicted: "But the Spirit saith expressly, that in later times some shall fall away from the faith, giving heed to seducing spirits and doctrines of demons, through the hypocrisy of men that speak lies, branded in their own conscience as with a hot iron; forbidding to marry, and commanding to abstain from meats which God created to be received with thanksgiving by them that believe and know the truth" (1 Tim. 4:1-3).

The only way the church can survive the threat of a diluted message is to refuse for it to be diluted. Paul wrote the Galatians saying that some were preaching another gospel (Gal. 1:6). He pointed out, however, that there is no such thing as a different gospel, but that men were seeking to pervert the gospel of Christ (Gal. 1:7). His warning was: "Though we, or an angel from heaven, should preach unto you any gospel other than that which we preached unto you, let him be anathema. As we have said before, so say I now again, If any man preacheth unto you any gospel other than that which you received, let him be anathema" (Gal. 1:8-9). A perverted gospel is not the saving gospel.

Paul determined to know nothing among the Corinthians save Jesus Christ and Him crucified (1 Cor. 2:2). He said, "My speech and my preaching were not in persuasive words of wisdom, but in demonstration of the Spirit and of power: that your faith should not stand in the wisdom of men, but in the power of God" (1 Cor. 2:4-5). Only the gospel of Christ crucified is the power of God unto salvation (Rom. 1:16).

Paul's instructions to Timothy were to hold the pattern of sound words (2 Tim. 1:13) and to commit the things he had heard from Paul to faithful men who would be able to teach others also (2 Tim. 2:2). He told Titus to speak the things which befit the sound doctrine (Tit. 2:1). An altered gospel is not sound but contaminated and defiled.

No congregation can remain faithful with a diluted gospel being preached, and history is littered with the debris of churches that were destroyed and had their candlesticks removed because of a diluted gospel. When we say the church can survive the threat of a diluted message, we must distinguish whether we mean an individual congregation, whether we are thinking of individual congregations in a generic sense or whether we are thinking of the universal church. With regard to a congregation, we must emphasize that the survival of any local church is based on its enduring sound doctrine and not turning aside to fables (2 Tim. 4:4). When we say "the church," meaning the church universal, the one body, of which Christ is the Head (Eph. 1:22-23; 4:4), we are referring, not to an organization, but to a relationship. The church universal is not confined to the living but includes the dead. Therefore its survival is assured whether there are any living saints or not.

Long ago God said that He would set up a kingdom that would never be destroyed, nor would the sovereignty thereof be left to another people, but it would break in pieces and consume all other nations (Dan. 2:44). Throughout the many centuries God has ruled over men, and the Messiah's rule is over all the dominion of God except for the Father Himself (1 Cor. 15:27). The Messianic kingdom is the one referred to in Daniel 2:44. The kingdom of Christ would exist whether a single Christian lived. When we think about *Christianity* failing or succeeding, we are not necessarily saying that the *Messianic kingdom* has succeeded or failed. The rule of Christ is accomplishing the will of God in every generation regardless of how many Christians there are. And as long as the seed of the kingdom, the word (Luke 8:11), lasts the children of the kingdom can be born. Although I think it is likely that there has never been a time when Christians did not exist, the continuity of living Christians is not what makes the kingdom endure. It is the germinating power of the seed, the gospel, that enables the kingdom to last for ever. As long as the generative power of the gospel lasts, Christianity can be spread (1 Pet. 1:22-25).

Other topics in this series deal with obstacles Christianity faces. My subject is the threat of a diluted message. Denominationalism furnishes us with a good example of what happens when the gospel message is diluted. The classic doctrine of "faith only" has characterized denominations from their beginnings, but they have gone far beyond this doctrine. Rationalism has destroyed the faith of the mainline denominations so that they have abandoned any moral stance on abortion, on homosexuality, and have taken positions of unbelief on many cardinal doctrines such as the Deity of Christ, and the inspiration of the Scriptures. All of these positions are the result of the diluted gospel that has characterized denominationalism from its inception.

We could discuss examples of a diluted gospel, and we could look at things without end that will promote a diluted message, but I have chosen five: Personal ambition, lack of faith in the word, faulty exegesis, carelessness in preaching, and emphasis on presenting pleasant sermons. Since preachers have a very great impact on what is preached, my comments will mainly concern preachers and their preaching. My aim is to deal with things that lead to a diluted message.

Personal Ambition
Men come to preaching through various doors. Few men ever have the opportunity to be a leader, to be prominent. For some, preaching is an opportunity to have that prominence when it will be available no other way. I have known men who achieved a certain standing among brethren and then found that there were other callings in which they could gain prominence, and they promptly abandoned preaching and transferred to something they could really put their hearts into.

As men who know nothing about preaching endeavor to become preachers, some tend to emphasize externals such as their libraries, preaching for large churches, and having cushy offices. Some young men observe older, more mature men, who have obtained a large library, etc., and determine that nothing will do but for them to have a large library, and to know all the right men, and travel among the movers and shakers of the brotherhood. Televangelists have comprehensive organizations that treat the preacher as the head of a multi-milion dollar corporation. He is surrounded by assistants as he administers schools, counseling services, and real estate arrangements. Too often role models are chosen consciously or unconsciously from televangelists among whom preaching is a public performance with emphasis on crowd-pleasing and lessons that are relevant to the working man such as dieting, and learning how to balance a checkbook. This kind of preaching will create swollen churches, with Joel Osteen and Max Lucado-like preachers. Precious little is left of the gospel in the messages preached by such men. As preachers of the gospel we must preach Jesus Christ and Him crucified (1 Cor. 2:2). Let our role models be Moses, Samuel, Elijah, Isaiah, Jeremiah, and, above all else, Jesus.

A competitive spirit and the desire to establish a reputation can lead to disaster. One of the most harmful spirits through the years has been the desire to establish one's intellect. This has led some to think that which entered not into the heart of man (1 Cor. 2:9) or of God (Jer. 19:5; 32:35). Doctrines are invented by men who gather to themselves a following. They have come up with things such as the A.D. 70 doctrine advocated by Max King and others and many other destructive heresies. The goal of every Bible student should be to think what God has thought before, not to discover new truths and lead some movement.

Paul used himself and Apollos as examples. He said others may seek to create a party centered around Paul or Apollos, but what are men but servants (1 Cor. 3:4-7)? Apollos himself was not mighty, but mighty *in the Scriptures* (Acts 18:24). Timothy was instructed to study the Scriptures, to know them (2 Tim. 2:15). Our chief emphasis as men of God should be to lay up God's word in our hearts so that we can preach it to others (2 Tim. 2:15) and that we might not sin against God (Ps. 119:11). We must take heed to our teaching for in doing this we will save both ourselves and them that hear us (1 Tim. 4:16). We need to emphasize the holy Scriptures in our studies. In dealing with personal ambition we must ask, "If Jesus had been dealing with a group of gospel preachers, would He have had to wash our feet?"

Faulty Exegesis

If you are a church-going person, you might ask yourself when was the last time you heard a preacher preach a lesson that was an explanation of some Bible passage. Very few churches today have the Bible used in their preaching. Their preachers not only do not use the scriptures in preaching, many of them actually do not believe the scriptures. When did you hear a lesson on pleasing God by doing the things that he said?

Merely calling oneself a preacher does not mean he automatically knows how to expound written material, much less Scripture. Good exegesis requires the ability to read well, and good expositional skills come more readily for one who is by nature a reader. But if one undertakes to preach the word, he must take it in hand to qualify himself to interpret written material. In speaking of the commentaries of Hugo Grotius (1583-1645), R. K. Harrison said, "His commentaries were of importance in that they espoused the principles adopted by the Reformers in their endeavor to interpret Scripture solely by the application of grammatical rules independently of *a priori* dogmatic assumptions" (Harrison, 8). This attitude led to the Latin expression, *Sola Scriptura* – only Scripture.

In all the study we do, the Scripture needs to be far and away our chief emphasis. Too many men make the Internet the source of their information, choosing anecdotes and statistics that constitute the bulk of the sermon. We spend more time cruising the Internet than we do studying Scripture. Once I was asked what is the main book I use besides my Bible. The answer is *Young's Analytical Concordance*.

Know the word of God. When we study, the first thing we must do is confront the text. Instead of keying in on one word too quickly we need to survey the book or passage as a whole. As we begin to study the sentences, be sure to understand the words, but don't let word studies become the tail that wags the dog; they are a means to an end. Since God taught His wisdom in words which the Spirit taught, combining spiritual things with spiritual words, He intends for us to interpret Scripture by the rules of grammar and syntax that govern any study of textual material. More than books about the Bible, men need to know the Scriptures themselves, whole books, and verses, and words.

Each expounder of God's word must come to the Scripture knowing that he will receive heavier judgment (James 3:1). We must be very careful when we deal with Holy Writ. We must not concentrate on the hidden things that only the elite can know, nor seek for original interpretations just to be original. I believe that Scripture always makes sense. When I don't understand Scripture, I haven't studied it long enough to see the point. One of the most important things in exegesis is to respect the context – always. When Jesus or an apostle quoted from the Old Testament, they knew and respected the context. Jesus respected the context of passages He quoted and set an example for us to do likewise.

Failures to expound Scripture properly has resulted in the denominational doctrine of "faith only" by affirming that "faith" means "faith only" in spite of an express statement in God's word that it is "not by faith only" (James 2:24). James 2:24 is set aside on the basis that it is talking about one who is already a child of God, in spite of the fact that Rahab the harlot is one of the examples in the context (James 2:25).

Premillennialism is based on one passage that mentions a reign of a thousand years, though it does not mention the second coming of Christ, nor a reign on earth, and only the righteous dead are involved (Rev. 20:1-6). A whole Christian mythology is spun out of such meager fibers.

One eternal covenant is advocated on the basis that the moral law of God has always been the same, in spite of the fact that capital punishment was not a part of that law until after the flood (Gen. 9:6), and polygamy was tolerated in the patriarchal age and under the Mosaic law, but not in the Gospel age (1 Cor. 7:2). In seeking to apply Deuteronomy 24:1-4 to Christians, there is a failure to understand that Deuteronomy was contingency legislation, not a statement of what God desired. One of the arguments made is to show how many New Testament principles can be found in the Old Testament. That similar commandments are found the Old Testament and the New Testament does not mean that there is only one covenant. In the United States, many of our laws were also found in the colonies and in Great Britain, but that does not mean that there has only been one constant law. Commandments which we obey are obeyed because they are part of our current laws, not because they were once a part of colonial law.

Carelessness in Preaching

The stock in trade of a preacher is truth. One's own integrity has a lot to do with his treatment of truth. If a man is not careful with truth generally, neither will he respect the truth of God's word as he should. I have known of preachers who were good men, but they did not recognize truth as sacred, but were willing to bolster their case with faulty reasoning and support their claims with fictional facts. We simply must not twist the meaning of verses to support an idea we want to present. When we bring evidence to our lesson, it needs to be honestly used and accurately quoted. To do otherwise is to dilute the gospel message, to destroy our standing with God, and to destroy the souls of our listeners.

To be poorly prepared or unprepared also leads to a diluted message. One of the things I deplore most is to see some brother get on line Tuesday and say that he wants to preach on the Holy Spirit the coming Lord's Day – does anyone have an outline he could use? Once I saw a cartoon the caption of which was "The Man of God on His Knees Seeking Guidance." He was casting dice, using them to choose at random an outline from a volume of printed sermons. You are not ready to preach on anything until you have thoroughly studied it yourself. If you merely take somebody else's work, you will not have evaluated it thoroughly and made it your own. If error is present, you buy into it without ever realizing that it is there.

Preaching needs to arise from the well of Scripture itself. We need to be aware of the needs of people whether it be doctrine, reproof, correction, or instruction which is in righteousness (2 Tim. 3:16). The prophetic spirit of preaching is a fervent application of the divine word to the needs of men.

Presenting Pleasant Sermons

One of our greatest dangers is to cater to the desires of men rather than preach the word of God. There have been men who thought that the test of whether a sermon was good or not was how harsh it was, but the most constantly imminent danger is to preach what people want. When Ezekiel began his preaching among the captives, God told him: "For all the house of Israel are of a hard forehead and of a stiff heart. Behold, I have made thy face hard against their faces, and thy forehead hard against their foreheads. As an adamant harder than flint have I made thy forehead: fear them not, neither be dismayed at their looks, though they are a rebellious house" (Ezek. 3:7b-9). After the destruction of Jerusalem, when Ezekiel's prophecies had come true, the conduct of the people changed, their conduct toward Ezekiel, but not their attitude. God warned Ezekiel:

> And as for thee, son of man, the children of thy people talk of thee by the walls and in the doors of the houses, and speak to one another, every one to his brother, saying, Come, I pray you, and hear what is the word that cometh forth from Jehovah. And they shall come unto thee as the people cometh, and they sit before thee as my people, and they hear thy words, but do them not; for with their mouth they show much love, but their heart goeth after their gain. And, lo, thou art unto them as a very lovely song of one that hath a pleasant voice, and can play well on an instrument; for they hear thy words, but they do them not. And when this cometh to pass (behold it cometh) then shall they know that a prophet hath been among them (Ezek. 33:30-33).

In Isaiah's day God said of Israel: "For it is a rebellious people, lying children, children that will not hear the law of Jehovah; that say to the Seers, See not; and to the prophets, Prophesy not unto us right things, speak unto us smooth things, prophesy deceits, get you out of the way, turn aside out of the path, cause the Holy One of Israel to cease from before us" (30:9-11).

Paul told Timothy, "Preach the word; be urgent in season, out of season; reprove, rebuke, exhort with all longsuffering and teaching. For the time will come when they will not endure sound doctrine; but having itching ears, will heap to themselves teachers after their own lusts; and will turn away their ears from the truth, and turn aside to fables" (2 Tim. 4:2-4).

No preaching should set out to be offensive, but many churches will not have a man without polish and a pleasant voice. Preachers are chosen on this basis, not upon their character and their dedication to God. Any capable speaker knows how to play the audience; it is not hard, and there is no burden of responsibility when all one has to do is present a little philosophy, a little psychology, tell a few stories about himself, and make everyone go out of the building happy all over and thrilled with the preacher.

Preaching like this will cause a church to drift, and the tendency will be to cater to the members more and more providing the things they like. This has already happened in the denominations and among institutional brethren. The church becomes a social club, with gymnasium and dining hall. This is a great danger, and among so-called conservative churches, the tendency is alive and well. Have you ever heard the old saying that someone was as poor as a church mouse? This saying used to be common. A church mouse was poor because there were no cupboards bulging with food, no dining rooms and kitchens. It really was not that long ago when churches did not have such things, but gathered to worship God. The social gospel, substituting earthly objectives for heavenly goals, has almost completely diverted denominational energy from spiritual purposes to merely social ones.

Lack of Faith in the Word

Too many men begin to preach without deep abiding faith in the word. Apparently some have not decided whether the inspired word is sufficient. Some preachers and elders have not made up their minds about what they think constitutes Scripture. Paul said, "All scripture is given by the inspiration of God *and* is profitable" (2 Tim. 3:16-17). Thus we neglect the Old Testament and preach very limited amounts of the New Testament. We need to take a look at what we have been preaching. Some men have not yet made it to first base, not having yet determined how much of the New Testament is inspired.

Lack of faith in the word leads to preaching one's own ideas instead of Scripture. One begins discoursing on philosophy and other subjects while convincing himself that it is gospel. Lack of faith in the word leads us to read other books so much that we forget to return to the fount of inspiration. Our preaching becomes diluted and convoluted.

We use the Scriptures according to the power we attribute to them. When we are spending all our time trying to determine whether the word is inspired, we preach our questions instead of answers.

Conclusion

Our task as the living is to preach the word and to refuse to pervert the gospel of Christ, but to love the holy word and proclaim it in all the world. Only by this means can we maintain the purity of the congregations of which we are a part and with which we preach the word. "Whosoever goeth onward and abideth not in the teaching of Christ, hath not God: he that abideth in the teaching, the same hath both the Father and the Son" (2 John 9).

Bibliography

R. K. Harrison. *Introduction to the Old Testament*. Peabody, Massachusetts: Hendrickson Publishers, Inc., 2004. Reprinted by arrangement with William B. Eerdmans Publishing Company, 1969.

Christianity Will Be Victorious

Joshua B. Gurtler

Preface

All Biblical quotations have been taken from the NKJV, unless noted otherwise. Other quotations that are included in this manuscript (many from those who believe the doctrine of Calvinism) should not be considered as my blanket endorsement of all of their beliefs or practices. Nowhere in this lecture do I intimate that America is a "Christian nation." Any description used of evangelicals as "believers" does not necessarily imply that they are in a covenantal relationship with Jesus Christ, per John 8:30-32;

Joshua Gurtler was born in Anniston, AL to John and Joan (Hammonds) Gurtler in 1974. He is married to Jana (Godwin), also from Alabama, and they currently live outside of Philadelphia, PA with their children, Tristan, McKenna, and Landon. Joshua has preached the gospel in the U.S., overseas, and for the Eastside church of Christ in Newnan, GA from 1999-2007. The Guardian of Truth foundation has published his workbook, *Unraveling Evolution,* suitable for teenagers or adults. Joshua studied at Florida College, Wallace State Community College, Auburn University, and the University of Georgia, where he earned his Ph.D. in food microbiology in 2006. He conducted post-doctoral research in 2006 and 2007 at UGA, while also being employed by *Kornacki Microbiology Solutions.* Joshua has lectured on food microbiology issues in the U.S., Canada, and China and has published three scientific book chapters and twenty-six peer-reviewed articles in scientific journals. He currently serves on graduate advisory committees for M.S. and Ph.D. students at Virginia Tech, Delaware State University, and Drexel University. He also serves on the editorial board of the referred scientific journals, *Applied and Environmental Microbiology and the Journal of Food Protection.* In 2010, Joshua was the youngest member appointed to the *International Association of Food Protection* Program Committee. Since 2007, Joshua has been employed as a research scientist for the USDA, Agricultural Research Service, Eastern Regional Research Center in Wyndmoor, PA. He is the primary USDA research collaborator on a multi-university team that recently won a $5 million, five-year AFRI grant to study the inactivation of viruses in foods.

12:42, 43; Acts 26:27-28 and James 2:18-20. I would like to thank those who reviewed this manuscript and provided helpful feedback: David Dann, Jesse Flowers, Marc W. Gibson, Matthew Harber, Daniel H. King, Kevin Maxey, Bill McIlvain, Allen McLellan, Joe Price, Dennis Scroggins, Jeffrey Smelser, Mike Willis, and Alan Yeater. I also want to thank Al McLellan for introducing me, some time back, to M. Stanton Evans' work, The Theme is Freedom, *which details the historical, socio-political backdrop for America's religious heritage. By acknowledging these reviewers, I do not imply that everyone agreed with all of my opinions. I did not include, nor will I reveal names of churches, places, or people used as subject illustrations in this manuscript.*

Introduction

Will Christianity be victorious? In America? Why would we ask the question? Doubters notwithstanding, the present state of spiritual disintegration in our country, in many ways, is a harbinger of more to come. This is not to say there are no areas of American society that haven't improved with the application of Biblical principles. Race relations, civil rights, including respect for minorities, women, children, and employees, all reflect positive societal progress in application of Bible principles. In the mean time, American culture has simultaneously regressed from its religious heritage in many areas, including:

1. The murder of 1,000,000 infants per year, since Roe v. Wade in 1973.
2. Ever-increasing disbelief in the inspiration and veracity of the Holy Scriptures.
3. Permeation of educational institutions with the teaching of Darwinian evolution.
4. The advent of no-fault divorces and a general disdain for the idea of permanency in marriage.
5. The 1960's sexual revolution, leading to the promotion of homosexuality, romanticizing extramarital affairs, the popularity of "open marriages," non-Biblical sex education in schools, and record levels of promiscuity among adolescents.
6. Increasing rights of criminals (especially murderers, thieves, perjurers, drug traffickers and abusers, pedophiles and sexually deviants) and ever diminishing rights of victims and their families.
7. Disintegration of respect for authority (e.g., parental, civil, judicial, federal, academic, employer, etc.).
8. Outlawing public prayer in schools and at school events.

9. Petitions to remove "God" from schools, currency, public buildings, the pledge of allegiance, etc.
10. Attempts (often successful) to remove the term "Christmas" or any references to the birth or resurrection of Jesus Christ (e.g., nativity scenes, songs, celebrations, greetings) from American culture.
11. Replacing the designations B.C. (before Christ) and *Anno Domini* (in the year of our Lord) with B.C.E (before the Common Era) and C.E. (Common Era).
12. Worship of the human body and the "unclothing of America," especially by the young (see *Christian Modesty and the Public Undressing of America* by Jeff Pollard).
13. Interest in Eastern religions, Buddhism, Hinduism, mysticism, new age movement, Islam, Wicca, etc.
14. The downward spiral of depraved entertainment in the cinema, TV, internet, magazines, music, books, tabloids, billboards, etc. (Note: 82% of Americans now have the internet.)
15. Various agencies within the U.S. Government spending thousands of tax dollars celebrating GLBT (Gay, Lesbian, Bisexual, and Transgender) Pride month (see references for Library of Congress; and Obama).
16. Liberal, non-christian judiciaries ruling in favor of all of the above.
17. The YMCA, in 2010, changing their name to "The Y" to remove any reference to the Christ.
18. President Obama sending ~$700 million/year of U.S. taxpayers' money to support abortions overseas, including funding for UNFPA.
19. A physician in Philadelphia, PA performing abortions on late term children after they were born, joking that one of the girls was big enough to walk out of his clinic.
20. And, lest you think the Republican Party will save you, even the Republican party is giving a nod to homosexuality (viz., George W. Bush's support of the "Log Cabin Republicans," the New York State movement to legalize same sex marriage, which was majority-funded by Republicans such as Michael Bloomberg. Also, the support of homosexuality and same-sex unions by Laura Bush, Barbara Bush, Cindy McCain, Meghan McCain, and Rudy Giuliani).

America has become a cornucopia of anti-christian sentiment and practices. We are inundated by a myriad of philosophies and temptations that threaten to destroy our faith which are all simultaneously saying, "Don't take your faith in Jesus so seriously. He isn't important."

While each digressive step appears to be *new*, as Christians, we know truly "there is nothing new under the sun" (Eccl. 1:4-10). Regardless of the depths of America's depravity, there is nothing novel about this behavior or about the inevitable outcome. America's sin is only the predictable and cyclical return to mankind's oft-repeated pagan tradition – the natural consequence of society's oscillation and undulation of spirituality. This pattern began in the Garden, continued through the patriarchs, into the Judges and Kingdom years, and was witnessed throughout the first few decades of the early church.

It is not as if all is lost, though. Understanding the historical precedents set by earlier societies will help us realize that Christians have always faced similar challenges. Biblically-recorded trials were often more difficult and discouraging than those we currently face. The Old Testament (O.T.) resounds with the theme of a remnant overcoming through faithful perseverance, while the New Testament (N.T.) of our Lord provides a panorama of hope and encouragement to overcome and stand victorious through our faith in Jesus Christ. Large sections of scripture (e.g., the letters to the Romans, Galatians, Philippians, Colossians, Thessalonians, Hebrews, and the writings of James, Peter, John, Jude and Revelation) were written so that we might have the confidence to endure the hardships, discouragements, oppressions, and trials that result from the battles that Satan is winning all around us. Notwithstanding Satan's triumphs, do not be discouraged, *the final victory belongs to the Lord.* (See Deut. 1:21; 20:4; Psa. 44:6-8; Matt. 16:18; Rom. 8:28, 35-37; 1 Cor. 15:57; 2 Thess. 3:3; 2 Tim. 2:19; 4:18; Heb. 2:18, 12:3; 13:5; 1 Pet. 5:9, 10; 1 John 4:4; 5:3-5; Rev. 3:21; 12:11; 15:1-3.)

If christianity is to survive in America, we must awaken ourselves, our children, family, and brethren to authentic faith, beginning and ending in the heart of remnant believers. Be prepared to be unpopular, even among christians, in order to be true to Jesus. Our desire, hunger, appetite, and "meat" must be to do the will of the Lord (John 4:33, 34, KJV). This lecture will be divided into six sections, pertaining to the survival of christianity in our spiritually-eroding American climate:

I.   Historical Precedents for Spiritual Erosion of Society
II. America: A Nation Founded on the *Influence* of the Bible
III. Attempts to Undermine Faith by Whitewashing American History (or, Rewriting History Concerning Biblical Influence on American Social Reform)

IV. The Effects of Spiritual Erosion on Traditional Religious Culture in America

V. Some Suggestions for Faithfulness to Christ in Our Present Culture

VI. Conclusion: Christ Will Be Victorious

I. Historical Precedents for Spiritual Erosion of Society

If you believe that America's pagan tendencies 100 or 200 years ago were just as bad as they are today (as I've been told), I respectfully disagree, and ask you to consider an alternative point of view. Apart from divine revelation, predictions are inevitably flawed (John 14:29). This is not to imply that it is wrong to examine cultural trends *in light* of historic societies. It should, however, compel us to approach the subject with humility. Consider that the law of diminishing returns highly influences ungodly behavior. For example, when a sinful practice demands more of a person than the supposed benefits, people sometimes return penitently to the Lord; or, at least cease their destructive behavior. Thus, any attempt to predict a spiritual movement is subject to unforeseen events or circumstances (e.g., war, famine, disease, natural disasters, intra-governmental and political turmoil, oppression or invasion by warring nations or parties, internal oppression by creditors, landlords, ruling classes, etc., economic recessions, depressions, familial upheaval or disintegration, etc.).

An Analogy for Predicting Spiritual Movements

One analogy to illustrate the difficulty of predicting group or societal spiritual outcomes may be taken from financial market investments, where the United States Securities and Exchange Commission (2010) advises the following:

> You can't open a newspaper or read a magazine without seeing ads promoting the stellar performance of "hot" mutual funds. But past performance is not as important as you may think, especially the short-term performance of relatively new or small funds. As with any investment, a fund's past performance is no guarantee of its future success. Over the long-term, the success (or failure) of your investment in a fund also will depend on factors such as:
>
> • The fund's sales charges, fees, and expenses;
> • The taxes you may have to pay when you receive a distribution;
> • The age and size of the fund;
> • The fund's risks and volatility; and
> • Recent changes in the fund's operations.

Likewise, we might say the following about forecasting a society's spiritual outcome, based on their current overall moral interest or vacillating individual relationships with the Lord:

> You can't open a religious newspaper or read a religious magazine without seeing articles detailing some "hot" ungodly American fad. But predicting the future based on *past outcomes* of ungodly behavior is not always as important as you may think, especially with regard to the short-term behavior of a relatively new or small sinful trend. As with any ungodly behavior, *other societies' past outcomes are no guarantee of another society's future failure or success.* Over the long-term, the success (or failure) of an irreligious movement in a culture, and that of the society itself or subgroups within the society, will depend on factors such as:

- The sinful behaviors' spiritual, physical, and financial charges, fees, and expenses it demands on individuals engaging in the sin.
- The consequences suffered from a supposed reward from the sinful behavior;
- The age and size of the ungodly societal fad;
- The sins' overall risks to an individual and the volatile position it places them in; and
- Recent changes in the ungodly movement's popularity.

Examples of National Contrition
There are many examples of (so-called) national repentance following societal turbulence.

- Repentance of Nineveh after Jonah's preaching (Jon. 3).
- Multiple returns to Jehovah by apostate Israel in the book of Judges and throughout the reign of the kings, the captivities and return of the exiles
- The heightened religious interest (for a period of weeks) following the 9/11 attack in the U.S.

Catalysts for National Contrition
Although only God can know the hearts of men (1 Chron. 28:9; Prov. 21:2; 16:2; Rom. 8:27; 1 Cor. 2:11), and despite accounts of seeming national penitence, it is possible that some returns to God are not based on personal contrition. Groupthink behavior, grounded less in individual penitence and more often a by-product of attrition to group-cohesiveness and consensus, often overtakes society, moving participants in lockstep with swelling national fervor. After all, hasn't Jehovah always only preserved a *remnant*? (see 2 Kings 19:3-5, 30-32; 2 Chron. 30:5-7; 34:8-10; Ezra 3:8; 9:8; Neh. 1:3;

Isa. 1:9; 10:20-22; 11:10-12, 15, 16; 37:30-33; 46:2-4; Jer. 23:2-4; 31:6-8; Ezek. 14:22; Joel 2:31, 32; Mic. 4:6-8; 5:2-4, 7, 8; 7:18, 19; Zeph. 2:6, 7; 3:12-14; Hag. 1:12-14; Zech. 8:11-13; Rom. 9:27; 11:1-5; Rev. 12:16, 17). Trials and hardships may be the best-documented catalysts for widespread repentance in society. During the depression era decade in America (i.e., 1930–1940) harsh conditions led to the lowest growth in U.S. population since the founding of the country (only a 7.3% increase). Yet, it may be argued that the overwhelming spiritual renewal occurring during these years was inversely proportional to the decreased population growth. It is also interesting that "churches of Christ" were one of the fastest-growing religious groups during this era. Contrast the 1930's, however, with the unprecedented prosperity of the baby-boom years (particularly between 1950 and 1960), contributing to the largest increase in U.S. population of any decade between 1920 and 2010 (i.e., an 18.5% increase in ten years). Unfortunately, these years also marked the beginning of a period of waning spiritual interest among Americans. Church attendance plummeted and, for the first time ever, American's spent more time kneeling at the altar of the television and cinema than at the altar of God – a practice that continues to this day.

A Word Concerning the Use of Models

George E. P. Box said, "Essentially, all models are wrong, but some are useful" (Box and Draper, 424). Likewise, any historic events we use as case-in-point models to make predictions, although highly logical, are imperfect – however; they may be *useful*. That is, *the practice of examining the past to elucidate potential group outcomes may be useful in calling attention to this stark and undeniable truth: Nations that continue unabated down a road of religious disinterest, spiritual slumber and rebellion against divine principles, without exception, will eventually suffer the logical, spiritual, and prophetic consequences of their misdeeds,* forewarned by Jehovah.

Scriptural Warnings Concerning Retribution by God on a Society

Although most of the following scriptures deal either with individual behavior, or more specifically with God's covenantal relationship with Israel and that of surrounding idolatrous tribes, history records that spiritual corruption of any society results in the same consequences as those that Jehovah meted out on Israel (Prov. 14:34; Job 4:8; Hos. 8:7; Rom. 6:23; Gal. 6:7, 8; Jer. 12:12-17; 18:5-11; Hos. 13:8, 9 [KJV]; Lev. 18:24-28; 2 Chron. 7:14; Ps. 81:13, 14). No culture has escaped these woes following apostasy and depravation. Although wrath may be delayed for a period of time, amounting to years or generations, judgment always comes.

Biblical Examples of Divine Retribution on Nations

A. Banishment of man from the Garden and other curses as a result of the fall in Genesis 3.
B. Destruction of mankind in the flood, based on the moral depravity detailed in Genesis 6:1-8.
C. Confounding the languages of men because of humanism, as described in Genesis 11:1-9.
D. Oppression of Israel by nations in *Judges* based on (1) Israel's failure to drive pagans from the land, as directed by Jehovah, and (2) recurrent spiritual apostasy.
E. Destruction of pagan peoples after Jehovah declared that their sin was "full."
    1. An instance where the sin of the people was not yet full: Genesis 15:16
    2. Instances where the sin of the people was now full (Gen. 15:16 coupled with Deut. 7:1, 2. Also, see Lev. 18:24-28 and Gen. chs. 18 and 19).
E. The suffering and death of the liberated Israelites in the wilderness in response to their ungratefulness, obstinacy, and self-indulgence as reflected upon in 1 Corinthians 10:5-10. Paul acknowledges the last example as an inspired model for christians to learn from. This behavior will result in similar consequences for us (1 Cor. 10:11-14).

II. America: As a Nation Founded on the *Influence* of the Bible
Although not a "Christian Nation," Historical America Bears the Signature of Biblical Principles

The western European Reformation movement was precipitated by and further propagated by a culture that questioned the orthodox ecclesiastical authority of the day. Debating societies were set up and faith was steered away from parish priests and toward a deeper understanding of scripture. This fervor constituted a movement toward a more perfect understanding of N.T. principles, which arguably culminated in the restoration movement in America at the turn of the 19th century. This "restoration" was preceded by similar rumblings in Scotland, England, Germany, etc. during earlier decades. The fact that these political/cultural trends influenced many to come to the truth of God's word cannot be denied. Today it is different. As morality and spiritual interest in a culture declines, unfortunately, the church often carries much of the excess spiritual baggage with it. This is presently occurring in America through a combination of factors, such as spiritual entropy and attrition, as well as the advent of "Christian" professionalism and commercialization. The latter treats the local church as a business where members are not disciplined, exacerbating corruption within these churches (Matt. 18:15-17; Rom. 16:17; 1 Cor. 5; 2 Thess. 3; Tit. 1:10-13; 3:10; 2 John 9-11). Incidentally, the same thing occurs when families make *exceptions* to personally withdrawing from a christian based on familial relationships.

As documented earlier, the scripture promises blessings to nations in response to their penitence, while warning of withdrawing blessings following their rebellion. Should it be surprising, then, if America's spiritual disinterest is concomitant with a general decline in political and economic prosperity and freedom, or military might and world dominance? The fact that America was conceived by those holding a faith in Jehovah is not debatable. Were there abuses and violations by Americans along the way? Certainly. Was the knowledge of God's word and the execution of Biblical truths perfect? No. However, this does not erase the fact that that the general sentiment of society in that day, to some degree precipitated by persecuted Protestants (e.g., Puritans, Quakers, Presbyterians, Lutherans, Mennonites, Amish, etc.) and even Roman Catholics and Jews who came to America for religious freedom, was reverence and service to Jesus Christ and/or Jehovah. Even those not persecuted in their home lands, such as the Anglicans who settled in Virginia and further south, were generally devout in their personal faith. Although modern historians are whitewashing the faith of the "founding fathers" of America from text books, their indelible historical records are well preserved.

America's Founding Fathers Speak on the Bible and Religion
George Washington's Inaugural Address
1732-1799 (First President of the United States)

> . . . No people can be bound to acknowledge and adore the Invisible Hand which conducts the affairs of men more than those of the United States. Every step by which they have advanced to the character of an independent nation seems to have been distinguished by some token of Providential Agency; (T)he foundation of our national policy will be laid in the pure and immutable principles of private morality . . . since we ought to be no less persuaded that the propitious (favorable) smiles of Heaven can never be expected on a nation that disregards the eternal rules of order and right which Heaven itself has ordained (Debates and Proceedings, 27-29).

George Washington's Farewell Address

> Of all the dispositions and habits which lead to political prosperity, religion and morality are indispensable supports. . . .Let it simply be asked, Where is the security for property, for reputation, for life, if the sense of religious obligation desert the oaths, which are the instruments of investigation in Courts of Justice? And let us with caution indulge the supposition that morality can be maintained without religion. Whatever may be conceded to the influence of refined education on minds of peculiar structure, reason and experience both forbid us to expect that national morality can prevail in exclusion of religious principle (Washington, 22, 23)

Thomas Jefferson

1743-1826 (Principle author of the *Declaration of Independence*; Third President of the United States; Second Vice President of the U.S.; First U.S. Secretary of State; Governor of Virginia).

> Can the liberties of a nation be thought secure when we have removed their only firm basis, *a conviction in the minds of the people that these liberties are of the gift of God?* (Koch and Peden, 278).

John Adams

1735-1826 (Second President of the United States; First Vice President of the United States)

> (I)t is religion and morality alone which can establish the principles upon which freedom can securely stand. The only foundation of a free constitution is pure virtue. . . .*Our constitution was made only for a moral and religious people. It is wholly inadequate to the government of any other* (John Adams, 229, 401).

John Quincy Adams

1767-1848 (Sixth president of the United States, Eighth U.S. Secretary of State; Opponent of Slavery; son to the second U.S. president, John Adams)

> *There are three points of doctrine the belief of which forms the foundation of all morality. The first is the existence of God; the second is the immortality of the human soul; and the third is a future state of rewards and punishments.* Suppose it possible for a man to disbelieve either of these three articles of faith and that man will have no conscience, he will have no other law than that of the tiger or the shark (John Q. Adams, 22-23).

Daniel Webster

1782-1852 (U.S. Secretary of State, served as U.S. Senator and U.S. Representative to House from Massachusetts and in U.S. House of Representatives from New Hampshire).

> (I)f we and our posterity *reject religious instruction and authority*, violate the rules of eternal justice, trifle with the injunctions of morality, and recklessly destroy the political constitution which holds us together, *no man can tell how sudden a catastrophe may overwhelm us* that shall bury all our glory in profound obscurity (D. Webster, 492).

Noah Webster
1758-1843 (Father of U.S. Scholarship and Education and Early Opponent to Slavery)

> The most perfect maxims and examples for regulating your social conduct and domestic economy, as well as the best rules of morality and religion, are to be found in the Bible. . . .The moral principles and precepts found in the scriptures ought to form the basis of all our civil constitutions and laws. . . . All the evils which men suffer from vice, crime, ambition, injustice, oppression, slavery and war, proceed from their despising or neglecting the precepts contained in the Bible (N. Webster, 338-340, par. 51, 53, 56).

Charles Carroll of Carrollton
1737-1832 (Maryland Delegate to the Continental Congress; Signer of the Declaration of Independence; U.S. Senator from Maryland)

> Without morals a republic cannot subsist any length of time; they therefore who are decrying the Christian religion . . . are undermining the solid foundation of morals, the best security for the duration of free governments (Steiner, 1907, p. 457).

William Penn
1644-1718 (Founder of Pennsylvania; Persecuted for and staunch defender of Quakerism)

> (I)t is impossible that any people of government should ever prosper, where men render not unto God, that which is God's, as well as to Caesar, that which is Caesar's.

James McHenry of Maryland
1753-1816 (Signer of the U.S. Constitution; Appointed 3rd Secretary of War by George Washington)

> (P)ublic utility pleads most forcibly for the general distribution of the Holy Scriptures. The doctrine they preach, the obligations they impose, the punishment they threaten, the rewards they promise, the stamp and image of divinity they bear, which produces a conviction of their truths,

can alone secure to society, order and peace, and to our courts of justice and constitutions of government, purity, stability and usefulness. In vain, without the Bible, we increase penal laws and draw entrenchments around our institutions (Steiner, 1921, p. 14).

Benjamin Rush of Philadelphia, Pennsylvania
1746-1813 (Signer of the Declaration of Independence; Physician, Writer, Educator, Humanitarian, and Early Abolitionist)

By renouncing the Bible, philosophers swing from their moorings upon all moral subjects. . . .All systems of religion, morals, and government not founded upon it (the Bible) must perish, and how consoling the thought, it will not only survive the wreck of these systems but the world itself. "The Gates of Hell shall not prevail against it" (Matthew 1:18) (Rush, 1807, p. 936). We profess to be republicans, and yet we neglect the only means of establishing and perpetuating our republican forms of government, that is, the universal education of our youth in the principles of Christianity by the means of the Bible (Rush, 1806, pp. 93-94).

Some Thoughts on America's Religious Fervor by an Outside Observer: Alexis de Tocqueville
In 1835, the French historian Alexis de Tocqueville describes America, less than sixty years old at the time, as follows,

Upon my arrival in the United States the religious aspect of the country was the first thing that struck my attention. . . .In France I had almost always seen the spirit of religion and the spirit of freedom marching in opposite directions. But in America I found they were intimately united and that they reigned in common over the same country. Religion in America. . . must be regarded as the foremost of the political institutions of that country; for if it does not impart a taste for freedom, it facilitates the use of it. Indeed, it is in this same point of view that the inhabitants of the United States themselves look upon religious belief. I do not know whether all Americans have a sincere faith in their religion—for who can search the human heart?—But I am certain that they hold it to be indispensable to the maintenance of republican institutions. This opinion is not peculiar to a class of citizens or a party, but it belongs to the whole nation and to every rank of society. The sects that exist in the United States are innumerable. They all differ in respect to the worship which is due to the Creator; but they all agree in respect to the duties which are due from man to man. . . .In the United States the sovereign authority is religious, . . . there is no country in the world where the Christian religion retains a greater influence over the souls of men than in America, and there can be no greater proof of its utility and of its conformity to human nature than that its influence is powerfully felt over the most enlightened and free nation of the earth. In the United States, if a political character attacks a sect (denomination), this may not prevent even the partisans of that very sect, from supporting him; but if he attacks all the sects together (christianity), every one abandons him and he remains alone. There is certainly no country in the world where the tie of marriage is more respected than in America or where conjugal happiness is more highly or worthily appreciated. . . . .In the United States the influence of religion is not confined to the manners, but it extends to the intelligence of the people. . . . .Christianity, therefore reigns without obstacle, by universal consent; . . . . .I sought for the key to the greatness and genius of America in her harbors . . . in her fertile fields and boundless forests; in her rich mines and vast world commerce; in her public school system and institutions of learning. I sought for it in her democratic Congress and in her matchless Constitution. *Not until I went into the churches of America and heard her pulpits flame with righteousness did I understand the secret of her genius and power. . . . .The Americans combine the notions of Christianity and of liberty so intimately in their minds, that it is impossible to make them conceive the one without the other* (excerpted from Tocqueville's *Democracy in America*).

M. Stanton Evans, in 1994, further elaborates on the theme of the religious fortitude of early Americans as follows,

Such, in brief compass, is the argument of this essay: Not only that faith and freedom "can" go together, but that they have to do so. The point is argued on a twofold basis: that religious belief and its associated values are conceptually indispensable to a regime of freedom; and that, as a matter of historical fact, our institutions of free government were developed on the basis of religious precept. Considered either way, the evidence shows that freedom is coterminous with faith – precisely as the founding fathers, along with such as Burke and Tocqueville, so frequently contended. . . . .The point is not that liberty and religious value can be "fused" by some ingenious method, but rather that they are a necessary unity – hemispheres that form a whole, thematically and in the development of our institutions. *Western freedom is the product of our faith, and the precepts of that faith are essential to its survival* (Evans, 37, 38).

III. Attempts to Undermine Faith by Whitewashing American History (or, Rewriting History Concerning Biblical Influence on American Social Reform)

In the attempt of secularists to scrub America of all things religious, or rather of all things "Christian," history is being rewritten. Americans today fail to understand the impact that the Bible has played in (and often the driving force behind) magnitudinal social reforms in this country.

American Social Reforms Resulting from the Application of Biblical Principles

Many of the greatest American social reforms were spearheaded by the (accurate or inaccurate) *application of Biblical principles.* Some of these events include, (1) scientific discovery based on the Biblical principles of creation, divine design, a worldwide flood, etc., (2) secession and emancipation from England, (3) abolitionist anti-slavery movements ending the slave trade, first in England and then in the U.S., (4) the women's suffrage movement, and (5) the civil rights movement. While anti-religious secularists want to take credit for these reforms, we should not let them rob us of our religious history. Unbiased, historical records reveal that the seeds of change for all of these social reforms were initially planted by those who claimed Jehovah as God and His word as their guiding edict. This does not imply that all of these individuals (1) were truly christians or (2) didn't fall far short of God's will in many areas (e.g., manstealing [kidnapping, 1 Tim. 1:10a], abuse of one's fellow man, insubordination to governing authorities, and sometimes blatantly wicked tactics used to accomplish their ends).

M. Stanton Evans comments on the re-writing of history to exclude Biblical influences as follows,

> An age intensely hostile to religion sees events through secular lenses, ignoring the role of biblical precept in Western institutions, American institutions most of all. The (anti-christian) historian surveys the evidence (at least sometimes), but fails to see it. . . .It is impossible, for example, to understand our revolution or constitutional founding without some knowledge of the original settlers and their faith, the English common law experience that lay behind them, and the medieval background from which all this developed. Typically, these are glossed over or ignored entirely in our histories (Evans, 19, 20).

Western Culture Owes Its Success to Biblical Faith

To push this thought further, consider the social, political, medical, technological, and industrial advancements as well as revolutions for personal liberty that the world has welcomed in the last 250 years. Most of these stemmed from western civilization (a.k.a., European "Christendom"). While we cannot deny egregious violations against mankind perpetrated by Western culture (as well as any other historical culture, for that matter), the advancement of science, technology, agriculture, medicine, increased average lifespan, personal liberty, and modern comforts enjoyed by billions today are owed to Western thought. While some argue that these advances are a result of freedom from the "christian dark ages," a stronger argument is made that these events coincide with unshackling human minds from medieval pagan superstition, illiteracy, and ignorance (unfortunately, often a by-product of European Roman Catholicism), via the Protestant reformation. The reformation clearly led to free thought, increased literacy and education, and removal of many "pagan-christian" beliefs, superstition, and mysticism. The reformation also provided Europeans more freedom and theoretical space to explore science, culture, history, industry, personal liberty, religion, and truth.

Christopher Dawson explains it this way:

> Without Christianity, there would no doubt have been some kind of civilization in the West, but it would have been quite a different civilization from that which we know; for it was only as Christendom – the society of Christian people – that tribes and people and nations of the West acquired a common consciousness and sense of cultural and spiritual unity (35).

After a lecture on creation vs. Darwinian evolution in 2010, I was confronted by an atheist from a university who had attended two nights. (Incidentally, he was very congenial and we remain on friendly terms.) His theme was "the superiority of society rooted in permissive paganism as opposed to regressive christianity." His model was the Greek state, which he claimed was more advanced, providing more personal liberty and a higher quality of life than "Christian America." He claimed that citizens in ancient Greece experienced less stress, and devoted more time to relaxation, wine, and philosophy. To paraphrase my response, I asked him if this was the same society where slaves, in almost every household in Athens, were often beaten, raped, and murdered, as well as bought and sold as chattel? Was this the same Greece where 20th century medicine and antibiotics were unknown, infant mortality was astronomical, women often died in child-bearing, and viruses and bacteria killed a large percentage of the population each year? Incidentally, for our humanist friends, this is the same Grecian society where animal welfare was non-existent, and where torture was sport and high entertainment. This was the same society that conquered nations around the known world while Greek soldiers commonly sodomized the prisoners as a final act of humiliation before execution or enslavement. This is the same Greece that applauded pedophilia of men and boys (pederasty) as a rite of passage; all a matter of undisputed historical record. Is this the culture we want to return to? We can only assume that such behavior is included in the apostle's admonition in Ephesians 5:11, 12.

Historic American laws pertaining to sexual conduct, including pedophilia, homosexuality, and polygamy (which are currently being removed, altered, or reinterpreted to permit more permissive behavior or lighten judicial sentences) were originally borne out of Bible principles.

Evans elaborates further:

> That biblical teaching was the formative influence in the creation of Europe, and that Europe was the nursery of freedom as we know it, are both established facts of record. This is not the linkage, after all, suggested by the usual story; the notion that Christianity equals Europe equals freedom is, indeed, the reverse of what should be expected. *If Christian doctrine is opposed to freedom, then liberty ought to flourish where Christianity has had the smallest degree of influence, and languish where that influence is the greatest. That a general survey prima facie says the opposite suggests that something in the conventional history is mistaken.* As shall be seen, this correlation of Christianity with the rise of freedom is anything but accidental. In fact, the precepts of our religion provided the conceptual building blocks for the free societies of the West – including the very idea of liberty as we know it, limits on the power of the state, and institutions that gave these practical expression (29, 30).

Nevertheless, the predominant secular agenda, currently wielded to destroy faith in the American culture goes something like this:

> Since archaic, superstitious, religious zealots bring about oppression and regression of society, an absence of Christian fervor, not only in the government but also of the populace in general, will lead to greater social progress.

Thus, the popular prevailing secular themes of the day, in post-modern America, are *tolerance, inclusion, diversity, rationalism, pluralism, amorality, irreligion, existentialism* (God is dead), *nihilism,* and *cultural, historical,* and *moral relativism.* The glaring irony and paradox of this politically-correct American philosophy is that *no known governmental systems of freedom and individual liberty have ever been established on the foundation of irreligion and amorality.*

The Bitter Fruit of Nations Founded in Humanism

Conversely, the most despotic and genocidal regimes ever known (responsible for the death of tens of millions) have been founded on the premise that God (especially Jesus Christ) must be scoured from the culture. This includes murder by the Soviet Union (up to 20 million during the Stalin era alone), Nazi Germany (up to 10 million), the killing fields of Cambodia's

Saloth Sar's (Pol Pot's) Khmer Rouge (up to 2.5 million), Mao Tze-Tung's little red book and Red China (40-70 million between 1949 and 1976), North Korea, Cuba, and communist Vietnam. Any system of government void of morally-grounded legislation and judgment will inevitably erode personal liberty until it, too, becomes a despotic regime. Why? Consider this: If no moral absolutes exist, then the conviction that *the right to life, liberty, and the pursuit of happiness cannot be an absolute*, which leads those in power to rule based on *personal gratification* rather than a higher moral law – read despotism/totalitarianism. Thus, we come full circle to social Darwinism that teaches "survival of the fittest," motivated by Richard Dawkins' "selfish gene," driven to promote one's personal interests at the expense of fellow citizens and/or society. This always leads to the moral collapse of cultures, such as the former USSR where love, charity, and personal interest in and sacrifice for the well-being of one's fellow man frequently dissipated, leaving in its Godless wake a simmering subculture of jealousy, betrayal, and general distrust among fellow citizens – the very problems the communists set out to resolve when they ousted Tsar Nicholas II in the 1917 revolution. The Bolsheviks were, of course, heavily influenced by Marx and Engels' doctrine of egalitarianism. Their very philosophy, however, contains many self-contradictory elements, precluding the sustainability of their workers' paradise. As Friedrich Engels' stated:

> We . . . reject every attempt to impose on us any moral dogma whatever as eternal, ultimate and forever immutable moral law. . . .We maintain on the contrary that all former moral theories are the product, in the last analysis, of the economic stage which society had reached at that particular epoch. And as society has hitherto moved in class antagonisms, morality was always a class morality (Feuer, 272).

Marx further elaborated:

> Man makes religion, religion does not make man. . . .Religion is the sigh of the oppressed creature, the heart of the heartless world, just as it is the spirit of an unspiritual situation. It is the opium of the people. The abolition of religion as an illusory happiness of the people is required for their real happiness. . . .Religion is only the illusory sun, which revolves around man as long as he does not revolve around himself. The task of history, therefore, once the world beyond truth has disappeared, is to establish the truth of this world (Feuer, 262, 263).

Why Humanism Fails in Society

It is inconceivable that a government, which denies moral absolutes and has banished acknowledgement of the divine from public institutions, could maintain a perfect commune of beneficence. A rebirth of this sentiment in American neo-socialism is being taken up by the current U.S. presidential administration, who are spokesmen for millions that hold the same philosophy. Consider the president's oft-stated desire to exploit the financially-successful through heavy taxation, best articulated in his agenda to "spread the wealth around." Couple these views with his description of traditional rural American conservatives in Pennsylvania and the Midwest (because they didn't support his ideology) as those who "cling to their guns or religion or antipathy" and you have sentiments not too far removed from Marx and Engels.

Two ways socialists have tried to "level the economic playing field" are through heavy taxation and large national debt: the latter inevitably leading to inflation and devaluation of currency held by the wealthy. To believe that a movement motivated by class-envy, which politically extorts wealth from the "bourgeoisie" will not lead these socialist extortionists to the same greed and corruption that they condemn in the wealthy, is irrational. The current anti-religious, Darwinian, secular/socialist fervor sweeping the ranks of Americans today echoes eerily back to 19th and 20th century communist pulpits. Compare today's popular, secular, materialist, neo-socialist, Hollywood, American rhetoric with well-known communist quotes of the not-so-distant past.

Vladimir Lenin

Human thought by its nature is capable of giving, and does give, absolute truth, which is compounded of a sum-total of relative truths. . . . The world is eternally moving and developing matter, reflected by the developing of human consciousness (Lenin, 1909). The way to *crush the bourgeoisie* is to grind them between the millstones of *taxation and inflation* (Lenin quoted by Wikipedia). Only *by abolishing private property* in land and building cheap and hygienic dwellings can the housing problem be solved (Lenin, 1916, vol. 24, pp. 455-480). Disarmament is the ideal of socialism (Lenin, 1916, pp. 94-104).

Joseph Stalin

Ideas are more powerful than guns. We would not let our enemies have guns, *why should we let them have ideas* (Torricelli, 121).

Karl Marx

The theory of Communism may be summed up in one sentence: *Abolish all private property* (Marx and Engels, sec. 3, par. 13). We should not say that one man's hour is worth another man's hour, but rather that one man during an hour is worth just as much as another man during an hour. *Time is everything, man is nothing: he is at the most time's carcass* (Marx, 1972, p. 89). The first requisite for the happiness of the people is the *abolition of religion* (as quoted by ThinkExist.com).

Friedrich Engels

We repudiate *all morality derived from non-human and non-class concepts.* We say it is deception, a fraud in the interest of the landlords and the capitalists. We say that *morality is entirely subordinated to the interests of the class struggle of the proletariat.* . . .We say: morality is what serves to destroy the old exploiting society and to unite all the toilers around the proletariat, which is creating a new communist society. . . .*We do not believe in an eternal morality* (Hunt, 113, 114). We are now approaching a social revolution, in which *the old economic foundations of monogamy will disappear* just as surely as those of its complement, prostitution. Monogamy arose through the concentration of considerable wealth in one hand — a man's hand — and from the endeavor to bequeath this wealth to the children of this man to the exclusion of all others. . . .Now, the impending social revolution will reduce this whole care of inheritance to a minimum by changing at least the overwhelming part of permanent and *inheritable wealth*—the means of production—*into social property. Since monogamy was caused by economic conditions, will it disappear when these causes are abolished?* One might reply. . . not only will it not disappear, but it will rather be perfectly realized. For with the transformation of the means of production into *collective property, wagelabor will also disappear* . . . With the transformation of the means of production into *collective property the monogamous family ceases to be the economic unit of society. The private household changes to a social industry. The care and education of children become a public matter.* . . .Will not this be sufficient cause for a gradual rise of a more unconventional intercourse of the sexes and a more lenient public opinion regarding virgin honor and female shame? (Engels).

Leon Trotsky

We must rid ourselves once and for all of the Quaker-Papist babble about *the sanctity of human life* (1930). For forty-three years of my conscious life I have remained a revolutionist; for forty-two of them I have fought under the banner of Marxism. If I had to begin all over again I would of course try to avoid this or that mistake, but the main course of my life would remain unchanged. I shall die a proletarian revolutionist, *a Marxist, a dialectical materialist, and, consequently, an irreconcilable atheist* (1940).

The socialist agenda today is blatantly antagonistic toward Jehovah, inasmuch as His laws demand a higher standard of authority than humanism — which is really freedom *from social, economic, or spiritual inequality* among men. Biblical teaching, however, supports systems of individual spiritual liberty (read *free will*) whereby one may pursue his destiny by his own volition. The current wave of antireligious American politicism is based on *selfishness*, rather than personal self-sacrifice, encouraged by political progressives such as Abraham Lincoln, John F. Kennedy, and Dr. Martin Luther King, Jr. Today, the speeches of all three of these men in their appeals to God would be considered right-wing religious propaganda by the socialist left.

Antireligious Humanism Contrasted with Historical America
Contrast this new socialist paradigm with the American *Declaration of Independence*, which makes clear references to a divine creator,

> We hold these truths to be self-evident, that all men are created equal, that they are endowed by their *Creator* with certain unalienable Rights, that among these are Life, Liberty, and the Pursuit of Happiness . . . the laws of nature and of *nature's God*. . . .And for the support of this declaration, with a firm reliance on the protection of *Divine Providence.*

Some argue that Americans were just as carnal 235 years ago as they are today. However, are citizens as *interested* in the worship, esteem, and good pleasure of Jehovah today as they were then? Could the sentiments expressed by de Tocqueville, above, be made today? Would our founding fathers' statements of faith represent the convictions of our current leaders? While marital infidelity certainly occurred in the 18th century, can we say that it was committed as brazenly by leaders and politicians and with as much fanfare and re-telling as it is presently?

IV. The Effects of Spiritual Erosion
on Traditional Religious Culture in America
What is Traditional Religious Culture?
By "traditional religious culture," I am referring to the religious and Biblical principles upon which America was founded, as detailed in sections II and III, above. This traditional religious culture includes Judeo-Christian beliefs and practices that have characterized and shaped much of American society, culture, customs, habits, and law. Traditional religious culture includes denominations of believers who profess Jesus Christ as Lord, although their theology may not accurately reflect that found in the N.T. Most major "non-cult," "Christian" groups in America (e.g., Ana-baptist and Baptist, Presbyterian, Wesleyan, Methodist, and Pentecostal or charismatic outgrowths, Anglican, Episcopal, Lutheran, Quaker, even some Catholics, and followers of what is commonly called the "Stone-

Campbell" movement) have historically maintained particular areas of Biblical common ground.

Commonly Held Biblical Beliefs among Most Protestant Denominations

1. The divine inspiration and authority of the Bible (denominational creeds notwithstanding).
2. Sin-separation from Jehovah, and the need for a mediator between Jehovah and man.
3. Divine incarnation in the form of Jesus Christ via the virgin birth.
4. The death, burial, resurrection, ascension, and eventual return of Jesus Christ as savior.
5. A day of reckoning before God to give an account for the deeds done in the body, including the reward of heaven for the justified in Christ and eternal punishment for the unfaithful.
6. The Biblical role of the male as head of the marriage, family, and as church leaders.
7. Respect for marriage, providing divorce and remarriage by the faithful spouse only for fornication (although, most have changed their practices in the 20th century based on the rising divorce rate in America and the commercialization of churches. For full documentation, see *Living Together: Myths, Risks and Answers* by McManus and McManus).
8. Disapproval of morally-deviant behavior (e.g., fornication, prostitution, adultery, pornography, homosexuality, polygamy, bigamy, gambling, profanity, drunkenness, etc.).
9. Some have similar convictions against recreational use of alcohol and other forms of drugs.

Signs of Religious Post-Modernism in America

In modern times, especially since the humanistic social-gospel move-ment of the post Civil War era, however, there has been a shift away from emphases on these spiritual fundamentals and toward the physical, social, "self actualization," and "felt needs" of man. No longer paramount is (1) the spiritual health of man, (2) saving the lost, and (3) preparation for divine judgment and eternity. The infusion of humanistic philosophy into churches has resulted in undermining any accurate Biblical theology that may have remained in these denominations. What has resulted is the homogenization of these churches with all things popular in contemporary culture, which has resulted in a denial of Biblical doctrines and an endorsement of the following accompanying beliefs and practices:

1. Denial of the inspiration, transmission, and preservation of the Bible as God's inerrant word.
2. Women assuming leadership positions and roles of "clergy" in local churches.
3. Church-sanctioned divorce and remarriage for reasons other than for fornication.
4. Accepting and/or supporting the abortion of unborn human beings.
5. Embracing the tenets of the sexual revolution, including either turning a blind eye to or outright acceptance of fornication, adultery, pornography, homosexuality, etc.

The fallout has been fissures in these groups (e.g., Presbyterian, Episcopal, Lutheran, United Churches of Christ, etc.) with dissenters starting more conservative splinter groups, or converting to different, more conservative denominations. Liberal-leaning groups have joined hands with socio-political movements, which has resulted in dramatic losses in membership. The United Church of Christ, one of the more prominent supporters of homosexuality, has seen its membership plummet by 45% from 2 million to 1.1 million in the past fifty years, and is currently losing ca. 3% per year. The Presbyterian church in America (openly welcoming "gays and lesbians" into its body), has lost its "reformed theology" emphasis and, despite a membership of 2 million, support only 215 total international missionaries. They are also losing ca. 3% of their membership per year. The humanistic Episcopal church, in 1976, declared that homosexuals are "children of God" and "entitled to full civil rights," while in 2009 they ruled that homosexuals may serve in any ordained position of the church. The denomination is losing 3% per year and has lost 1.4 million members in the last forty-four years.

Here is the Point: Conservative Warnings against Spiritual Erosion Were Correct All Along

Here is the point: Since at least the era of reconstruction, churches of Christ in America have been sounding the alarm to their leftist denominational friends regarding the social gospel. Brethren have warned that this twisted doctrine, which shifted emphasis away from the spiritual needs of man and turned these churches into little more than benevolent relief organizations was (A) wrong and (B) headed for disaster. Let's take this one step further. For at least the last fifty years, many in "non-institutional" churches of Christ have been sounding the alarm to their leftist (i.e., "institutional") brethren that church involvement in human institutions, the social gospel, and church-supported "food fun and frolic" is transforming local churches into social institutions that are (A) wrong and (B) headed for disaster.

Today, both the leftist denominations and leftist churches of Christ have created a social gospel tsunami, while conservatives in both camps are doing everything they can to stem the tide. But, it's too late for many. In 1785 or 1885, Episcopal churches in Philadelphia, PA could not have guessed that in 2010 their numbers would be dwindling, their evangelism stagnant, and they would be openly accepting homosexuality. Likewise, in 1960, many of our institutional brethren (although having been duly warned) would have never guessed that 50 years later, their ranks would be infiltrated by the current ecumenical teaching of Max Lucado, Rubel Shelly, Al Maxey, C. Leonard Allen, Mike Cope, Lynn Anderson, Rick Atchley, Ed Fudge, and others associated with *New Wineskins Magazine*. The teaching of this latter loose conflagration of brethren essentially says "churches of Christ" in America have been too narrow and legalistic, and should interpret the Bible more liberally, not requiring command, example, or necessary implication for authority in religion. This more-lenient method of interpreting the scripture (a.k.a., "new hermeneutic") allows for heretofore forbidden practices in churches of Christ, such as women assuming leadership roles (e.g., leading public prayer and teaching men publicly), the use of musical instruments in worship, partaking of the Lord's supper on days other than the first day of the week, solos, choirs, musicals and dramas, "spiritual dancing," joint fellowship assemblies with Calvinistic denominations, and more permissive views regarding divorce and remarriage, immodest dress, and enjoying recreational (social) inebriation with ethyl alcohol. The goal is to overturn the "old traditional archaic" teachings among churches of Christ and establish a "new hermeneutic" or new Bible interpretation. They shun ideas such as "speak where the Bible speaks and be silent where the Bible is silent" and "have book chapter and verse for everything we do" and "do Bible things in Bible ways and call Bible things by Bible names."

One Example of the Fruits of Spiritual Erosion: Biblical Liberalism
Liberal Biblical interpretation is the historical descriptor for the modernist movement away from a fundamental interpretation of the Bible as the inerrant word of God. Many of today's liberal Protestant groups (e.g., Episcopal, Presbyterian, Lutheran, United Churches of Christ, and some Methodist) accept some form of this hermeneutic and are much too liberal for even some Catholics. (Imagine that.) A taste of what is coming out of these camps is well-documented in a 2005 *Washington Times* Article entitled,

"Gay Bishop Backs Planned Parenthood," based on a speech given at the abortionist group's annual prayer breakfast (Ward). The website *Catholic Answers* has received over two dozen responses by Catholics condemning the Episcopal Bishop and calling him to repentance (Catholic Answers). The irony cannot be overlooked that we are now in an age where *Catholics are protesting the ungodliness of Protestants.*

Spiritual Erosion in America Follows the British and Western European Model

Protestant denominations that continue to experience growth in America today are those that hold firm many of the *Commonly Held Biblical Beliefs among Protestant Denominations* that were presented above. These groups are sometimes described as "evangelical," still placing a major emphasis on evangelizing the lost, the return of the Christ, a final day of judgment and eternal sentences of heaven or hell for the righteous in Christ and unrighteous, respectively. How the rise of neo-paganism in America will affect the long-term stability of these groups is up for debate; however, in recent years, by their own admissions, secularization is taking its toll on the fidelity of their membership. John MacArthur often warns against following in the footsteps of historic European digression and in his book, *Can God Bless America?* he says,

It is not just an American problem, however. . . .Every nation has gone this way. Examine Western Europe, for example, where the gospel first spread and from which it went out to the rest of the world. *Europe was also the birthplace of the Protestant Reformation less than 500 years ago. But Western Europe today is a spiritual wasteland, overrun with agnosticism, humanism, and widespread ignorance of God's word.* Europe followed the path described in Romans 1 step by step. Notice carefully the steps of decline Paul outlines in Romans 1. When a nation abandons God and turns to idols, God abandons them (Romans 1:24). First they sink to immorality (v. 24). Then they sink deeper to homosexuality (vv. 26-27). So they start by embracing heterosexual sin, and then they turn to homosexual sin. Does anyone question that we are already there? You know society is reaching that point when people will not tolerate anyone making moral judgments. When people love and revel in things that are debased and depraved and twisted, God leaves them to what they love –"to do those things which are not fitting." . . . All sense of guilt is finally eradicated. "Knowing the righteous judgment of God, that those who practice such things are deserving of death, not only do the same but also approve of those who practice them" (v. 32). At that point, all hope for the society is gone. Media and public discourse become vile and profane. *The*

Jerry Springer Show becomes high entertainment in such a culture. The approval rating for an immoral politician skyrockets. That is what divine wrath looks like. . . .This is the *wrath of abandonment.* It is a frightening reality. God gives people over completely to their own sinful desires, steps back, and lets them go. They want their sin, so God allows them to have it without hindrance (MacArthur, 2002, pp. 56-60).

A Spiritual Famine of the Word: Biblical Ignorance among Protestants

Although there have always been professing "Christians" ignorant of basic Biblical facts, their numbers appear to be growing. Larry Fowler, in his book, *Raising a Modern-Day Joseph,* said,

> I asked Pat Blewett, Dean of the College at Columbian International University how he viewed the Bible knowledge of incoming college freshmen. He said that ten to fifteen years ago, the average score for freshman on the college's Bible knowledge test was about 60 percent; now it's less than 40 percent (Fowler, 28-30).

Regarding the famine of Bible knowledge among evangelicals, Chuck Swindoll stated,

> Perhaps the greater tragedy is the number of Christian colleges and universities who are no longer concerned enough about biblical knowledge even to test students on it. . . .In late 2005, Awana asked two questions of a hundred Bible colleges and seminaries: (1) "Do you measure the Bible knowledge of incoming freshmen?" (2) "If so, have you seen a trend in their scores over the past ten years?" Fifty-eight schools responded. A number of responses included comments such as these: "The general consensus of the Bible and theology faculty is that there has been a marked decrease in the level of Bible knowledge in recent years. It seems that even students who have gone to church all their lives are not as biblically literate as students in years gone by" (David Reese, Toccoa Falls College). "I have been teaching at Puget Sound Christian College for 23 years in the Bible department. The level of Bible knowledge for incoming students has decreased dramatically over this period. Our assumption now is that incoming freshman know nothing about the Bible, and that we must start at the most basic level" (Mark S. Krause, Dean, Puget Sound Christian College).

A Spiritual Famine of the Word: Biblical Ignorance among Brethren

A similar situation may be happening among our own brethren. A wave of "Vacation Bible Schools" among churches of Christ have very little to do with "school," and even less to do with the Bible. One VBS among non-institutional brethren that I attended was themed after "the old west." Hay bales were scattered throughout the church building. The teachers and the preacher were decked out in cowboy gear (the preacher, in fact, had some very cool and expensive-looking spurs on his boots). Cowboy hats, bandanas, ropes, etc. were the attire and many children were brought in from the community. The preacher stood up at the Lord's Supper table, welcomed everyone and described the great time they were going to have. He then came over to me and apologized, telling me he was sorry that he had forgotten to use any scripture. The rest of the morning was spent in games and activities. Children were running all around the yard at the direction of the cowgirl teachers. When I tried to leave prematurely, a member beckoned me to stay and see the preacher's "panning for gold" activity. I walked over to the preacher and the children were literally panning through sand and water with disposable aluminum pie pans for glittering metal buried in the sand. There was no Bible taught that day, to my knowledge.

One time, a classmate in college and I came to realize that we were both christians and sons of evangelists. He told me his father was a retired "youth minister" from a very large church of Christ where Rubel Shelly preached. When I told him the congregation I worshipped at, he said, "Oh, that's the church where the women wear those funny things on their heads isn't it?" In a very polite and respectful manner I said, "Yes there are some women that wear the head covering." I asked him, "So, what are your views on the covering described in 1 Corinthians 11?" He asked me what 1 Corinthians 11 said because he didn't know. After summarizing the chapter to him, he was still very confused, as if he'd never read it before. The new hermeneutics of Rubel Shelly and *New Wineskins Magazine* and Rubel's youth minister obviously must have overlooked studying 1 Corinthians with their youth as they were teaching them the Bible. Members of churches of Christ were at one time known among the world as "walking Bibles." These days, they are becoming more Biblically illiterate while *simultaneously joining hands with* Calvinists. Chuck Swindoll comments on this biblical illiteracy among evangelicals today in saying,

> We are not suffering from a famine of churches. We have them by the dozens. Some metropolitan areas have literally hundreds of churches within their city limits. . . . So why is there such a famine? The answer, quite simply, is that God's Word has been replaced with artificial food. The dinner bells ring each Sunday . . . and beautiful tables are set with fine china and silverware and fabulous décor – but there is no solid food served, only junk food. Everyone leaves hungry (237).

Steven J. Lawson goes further than Swindoll in his analysis,

> As the church advances into the twenty-first century, the stress to produce booming ministries has never been greater . . . pressure to produce bottom line results has led many ministries to sacrifice the centrality of biblical preaching on the altar of man-centered pragmatism. A new way of "doing" church is emerging. In this radical paradigm shift, exposition is being replaced with entertainment, preaching with performances, doctrine with drama, and theology with theatrics. The pulpit, once the focal point of the church, is now being overshadowed by a variety of church-growth techniques, everything from trendy worship styles to glitzy presentations to vaudeville-like pageantries. In seeking to capture the upper hand in church growth, a new wave of pastors is reinventing the church and repackaging the gospel into a product to be sold to "consumers." Whatever reportedly works in one church is being franchised out to various "markets" abroad. As when gold was discovered in the foothills of California, so ministers are beating a path to the doorsteps of exploding churches and super-hyped conferences where the latest "strike" has been reported. . . .In a strange twist, the preaching of the cross is now foolishness, not only to the world but also to the contemporary church (Lawson, 198, 199).

Spiritual Erosion among Churches of Christ

The influence of the current wave of American humanism, agnosticism and anti-christian fervor has not left members of the "church of Christ" untouched. Anecdotal evidence and surveys across the brotherhood have revealed the direction in which members are being influenced. Among more institutionally-minded brethren, the late Ron Brotherton was a professor at International Bible College (now Heritage Christian University, in Florence, AL). In the 1970s, brother Brotherton dedicated much of his teaching to warning institutionally-minded brethren about the slippery slope of worldliness and humanism, as a byproduct of drifting away from the Bible. I have a scathing expository sermon on cassette that Brotherton preached on Ephesians 4:25ff in which he takes the institutional churches of Christ to task in a manner unlike I've heard any non-institutional brethren do. At that time, Brotherton claimed that their groups were losing over 50% of all children brought up in families of members of the church. I have heard much higher figures tossed around among brethren today. One story I recently heard was of a non-institutional church where there were ten teenage friends. Today, only one of these adults has not fallen away. Connie W. Adams has said that you used to go to a church picnic at a local park and be able to distinguish the Christians from those of the world by their modest dress; however, today members of the church are often dressed just like the world.

Steve Wolfgang, weighing in on digression among Christians, and the ensuing debates among brethren, quotes from David Edwin Harrell's book, *Churches of Christ in the 20th Century*,

> But even good historians tread dangerous ground when they begin to describe contemporary events– especially when they themselves have been ardent participants in those events (as Ed himself notes in (his) Preface, pp. xi, xv-xvi). . . .As brother Harrell notes in the same context: *"As church growth accelerated and larger congregations multiplied, warnings about changing attitudes and doctrinal laxity could hardly be dismissed as figments of Ron Halbrook's imagination."* Who could have said it better? Probably not even Ron Halbrook himself could improve upon it. But if anyone wishes to try . . . have at it. "He that hath ears to hear, let him hear" (Wolfgang, 8).

Two Telltale Signs of Spiritual Erosion in Religious America

I will provide only two examples, which I feel are case-in-point illustrations of current spiritual erosion. There are, doubtless, hundreds of other examples that could have been used. I submit these two areas for your consideration as models upon which many other applications can be made in American culture as well as among christians.

A. Telltale signs of spiritual erosion in America: Failure of religious leaders and evangelists to warn christians about present dangers. Although "the Lord knows those who are his" (2 Tim. 2:19), and our Lord has established His church and "the gates of Hades shall not prevail against it" (Matt. 16:18), the Biblical admonition and example to warn our brethren stands. It would be just as neglectful on our part to ignore current activities that endanger the souls of fellow believers within our sphere of influence, as it would have been for Paul or John to ignore (1) The party of the circumcision, (2) The hypocrisy of Peter and Barnabas recounted in Galatians chapter 2, (3) The immorality, hypocrisy, and worldly attitudes among members at the church in Corinth, (4) The Gnostic influences, including denial of the deity and/or humanity of Christ, (5) Pagan doctrines and practices creeping in among the seven churches of Asia in the book of *Revelation.* Why? Because all of these practices lead to the destruction of souls and instability within the local church. While no one can claim apostolic authority today, we have no less a charge, "to contend earnestly for the faith which was once for all delivered to the saints" (Jude 3).

A Word Regarding Balance in Preaching and Teaching

Individuals who spend all of their time sounding warnings, are clearly unbalanced, not proclaiming the whole counsel of God (Acts 20:27). For, truly, "The kingdom of God is . . . righteousness and peace and joy in the Holy Spirit" (Rom. 14:17). However, an evangelist who spends 1, 3, 5, or even 10% of his evangelistic efforts (which will vary based on circumstances) warning against apostasy cannot be characterized as unbalanced. Rather, those who are charged with the task of, and yet spend no time, warning those within their sphere of influence will one day give an account to the Lord for blood that may be on their hands (Heb. 13:17).

Calvinists Sound Warnings While Non-Calvinists Do Not (?)

It is quite a conundrum how many brethren (who are not Calvinists and believe christians can fall from grace) spend less time warning against sin than many popular Calvinists I listen to on occasion (e.g., John MacArthur, Charles Colson, Charles Swindoll, the late Adrian Rogers, J. Bruce Sofia, Alistair Begg, James McDonald, Hank Hanegraaff, Michael Youseff, Tony Evans, Ravi Zacharias, David Jeremiah, Greg Laurie, Dennis Rainey, Joe Focht, Ray Comfort and Kirk Cameron, Philip Ryken, Billy and Franklin Graham, as well as James Dobson, Julie Slattery, Jim Daly and the *Focus on the Family* broadcast, and even Creflo Dollar). Listen to any of these teachers for any length of time and you will hear clear warnings against spiritual digression in society. They are doing their best to hold back an unrelenting tide of erosion in their groups.

A popular sentiment among some christians, however, is that certain inspired writings only had application to specific problems of the first century. These passages, as the argument goes, are not to be used for present day warnings. Are the following texts obsolete, or can they and should they be applied in targeted circumstances today? Acts 20:29-31; Titus 1:10-14; 2 Timothy 3:1-7; 4:3. While talking with a group of christian men in a home some years back, I was corrected for "worrying too much" about digression among brethren today. When I quoted Matthew 16:3 as to our need to warn christians regarding the "signs of the times," I was told very condescendingly, "Yes, but those were very special circumstances Jesus was addressing." Yes, they were. The circumstances were that God's people had turned away from Him and were riddled with hypocrisy. But of course, that doesn't occur today . . . does it?

Why Undermine Warnings among Brethren in an Age of Rapid Spiritual Erosion?

Why would christians today undermine spiritual warnings when the world is crashing down all around us, and we are losing the majority of children that are raised by members of the church? The scriptures in the previous paragraph wisely serve as blueprints into which modern digressions may be substituted, the faithful warned, and sinners rebuked. I am deeply indebted to those who taught sound doctrine to my parents and ancestors. I, by extension, have gleaned the spiritual benefits of their labor. I am also grateful for the Biblical warnings of my parents, grandparents, preachers, and friends that echo in my ears as I raise my children. If you feel the same way, please consider the straightforward warnings of the N.T. and those of your mentor/teachers and ask the question, "Does this same spirit of warning characterize my teaching to my children, or the Biblical teaching I am exposed to and exposing my children to today?" How many christians would be unfaithful today, or would have died unfaithful, were it not for the warnings of godly brethren? Among so-called "conservative" brethren, however, there are those who cringe at warnings against societal trends, or ungodly or unsound teaching, or practices among christians. Those who warn brethren are occasionally censured as over reactors, upsetting the peace and established traditions of some circle of christians or churches.

I am not advocating the formation of a party, clique, society, organization, creed, or otherwise human institution for the preservation of christianity. What I would encourage is walking "circumspectly" (Eph. 5:15), following the scriptures to warn others as you have the opportunity and ability, based on present dangers. Do the following admonitions given to the young evangelist Timothy not apply to us today? 2 Timothy 2:24-26; 3:16; 4:1-3.

Our More-Institutional Brethren Have Been Sounding These Warnings for Years

Despite obvious differences over the nature of the local church (and although I cannot vouch as to where they all stand today), I have great respect for individuals such as brother Wayne Jackson (formerly with Apologetics Press of Montgomery, AL), David Miller (author of *Piloting the Strait,* and currently with Apologetics Press), Goebel Music (author of *Behold the Pattern*) and various others who hail from Searcy, Arkansas as well as the Brown Trail School of Preaching, and the Memphis School of Preaching, etc. For decades, these brethren have been sounding the same warnings that Ron Brotherton did against digression and apostasy in the 1970s. However, among many *non-institutional* brethren, these types of warnings are sometimes frowned upon as too negative. While Wayne Jackson et al. were warning against the digressions of Max Lucado and the like, a christian preacher friend of mine attended a summer preacher training program in a *non-institutional* church of Christ. His assigned study text for the summer? Max Lucado's latest books. Is it any surprise to hear that my friend has now drifted off into ecumenism and is currently an interdenominational ministry consultant, having renounced traditional views of "main stream" churches of Christ as too narrow? He presently favors the "new hermeneutics," change-agent approach of teachers associated with *New Wineskins* Magazine. This story of my friend is just one anecdotal example that could be multiplied thousands of times over of those who, although brought up in the truth, have been swept away by what might be called the "peace where there is no peace" movement (Jer. 6:14-19).

An Evangelical Sounds the Warning

Jeremiah 6:14-19 clearly applies today on a number of levels. The same sentiment is repeated from the book of *Genesis* through the book of the *Apocalypse*. We must remember that the patriarchs, prophets, apostles, evangelists, pastors and teachers of the O.T. and N.T. had a specific charge to warn the people of God. Evangelicals in America today can plainly read the handwriting on the wall and Chuck Swindoll warns,

> Churches don't need to try so hard to be so creative and cute that folks miss the truth. No need for meaningless and silly substitutes that dumb down God's Word. These may entertain people – even encourage them— but rarely will they convict the lost or bring believers deeper in their maturity. Teaching the truth takes care of all of that. Remember Paul's words: "reprove, rebuke, exhort" (2 Tim. 4:2). Those are not politically correct terms. Why? Because God is not politically correct. He never intended to be. Sadly, in an alarming number of churches today God's people are being told what they *want* to hear rather than what they *need* to hear. They are being spoon-fed warm milk, not challenged to digest solid meat. A watered-down teaching ministry will usually attract crowds (for a while), but it has no eternal impact. . . .Satisfying the curious, scratching the itching ears of our postmodern audiences, is an exercise in futility. Like eating cotton candy, the experience may be delightful . . . but there's no food value (Swindoll, 89). Sermonettes are for Christianettes . . . instead of stretching and challenging them, we're entertaining them. Our congregations need pastors who study hard, pray hard, and prepare well-balanced meals, then open the Scriptures and teach people how to study the Word for themselves (Swindoll, 90). I am more convinced now than ever that when we enter into the Christian life, we enter a battleground, not a playground. Just because everything *appears* peaceful does not mean that everything is peaceful. . . .If we could slap a warning label across the

times in which we live, it might read, "Warning! Difficult times are upon us and they will never go away!" (Swindoll, 157).

I've said things much less critical than Swindoll concerning digression and have been accused by members of the church of Christ of "overreacting." Recently, a gospel preacher (who hasn't written for *Truth Magazine,* incidentally) presented a series of lessons warning against spiritual digression in churches of Christ. The following week in an unrelated conversation with a friend, I heard negative comments about the preacher's teaching, intimating that we just need to mind our own business. Years ago after a college "devotional" in which I was teaching from 1 Corinthians 14, a student approached me and said, "We don't need to hear that stuff. We've been hearing that since we were kids." He told me about a book that would help me become a better preacher and later gave me the copy that I still have today. It was former White House speech writer Roger Ailes' book, *You Are The Message.* While it may contain some good advice, I thought it odd that secular material should be substituted for expository preaching. That was eighteen years ago and I don't think those progressive attitudes have disappeared in the intervening years.

B. Telltale signs of spiritual erosion in America: Omitting one of the weekly assemblies of the local church. (Note: Lest I am labeled a hobbyist, let me clarify that this current trend in many churches *is only one example* of ways christians are vying for "more of self and less of Thee," so to speak. This model, and the admonitions I provide, *can be applied to many issues in the local church today.* Let me make myself clear *so as not to be misquoted*: not everyone who advocates omitting one of the weekly assemblies is carnally-motivated. In fact, sometimes there may be good reasons not to come together for another Bible study and worship period.)

Omitting one of Three Weekly Meetings of the Local Church:
A Matter of Opinion

My wife and I have personal convictions concerning meeting with the local church, which we would not bind on anyone. However, I ask you to consider whether the conclusions we have reached are *reasonable* (Rom. 12:1). We feel that, when we look for a place to move, our first consideration must be living close enough to a local church family so that we can attend their meetings. A family who doesn't know and/or interact with one another will quickly become dysfunctional. I did not apply for a job in one locale in the Western U.S. because we would have had to travel 2+ hours to meet with the brethren, thus the church wouldn't be "local" or very much a part of our daily lives. We feel it would be wrong, regardless of how good the job opportunity might be, for us to purposefully live a great distance from the meeting place of the congregation and then claim that making it to the assembly times is a "hardship," so brethren must cancel the service. In this situation, we would be placing our personal interests ahead of the edification of our brethren. If other members of the church are receiving great benefit from the activities that accompany a second service on Sunday, why would we want to eliminate their meeting? If it becomes an undue hardship for us, we could either stop attending the service, or make efforts to live closer. Three assemblies a week is an *extremely small sacrifice* compared to what others have made for the Lord (Heb. 11:32-12:1).

Examine our Motives for Omitting One of Three Assemblies

If coming together to meet with the local family of believers only three times a week is an imposition on christians, it calls into question just *what* is *more* important in their lives. Attendance doesn't *prove* Christlikeness, but placing the world *ahead* of our spiritual family certainly indicates a lack of commitment to the Lord. Are we hired laborers in the Master's kingdom, looking for the next paycheck, handout, incentive, or dividend? Or, are we His heirs? Hired laborers ask, "What do I *have* to do?" Heirs of the kingdom ask, "What *may* I do to help?"

How much driving are we willing to do to attend sporting events, concerts, hunting, fishing, hobbies, shopping, visiting family, taking vacations, going to work, seeing area sights and attractions? Are we tired after these trips? Certainly. But, we are happy and most willing to exhaust ourselves for the sake of the joy received. However, are we exhausted after serving the Lord? We should be. Are we happy and most willing to exhaust ourselves and sacrifice our conveniences for the Lord? Or, are we exhausted and *unhappy* because we feel it is something we "have to do" instead of something we "want to do"? Consider the following nine natural results of eliminating a second worship service on Sunday.

Nine Natural Consequences of Eliminating
a Second Worship Service on Sunday

1. Parents who stay home with a sick child on Sunday morning cannot worship with the saints on Sunday night, thus they have no opportunity to worship with brethren on Sunday.
2. This will eliminate another opportunity for non-christian visitors to worship with us.

3. This eliminates another opportunity for traveling christians to worship with us.

4. This will eliminate another opportunity to spend 15-30 minutes before and after the assembly with our fellow brethren and visitors, equivalent to 1-2 hours per month, 12-24 hours per year, or 120-240 hours in 10 years.

5. Families will almost certainly *spend less time together on Sundays* en route to these meetings. People will do things other than spending time together with their entire family.

6. In every place I have ever seen eliminate the second worship assembly on Sunday, the results are not *more* spiritual activity but less. You might say, "Well this shouldn't happen." Let's be honest, what do most christians do with that second half of the day? From what my wife and I have seen, this time is spent watching television, going to the movies, shopping, going out to eat, doing schoolwork, conducting business or preparing for work, playing sports, reading books, working around the house, engaging in hobbies, spending time on the internet, sleeping, etc. Eliminating one of the assemblies trades spiritual for *secular.* My wife and I have experience with eight churches that met only once on Sunday. In every case, time spent in spiritual activities *decreases and time spent in secular activities increases.*

7. Many churches, in the wake of eliminating their Sunday PM service, extend the Sunday AM service from two hours to three hours. In these cases, many people find it difficult to concentrate for three hours and end up attending only part of the Sunday AM service. In one church I know of, this became so much of a problem that, although the PM service was eliminated, the previously-extended services were eventually shortened to the original two-hour format.

8. Many churches have a number of capable men with the ability and desire to preach; however, eliminating one assembly further limits that opportunity.

9. This eliminates another opportunity to hear the word of God preached.

Correcting an Incorrect Mindset Regarding Church Assemblies: Binding Tradition versus Committing the Whole of Our Life to the Lord

The point here is that for whatever reason (e.g., historical precedent, denominational mentality, tradition, etc.) assembling with the local church is sometimes viewed and treated as the *whole* of christianity. Christians, who gauge their faithfulness to God by outward or established traditions, believe they are sinning if they fail to keep the local customs. Consider the following two hypothetical examples. *Family A* believes it is wrong to miss any of the weekly assemblies; thus, they may sometimes attend, not because they *want* to attend, but because they feel like they "have to." How do I know this? I often fell into this category during my college years. This same family, who would never think of missing an assembly, may never spend time in family Bible reading, prayer, worship, hymn singing and praise to God in their home. However, they may look down on *Family B* who is unable to make it to the assembly because they live two hours away (Note: although this isn't what we would choose to do, we all know cases where this occurs.) All the while, *Family B* has a great desire to assemble if they could and, in fact, has Bible studies in their home seven days a week. Which family is more committed to the Lord? *Family A* feels that they are more dedicated because they are keeping the tradition of the *brethren*, while *Family B* is just trying to do their best to serve God, although they may not be able to keep up with all the customs of the local brethren. Here is the take-home message: It would be wrong for *Family A* to tell *Family B* that they must keep all of the local church customs or else they are in sin. Likewise, it would be equally wrong for *Family B* to conclude that, if they miss the Sunday PM assembly, they are in sin; thus to rectify this situation, they *insist* that the church *cancel* the service so that they will not feel guilty. These scenarios are taking place today.

Judging Our Commitment to the Lord Based on Local Customs Rather Than by Biblical Faith

Not only is the above example plausible, many of us have seen this occur in churches around the country. It is also the situation we find ourselves in when we begin binding the traditions of men over the traditions of God (Mark 7:1-9). Granted, some practices, customs, or traditions fall clearly within the realm of divine. Paul (in 1 Cor. 7:10) was providing divine instruction, not to be confused with opinion. Some advice, however, is clearly personal and does not amount to divine fiat, or transgression if disregarded (1 Cor. 7:6-9, [see 21st Century, KJV]; 1 Cor. 7:25, 26, 40). Thus, a local custom is a matter of personal faith based on one's *"reasoning"* judgment (Rom. 12:1; Phil. 2:12). However, when brethren feel guilty that they can't make it to one of the assemblies that others are deriving great benefit from, why not simply be honest and say, "I just can't make it to this assembly anymore. You have to understand that I'm giving 100% to the Lord; however, because of X, Y, and Z factors, I'm not able to meet with the local family on this occasion." In this way, brethren could continue deriving great spiritual benefit from the meeting rather than having the *whole church eliminate* the assembly.

When is a local custom, tradition, practice, or habit viewed as equivalent to the word of the Lord? Answer: When Christians define their commitment to Christ *only* on the basis of local church customs, traditions, habits, and practices. This is religiosity. This contradiction turns the meaning of God's word on its head – a twisted theology that the Lord never intended. In this case, modern Christianity is judged on the basis of whether we are adhering to the traditions, customs, and habits of the local family of believers instead of an individual, heartfelt longing to know the Lord by understanding His will and serving Him in *all* aspects of our lives – not just for three hours on Sunday and one hour on Wednesday.

I recently heard someone ask the question, "If you removed the weekly assemblies, would Jesus still be a part of your life?" We might further ask, If you removed preparation for Bible class, and the two weekly sermons, would Jesus still be a part of your daily life? If you removed the opportunity to contribute to the local work of the church, would Jesus benefit at all from your financial prosperity? If you removed congregational prayers as well as prayers before meals, would you still pray to God without ceasing (1 Thess. 5:17)? What if you removed everything that others outwardly judge your service to Christ by? What if you removed all the local customs that we feel *compelled,* and *obligated* to do? Would there still be anything you would *want* to do for God? That is, if I removed things that I might do "grudgingly or of necessity" would I still be a "cheerful giver" (2 Cor. 9:7)? God judges us based on our personal sacrifice, dedication, and service to the Lord, rather than simple attrition to the will of the local church, elders or preacher. What part does Jesus share in your daily walk of life on Mondays, Tuesdays, Thursdays, Fridays, and Saturdays? Is there something that christians would rather be doing on Sunday nights in the place of worshipping God? One gospel preacher, formerly a Catholic, summed up the practice of eliminating one of three weekly services as follows,

> America IS an idolatrous and pagan country with a sprinkling of Christians (relatively speaking) providing enough salt to preserve it. What happens when the salt loses is savor? . . . Eliminating (worship) services to God is like taking salt out of a recipe – don't you think? Man can make a thousand "good reasons" for eliminating a second service while the underlying motives (if we are REALLY honest) are to serve ourselves (McIlvain).

V. Six Suggestions for Faithfulness to Christ in Our Present Culture
If christianity is to survive in America, it is contingent on the faithfulness
of believers. In light of the current spiritual recession in America, here are
six suggestions for faithfulness to Christ.

A. Get uncomfortable and sacrificial (Rom. 12:1, 2). In a recent interview, Dr. Kevin Leman, discussing his book, *Have a New Kid by Friday,*
said that he believes the most important line in the book is, "An unhappy
child is a healthy child." His point was that, if children are to grow and
mature, there will be difficulty involved, often leading to pain and unhap-
piness. If parents want children who are *always* happy, chances are, they
are not receiving appropriate discipline and instruction in the Lord (Eph.
6:4). In like manner, America is arguably the most satiated, pleasure-filled,
hedonistic society the world has ever known, in terms of the wealth spent
on self-gratification. As we have become wealthier and more comfortable
(in our attempt to be happy), our interest in God has waned. The history of
faithful christians in America and in the N.T., however, is one of toil, pain,
hardship, and *sacrifice.*

An Abridged Historical Background of Christian Sacrifice in America
     Our country has been blessed beyond our forefathers' wildest imagina-
tions. The 60-70 hour work weeks that were the rule in days gone by have
now been shortened, often to ca. 40-50 hours, providing most Americans
(not without exception) with free time to engage in personal interests or hobbies. We have more disposable/expendable income today than any previous
generation, which affords us luxuries our ancestors could not acquire (e.g.,
eating richer more expensive foods such as meat, eating out at restaurants,
temperature-controlled buildings and automobiles, home entertainment
centers, modern means of transportation, vacations, and leisure time). Yet,
are we sacrificing more for God today, or less? Are we giving more of our
time and energy to Jesus, or less? Honestly, what trials, inconveniences, or
sacrifices do we make for the Lord? It is a question that has brought me to
shame after reading works such as John Foxe's *Book of Martyrs,* or *China's
Christian Martyrs* (Hattaway). The times in which God's people have
multiplied the fastest were times of the greatest trial, hardship, sacrifice,
and discomfort (e.g., during Saul's persecution, Acts 8:1-4; and during the
great depression, ca. 1930-1941).

     History shows us that despite our American forefathers' arduous work
hours, and conditions, churches from yesteryear often devoted more time
to assembling and hearing God's word taught and worshiping than we do.

A preacher I know recalls how his grandfather's generation would plow the field for twelve hours a day, then walk a few miles to go to a gospel meeting, get up the next morning, and work for another twelve hours. This would go on for three weeks. My great great grandfather and his family in DeKalb county Alabama, before the turn of the 20th century, had to walk or ride a mule or wagon for miles just to attend the local assembly of saints. Stories like this are not rare, and can be corroborated in books such as *J. D. Tant Texas Preacher,* and *Preaching in a Changing World* by Irven Lee. Historians among our brethren have also dealt extensively with this subject, addressing the changing nature of local churches in the United States, which are, in many cases, moving from a spiritual emphasis to a more self-serving emphasis. Generally-speaking, we are shortening the amount of time the local church family meets together to worship. When I was a child in the 1970's, ten-day meetings were still held in some places and weekly ladies Bible classes were more common than today. This is not an indictment, but should stir us to ask, "Are we sacrificing more for God today, or less?"

The scripture is filled with examples of God's people upending, over-turning, and changing the world when they were called to step out of their comfort zones and sacrifice for the Lord. Jesus *never* called us to a life of ease and worldly satiation but to be *pilgrims* (1 Pet. 2:11). It is not surprising that when christians no longer see themselves as pilgrims and have no more of the challenges that sojourners face, worldliness, complacency, infighting, and apostasy take root. *There is no infighting during battle on the front lines!* Consider the following examples of Jesus calling christians *out* of comfort and *into* hardship.

1. The man who would have no place to lay his head.

   As they were walking along the road, a man said to him, "I will follow you wherever you go." Jesus replied, "Foxes have dens and birds have nests, but the Son of Man has no place to lay his head" (Luke 9:57, 58, NIV).

2. The man who would not be there to see his father die.

   He said to another man, "Follow me." But he replied, "Lord, first let me go and bury my father." Jesus said to him, "Let the dead bury their own dead, but you go and proclaim the kingdom of God" (Luke 9:59, 60, NIV).

3. The man who would have to turn his back on his own family.

   Still another said, "I will follow you, Lord; but first let me go back and say goodbye to my family." Jesus replied, "No one who puts a hand to the plow and looks back is fit for service in the kingdom of God" (Luke 9:61, 62, NIV).

An evangelical, Glenn Penner has personally known hundreds of people who have been persecuted and martyred around the world for belief in Jesus. He writes,

> Weakness, suffering and sacrifice are God's *modus operandi.* This is how God accomplishes his work: not through strength or compulsion but through love and invitation. . . .A cross-centered gospel requires cross-carrying messengers. When Jesus declared, "If anyone would come after me, let him deny himself and take up his cross and follow me" (Matt. 16:24) *we need to take his words much more literally than we are accustomed to doing.* . . .Romanian church leader Josef Ton . . . coined the phrase "Christ's cross was for propitiation. Our cross is for propagation." *To be called to follow Christ was to receive a call to suffer* (e.g. Acts 9:16; 14:22; 1 Thess. 3:3; 1 Pet. 2:21; 3:9, 17). . . .It was this understanding that sacrifice, suffering, and even death were the normal cost of discipleship that fuelled the evangelistic efforts of the first-century church. They did not expect to experience all of the blessing of heaven in this world. They knew that by their faithfulness, even unto death, they were storing up rewards in heaven. Contrary to our belief that it is a blessing *not* to be persecuted, they knew that it was the persecuted *who are blessed* (Matt. 5:10-12). . . .Rather than following our example of thanking God for the privilege of not suffering for him, they thanked God for the honor of suffering for his sake (Acts 5:41). They knew that in order to bring life to others, they must die; to see others experience peace with God, they would have to suffer the violence of the world; to bring the love of God to a dying world, they would have to face the hatred of those whom they were seeking to reach. It is in this context that they described spiritual *warfare*; not *freedom* over bad habits or psychological problems. . . .There is no glory for the sufferer. No hero worship. No merit for those who are able to endure hardship, no boasting of one's achievements (Penner, 19-21).

Although we are ready and willing to correct the doctrinal error of denominationalism, can I say that my personal faith and sacrifice are equivalent to those of my sectarian friends? Maybe so. Maybe not. However, if we expect to be emissaries of Christ, is there any good reason why we should be exempt from the same sacrifices as our first century and N.T. brethren? Do we really want to sacrifice, or do we want to remain comfortable and inert? If we want the comfort, ease, convenience, and unobtrusiveness of three-hour-a-week christianity, have we not redefined what it means to be a christian, and in the process, should we be surprised if the spread of the gospel ebbs in the wake of self-gratification? Do the martyrs' sacrifices compare to a 21st century member of the church in America who wants to *"go into all the world and preach the gospel to every creature"* as long as he can do it in a particular country, in a specified region of that country, in a particular state in that region, and in a specified county in that state? David Platt, an evangelical from Birmingham, Alabama, in his book, *Radical: Taking Back Your Faith from the American Dream,* says it better that I could,

> And this is where we need to pause. Because we are starting to redefine Christianity. We are giving in to the dangerous temptation to take the Jesus of the Bible and twist him into a version of Jesus we are more comfortable with. A nice, middle-class American Jesus. A Jesus who doesn't mind ma-terialism and who would never call us to give away everything we have. A Jesus who would not expect us to forsake our closest relationships so that he receives all our affection. A Jesus who is fine with nominal devo-tion that does not infringe on our comforts, because, after all, he loves us just the way we are. A Jesus who wants us to be balanced, who wants us to avoid dangerous extremes, and who, for that matter, wants us to avoid danger altogether. A Jesus who brings us comfort and prosperity as we live out our Christian spin on the American dream. But do you and I realize what we are doing at this point? We are molding Jesus into our image. He is beginning to look a lot like us because, after all, that is whom we are most comfortable with. And the danger now is that when we gather in our church buildings to sing . . . we may not actually be worshiping the Jesus of the Bible. Instead we may be worshiping ourselves (Platt, 13).

Biblical Precedent for Sacrificing More for God

Instead of a model designed to sacrifice less to God and preserve our excess time, energies, money, and talent for self gratification, Jesus sets a different standard: *Be used up for the Lord.* We should want to grow tired, be burdened, be spent up, and be used up in the service of God. Are we really used up for the Lord? Are we really sacrificing ourselves today? Or, do we become discouraged when our worship, service, sacrifice, or offering becomes an inconvenience? One reason two very close friends of mine have drifted off into interdenominational fellowships is that the brethren in their local churches sacrificed so little for the kingdom and considered my friends so "overzealous" that my friends found other places to worship where the people were much more motivated for service, despite being in doctrinal error. Many denominations have 6AM men's Bible studies. I suggested we do that in one locale and I was laughed at. One brother said to me, "No one would get up that early for a Bible study." Consider the following scriptures as you answer the question: "Does my sacrifice to God cost me anything?"

> I will most gladly *spend and be expended* for your souls. If I love you more, am I to be loved less? (2 Cor. 12:15, NASB).

> Now I rejoice in *my sufferings* for your sake, *and in my flesh* I do my share on behalf of His body, which is the church, in filling up what is lacking in Christ's afflictions (Col. 1:24).

Do we have the same willingness to be bruised and crushed for the Lord and our brethren (Isa. 53:5)? Whereas suffering is most commonly depicted as a bad thing, Paul says, for him, it was good! He *rejoiced* in it. Should we not rejoice for the *opportunity* to suffer for the Lord?

> Having so fond an affection for you, we were well-pleased to impart to you not only the gospel of God *but also our own lives*, because you had become very dear to us (1 Thess. 2:8).

Paul was willing to give his very life for the sake of, not only the Lord, but also for his brethren. Are we willing to do the same? "Suffer hardship with me, as a good soldier of Christ Jesus" (2 Tim. 2:3). Paul not only endured suffering, but pleaded with Timothy to endure the same with him. Do we exempt ourselves? Could we change the titles of hymns to better suit 21st century christianity? "Soldiers of Christ Arise. . . and Turn on the Television." Or, "I Want to Be A Worker for the Lord. . . for 3 Hours a Week." Or, "All to Jesus I Surrender. . . Unless He becomes a Burden." Paul said,

> . . .for which I *suffer hardship* even to imprisonment as a criminal; but the word of God is not imprisoned. For this reason I *endure all things* for the sake of those who are chosen, so that they also may obtain the salvation which is in Christ Jesus and with it eternal glory (2 Tim. 2:9, 10).

John the baptist was decapitated, James was murdered with a sword, our Lord was stripped, whipped, slapped, spit upon, and tacked to a piece of crude lumber for us, John was abandoned on a rocky island, Stephen was crushed to death, the apostles were slaughtered, Peter (according to historical tradition) was crucified upside down after watching his wife and daughter murdered, christians in China today worship God at the risk of their lives, even Catholics in Asia, Orthodox believers in the former Soviet Union, and Calvinists around the world have offered the last full excruciating measure in service to their Lord who died for them. What are we sacrificing today for the good of the Lord and our fellow brethren?

Some Concluding Thoughts on Self-Gratification versus Self-Sacrifice
The World Christian Database (2010) estimated that in 2006, worldwide, 468 people *per day* died for their faith in Jesus Christ. Certain elements in the countries of Indonesia, Iran, Pakistan, Laos, Cambodia, the Philippines, as well as Africa, etc. are highly hostile to believers. Many brethren among us have sacrificed greatly for God in Africa, India, China, the Philippines, Vietnam, the Caribbean, Central and South America, etc. However, are these sacrifices typical of 21st century christians in America? If not, don't be surprised as each successive generation of American christians becomes smaller and less interested in the Lord. Every day, 450+ people die for their faith in Jesus Christ while in America, churches of Christ are eliminating one of their three weekly assemblies, shortening seven day gospel meetings to two or three day events, chastising a preacher for having more than a few children because it will become a "financial drain on the church," *discouraging* sons from preaching the gospel or daughters from marrying preachers, and encouraging children to miss worship services in order to attend a school event, do homework, or work a job (Matt. 10:37-39; Luke 14:25-27).

B. Squeeze the world out and the Lord in. Beyond adhering to a list of prohibitions and commands, christians in America, now more than ever, need to break out of the mold of ritualism, and heartless religiosity and foster authentic heartfelt christianity; the kind of faith that squeezes the world out and the Lord into every facet of our lives. This is the kind of faith that will withstand (1) Propaganda at the secular state university, (2) Ungodly behavior, disputes, and factions in the local church, (3) Apostasy by one's family, friends, and brethren, (4) Trials, hardships, and sufferings of life, (5) 21st century lusts of the flesh, (6) Marital problems or unfaithfulness, and remain true to the Lord. Anyone of these could lead to unfaithfulness.

Am I demanding too much? What did the first century N.T. church look like? The question, rather, should be, what was the *ideal* for the N.T. christian that God left for us in His word? Was it a lackadaisical, worldly American christian who drags himself to worship, makes jokes about long and boring sermons, looks for any reason to get out of meeting with his spiritual family beyond three hours a week, and offers no more in service to the Lord and his brothers? Is it the saint who is more excited about the NFL, NBA, NHL, NCAA, or MLB than the spiritual growth of a new saint who recently obeyed the gospel? Consider the first church in Jerusalem,

And they continued steadfastly in the apostles' doctrine and fellowship, in the breaking of bread, and in prayers. . . .So continuing daily with one accord in the temple, and breaking bread from house to house, they ate their food with gladness and simplicity of heart, praising God and having favor with all the people (Acts 2:42, 46, 47a).

Here were people who had squeezed the world out and squeezed Jesus into the whole of their lives. Here were people who longed for (1) the teaching of the apostles, (2) spending time with their fellow brethren, (3) partaking of the Lord's supper and remembering His death, (4) talking with the Lord of the universe, (5) entertaining one another with meals in their homes, and (6) giving glory to God and in return received love and appreciation from their fellow man. What results can we expect today if we follow this same pattern instead of following the "American Dream"? "And the Lord added to the church daily those who were being saved" (Acts 2:47b).

Being a christian permeated every aspect of the Jerusalem church's lives. While I don't advocate their Calvinism, the Amish and certain sects of Mennonites demonstrate this quite effectively today. When I was a child, my family lived in proximity to a community of Holdeman Mennonites (who do not use instruments of music in worship, as we, and who are amillennialists). At a young age, I was perplexed as to how christians in various churches of Christ that I knew could be so worldly, while my Mennonite friends reflected the sanctification and spirit of the Lord that my father preached about. It took many years to reconcile this in my mind. As I grew older, I came to understand the distinction in the upbringing of Mennonite children and my peers in the church. My Mennonite friends had a family life characterized by Bible study, worship, and holiness. Most had no televisions or radios. While the churches I was associated with were doctrinally sound regarding salvation, baptism, the nature of the local church, etc., too many christians were emphasizing the wrong things. Christians, brought their children to the local assembly for four hours a week, but the other 164 hours in the week were dedicated to teaching the children all about *academics, athletics, baseball, football, soccer, basketball, the world series, the super bowl, hunting, fishing, dirt bikes, and four wheelers, 4H, band, voice lessons, business, real estate, attending the best college, getting the best grades, television, Hollywood, wrestling, dancing, NASCar, fashion, pop culture, rock and roll, etc.* Had all of this time and energy been put into teaching my church friends about about the Lord, more of them might be faithful today. Consider these thoughts in light of the following scriptures: Deuteronomy 6:6-8; Proverbs 22:6; 2 Timothy 1:5; 3:14, 15. If christianity is to survive

in America among current believers and their posterity, christian parents
need to make up their minds whether they want to have the "All American
Boy" or girl, or whether they want to squeeze the world out of their home
and have a humble servant of God (Josh. 24:14-16).

Twenty Recommendations for Squeezing the World Out and the Lord into Your Life

(Note: Although these are written primarily for parents and their children,
the same principles can be universally applied to families who do not have
children.)

1. Turn off the TV. . . Turn off the World. It has been said,

    > If we watch enough television, our senses are dulled and we become just
    > that stupid. We become passive and disconnected. Our ability to think
    > shrivels. Clear courageous thinking is now a rarity (Swindoll, 156).

    I like to put it this way: We like to watch TV because we get excited
    about watching other people *living their lives.* The irony, however, is
    almost painful . . . why don't we get up and start living our own lives
    (Phil. 4:13; Eph. 5:15, 16)?
2. Study the Bible with your family in your home at regular times during
    the week.
3. Ask your children what they learned in Bible class.
4. Use current news events as subject illustrations to teach your children
    Biblical principles.
5. Give your children instructions from a Biblical perspective with Bibli-
    cal explanations (when possible) rather than only always authoritative
    commands or worldly explanations.
6. Visit nursing homes and shut-ins.
7. Take your family to gospel meetings.
8. Volunteer for projects to help other members of the church.
9. Turn off secular music and turn on a capella hymns or sermons when
    traveling. (CD's can be purchased from a Bible bookstore or downloaded
    for free from *www.kleinwood.com.*)
10. Let your children see you studying the Bible and praying.
11. Pray that the Lord will make your children instruments for righteousness
    and the glory of God, even it if means going through hardships.
12. Live so that when you die, your children will say, "My father (or mother)
    loved the Lord."
13. Put up scriptures in your home (e.g., on the mirror in the bathroom, in

children's rooms, on the refrigerator, on doors, or in your vehicle or on your office wall).

14. Memorize scripture with your family and post these verses in your home.
15. Become evangelistic and take an interest in saving the souls of others.
16. Have regular periods of devotion, singing hymns, and praising God with your family.
17. Turn off ungodly commercials advertising beer, immodesty, sexual content, etc.
18. Don't laugh or make light of sin, lest you minimize its severity in the minds of your children.
19. Pray with your family every day.
20. LIVE THE LOVE OF JESUS (Matt. 25:31-46).

C. Teach, first, by example. If christianity is to survive among us and our posterity, we must *demonstrate* authentic lives of faith (Rom. 12:1, 2). Ralph Waldo Emerson is purported to have said, "Who you are speaks so loudly, I can't hear what you're saying." When our lives do not match our doctrine, we may do more harm than good. Remember Jesus' warning?

> Therefore whatever they tell you to observe, *that* observe and do, but do not do according to their works; for they say, and do not do (Matt. 23:3).

How many *unbelievers* have been turned off by hypocrisy in christians and how many *believers* have been driven away from God by poor and ungodly examples among brethren? Consider Romans 2:17-24. When people see our children or us, can they tell that we've "been with Jesus"?

> Now when they saw the boldness of Peter and John, and perceived that they were uneducated and untrained men, they marveled. And they realized that they had been with Jesus (Acts 4:13).

Godly Knowledge and a Godly Example are Essential
Certainly we should stress *knowledge*. Knowledge of God, His son, His spirit, His immutable plan devised before the foundation of the world, and His written revealed word. However, knowledge isn't enough. A christian or group of christians who have adequate knowledge of the Bible may still be castaway (1 Cor. 9:27). We are warned that knowledge puffs up, and that even someone with "all knowledge" may be considered "nothing" to God, in the absence of love (1 Cor. 8:1; 13:2). Many of us go through life hearing all the right things, learning Biblically accurate doctrine, yet we don't live

for the Lord, partially, because we've had poor examples, models, or mentors. Jesus taught by words, but often His most impactful statements were non-verbal. One clear example is the silent suffering servant (1 Pet. 2:23; Isa. 53:7). I've discussed the problem of negative examples with individuals before who make brash statements like, "Well, that's no excuse. Elijah served God alone." However, the very same individuals who make these statements may be christians today *because* of the example, modeling, and mentoring of other Christians! Is this not a theme that we see throughout scripture? (See John 13:14, 15; Phil. 3:17; 2 Thess. 3:8, 9; 1 Tim. 4:12; 1 Pet. 2:21; 1 Pet. 5:2, 3; 1 Cor. 11:1; 4:16.) We cannot underestimate the power of example. We must not rely too much on what we say while giving little heed to how we are being perceived by others. What our brethren, our children, and the world need to see is a reflection of Jesus. That is, we are to be people who live for the Lord, but do not do it *to be seen by men*. That may seem like an oxymoron, yet the Lord calls us to be light and salt to the world, while not looking for recognition, or the praise and glory of men (cf. Matt. 5:13-16 and 6:1-5, 16-18). Only that GOD gets the glory in all things and that people come to know Jesus as master and God.

Drop the Egos
Drop the egos. While godly examples are vitally important, the delicate balance is to be an example without seeking the glory of men. The christian who vaunts and parades his deeds to be seen undermines much of the good he could accomplish by his teaching. While we may seek the praise of others to (1) counter personal feelings of low self-worth, or maybe (2) to attract the attention of others (which is bad enough), there may be a more carnal reason. Could it be that we seek recognition for (3) our carnal longing for the glory and praise of men? Jesus had much to say on this subject. Consider Matthew 6:1-5, 16-18; Luke 18:9; Matthew 23:5, 6; 20:25-28; Luke 14:7-14. Yet, we all know people (maybe ourselves) who wear us out every time we see them, describing "all the good" they're doing for God. Drop the egos.

D. Preach *THE* word (2 Tim. 4:1-3). If christianity is to survive in America, the truth cannot be traded for a pseudo-gospel. There must be correction, rebuke, laying bare the deeds of darkness, and buffeting the soul and conscience that the spirit might be saved. Too many parents, grandparents, christians, preachers, elders, and teachers, wanting to satisfy, pacify, and placate people, may have forgotten that Jesus converts souls by pricking (poking, prodding, piercing) hearts with His word (Acts 2:37). Question: How did we or anyone truly come to Jesus? Did we come to Jesus out of triumph, success, personal self-fulfillment, satiety, victory, and comfort? Did we come to Jesus out of self-sufficiency, peace of mind and heart, and by accentuating the positive and eliminating the negative? Certainly not. All those who come to Jesus can only do so out of guilt and failure – by falling before eternal God in humble submission, admitting our sin, and pleading with the Lord for (or an answer to) a good conscience in baptism (1 Pet. 3:21). The Lord only ever calls the humble to Him, although pleading with the proud. Why? Because the Lord dwells among the humble (Isa. 57:15; Phil. 2:8). The word of God has the power to bring us to our knees, weeping and confessing before the Lord (Psa. 51:17). When Ezra read the word of God, the people responded with weeping, similar to the Jews on the day of Pentecost (Acts 2:36, 37; Neh. 8:9). For the faith of Jesus Christ to survive in this country, or anywhere in the world, the word of God must be the *central message*. Failing to adhere to the whole counsel of God will result in spiritual death and blood on the hands of teachers.

> Therefore I testify to you this day that I *am* innocent of the blood of all *men*. For I have not shunned to declare to you *the whole counsel of God* (Acts 20:26, 27).

American culture, however, shuns guilt, thus, there is the tendency, among some, to preach a limited, watered-down message consisting only of peace. Ann Landers seems to support such:

> One of the most painful, self-mutilating, time- and energy-consuming exercises in the human experience is guilt. . . .Guilt is a pollutant and we don't need any more of it in the world (Landers, 514-517).

Popular polytheistic, psychological guru Wayne Dyer, condemns guilt as,

> A futile waste of time. . . .Guilt is the most useless of all behaviors. It is by far the greatest waste of emotional energy. Guilt zones must be exterminated, spray-cleaned and sterilized forever (Dyer, 90, 91).

While *inappropriate* guilt feelings are not helpful and, at an extreme, may indicate mental illness, guilt, in its healthiest sense, is the emotional pain experienced as a result of improper behavior. Imagine life free from *any* pain. What if we experienced (1) No pain when touching something hot? (2) No pain when staring at a bright light or the sun? (3) No pain when hemorrhaging? (4) No pain when injured, gunshot, or physically ill? We wouldn't know to seek medical attention, which could result in further injury or death. Likewise, individuals who lack any guilt (without the forgiveness of Jesus) are destined to spiritual death. Our conscience (heart) is a very sensitive and precious gift – hand-crafted by God in His image. The popular American practice of anesthetizing the conscience, despite unresolved sin, will destroy the very part of man that leads him to Jesus (Rom. 10:10; Prov. 4:23). The message of the gospel is for man to recognize his fallen state and throw himself on the mercy of the Lord (Rom. 7:24). Following sanctification in Christ, surely there is no more need for guilt or conscience-piercing messages, is there? Although this is the mantra of many ministries today, it is not reflected in the N.T., which calls even the regenerated christian, sanctified, and redeemed in Christ, to ongoing reformation, restoration, and repentance (e.g., letters to Rome, Corinth, Galatia, Ephesus, Philippi (viz., Euodia and Syntyche), Colossae, Thessalonica, Timothy, Titus, the Hebrews, of James, of Peter, epistles of John, of Jude, and to the seven churches of Asia).

Christians, especially evangelists, with no capacity for guilt, despite their sin, begin to feel they "have arrived" and need no further correction. We may assume that since we have the whole truth, we need no further reformation, restoration, examining, searching, or studying of God's word (Acts 17:10, 11). In absence of continued spiritual growth, stasis and entropy set in and the last state is worse than the first (2 Pet. 2:20). The "we have arrived" mentality leads to the "don't tell me what to do" mentality, which leads to the "no I don't want to study" mentality and then to the "as long as it says church of Christ on the sign we're OK" mentality . . . shades of sectarianism? Chuck Swindoll, in his book *The Church Awakening: An Urgent Call for Renewal,* explains how this is occurring among denominations, which may have application for us as well,

> Some churches today have adopted a professional mind-set entirely. Like the consumer culture they live in, the people pay the pastors to do the work of the ministry, while they sit and watch and offer critiques. Where is *that* in the Bible? A pastor who allows this approach to occur has fallen for what I call the "Superman syndrome." I'm not talking about pulling on a pair of blue tights and a red cape and putting on a fancy "S" on his chest—though I heard of a pastor who did *exactly* that on Easter Sunday (I wish I were kidding). I'm talking about an attitude that says, "I am self-sufficient," "I need no one else," or "I will show no weakness or admit any inadequacy." These words betray the presence of the Superman syndrome—that particular peril for pastors who go it alone and become "the stars of the show" (Swindoll, 51).

For further documentation on removal of guilt, condemnation, and conscience from our religious culture or from denominations, see John MacArthur's book, *The Vanishing Conscience.*

"Professional" Preachers and Commercial Ministries

Another area of concern for preaching the gospel in 21st century American christianity is the evolution of the local church from a band of sympathetic Christ-followers to a commercial-like enterprise with goals, priorities, and practices that either distract from the mission of Christ, or are clearly antithetical to it. Former chaplain of the U.S. Senate, the late Richard C. Halverson, said,

> In the beginning the church was a fellowship of men and women centered on the living Christ. Then the church moved to Greece, where it became a philosophy. Then it moved to Rome, where it became an institution. Next, it moved to Europe, where it became a culture. And, finally, it moved to America, where it became an enterprise (Swindoll, 29).

A young preacher once told me, "I'm thinking about going into overseas evangelism. I hear there is good money in it." What members of non-institutional churches of Christ have been warning their more institutionally-minded brethren and denominational friends for years has now come of age – the more "conservative" among our institutional brethren as well as "conservative" evangelicals are shouting warnings against the evolution of their churches into entertainment and profit-driven organizations. One evangelical said,

> We pastors are being killed by the professionalizing of the pastoral ministry. The mentality of the professional is not the mentality of the prophet. It is not the mentality of the slave of Christ. Professionalism has nothing to do with the essence and heart of the Christian ministry. The more professional we long to be, the more spiritual death we will leave in our wake. For there is no professional childlikeness (Matt. 18:3); there is no professional tenderheartedness (Eph. 4:32); there is no professional panting after God (Ps. 42:1). . . .Our business is . . . to deny ourselves and take up the blood-splattered (sic.) cross daily (Luke 9:23). How do you carry a cross professionally? We have been crucified with Christ; yet now we live by faith in the one who loved us and gave Himself for us (Gal. 2:20). What is professional faith? We are to be filled not with wine but with the Spirit (Eph. 5:18). We are God-besotted lovers of Christ. How can you be drunk with Jesus professionally? Then, wonder of wonders, we were given the gospel treasure to carry in clay pots to show that the transcendent power belongs to God (2 Cor. 4:7). Is there a way to be a professional clay pot?. . . Banish professionalism from our

midst, Oh God, and in its place put passionate prayer, poverty of spirit, hunger for God, rigorous study of Holy things, white-hot devotion to Jesus Christ, utter indifference to all material gain, and unremitting labor to rescue the perishing, perfect the saints, and glorify our sovereign Lord (Piper, 1, 2, 4).

Replace the word "pastor" with "evangelist" in the two preceding paragraphs, and who could disagree? Just as the world creeps into denominations, too often, denominationalism creeps into the Lord's body. The work of the Lord must be one of heartfelt compassion, love, and desire to please Jehovah. A.W. Tozer well said,

> Familiarity may breed contempt even at the very altar of God. How frightful a thing it is for the preacher when he becomes accustomed to his work, when his sense of wonder departs, when he gets used to the unusual, when he loses his solemn fear in the presence of the High and Holy One; when, to put it bluntly, he gets a little bored with God and heavenly things.

We should have the same appetite for doing God's will as Jesus did for the father,

> Therefore said the disciples one to another, Hath any man brought him ought to eat? Jesus saith unto them, *My meat is to do the will of him that sent me*, and to finish his work (John 4:33, 34, KJV).

E. Couple correction with compassion (gentleness). In our passion to stand for the kingdom of God and to oppose all error in this new millennium, let us never forget that irreparable harm can easily be done by showing no compassion in our correction. Were there instances of stern rebuke in the N.T.? Certainly. But in every case, consider the context. Stern rebukes were, without exception, reserved for the religiously stiff-necked and not the alien sinner or young christian who were trying to understand and do the right thing. The admonition for compassionate (gentle) correction in the word of God cannot be overlooked (Gal. 6:1; 2 Tim. 2:24-26; Eph. 4:1-3; 1 Cor. 9:19-23; Col. 4:6; 1 Tim. 5:1, 2; Phil. 4:5; 2 Pet. 1:7; Col. 3:12, 13; Eph. 4:26, 27, 29, 31, 32).

F. Replace political militancy with the love, power and might of Jesus Christ. The early church's influence on the world was one of positive spiritual impact. Early christians were known as being non-violent, nonretaliatory, extremely generous, and highly sacrificial toward their non-christian neighbors. Early christians unintentionally shamed pagans around them by their example; showing more love to their pagan neighbors than the pagans did. The christians were known to retrieve pagan infants left for dead on the tops of hills and raise them as their own. Imagine the doors of opportunity to spread the gospel that this presented. The power of Christ was witnessed in the transformed lives and spiritually and socially magnanimous behavior of the converts, leading others to inquire of their change and seek the gospel,

> Wives, likewise, be submissive to your own husbands, that even if some do not obey the word, they, *without a word, may be won* by the conduct of their wives, when they observe your chaste conduct *accompanied* by fear (1 Pet. 3:1, 2).

When Julian became emperor of Rome in A.D. 361, his plan to revive paganism among the populace failed. Writing to the pagan priest Arcasius about the detested Christians, he said,

> The religion of the Greeks does not yet prosper as I would wish, on account of those who profess it. But the gifts of the gods are great and splendid, better than any prayer or any hope. . . . Why then do we think that this is sufficient and do not observe how the kindness of Christians to strangers, their care for the burial of their dead, and the sobriety of their lifestyle has done the most to advance their cause? For it is disgraceful when no Jew is a beggar and the impious (Julian's name for Christians) support our poor in addition to their own; everyone is able to see that our own religious people lack aid from us (Thenagain.info).

Early christians didn't have to start an institution, organization, society, relief fund, or civic club. As they saw a need arise within their sphere of influence, they simply met it, and revolutionized the world through Christ. They didn't have to parade, vaunt, publish, trumpet, or otherwise laud their good deeds among men. They simply lived it. This behavior turned the world's attention toward Jesus who, during His ministry, showed love and mercy to the most sinful, depraved, and pitiful that society had to offer (viz., children, widows, publicans, harlots, drunkards, Gentiles, lepers, lame, diseased, Samaritans, social outcasts, etc.), in stark contrast to the religiosity of the religious leaders of the day. The behavior of the early Christians was in fulfillment of the inspired writings of Jesus and the apostles (John 13:34, 35; Gal. 6:10; Matt. 5:38-48; 1 Pet. 2:12; Luke 10:25-36).

In light of these verses, it may be easier to contrast the Christ-filled life with one of conservative political militancy. Many christians believe they are accomplishing God's will by redirecting our efforts away from redeeming society *by the gospel* to redeeming society by *political protest*. The late

Jerry Falwell's religious right, while well-intentioned, is not a *replacement* for the gospel. As christians protest, debate, boycott, argue, and rebuke those on the political left, we may, in fact, be isolating ourselves from any chance to convert our political "opponents." Why create hostility between neighbors, co-workers, friends, family, and other social contacts by debating tax reform, foreign wars, embryonic stem cell research, homosexual marriage, prayer in school, and abortion, if our friends don't believe that Jesus is Lord in the first place?! The transforming power of the gospel wins these political battles without firing a partisan shot, when Jesus is recognized as savior, and is put on in baptism (Gal. 3:27). When individuals accept the Bible as the inspired word of God, their views on embryonic stem cell research, homosexual marriage, prayer in school, and abortion will come in line with God's.

"Fox News Christians"

Christians have been enthralled with conservative talk shows in the last two decades. When I first heard Rush Limbaugh in 1993 and Bill O'Reilly in 1999, I was enthusiastic. There were finally socio-political voices responding to the popular "anti-christian" left-wing rhetoric. Now there is Sean Hannity, Mark Levin, Michael Medved, Michael Savage, Glenn Beck, Laura Ingraham, Neil Boortz, Laura Schlessinger, Bill Bennett, G. Gordon Liddy, Dennis Prager, Mike Gallagher, Fred Thompson, Jordan (Jay) Sekulow, Mike McConnel, Cal Thomas, Stephen Baldwin, Mike Huckabee, and Joe Scarborough, just to name a few. As the 1990s progressed, there seemed to be a new wave of "Fox News Christians"— that is, christians who equated standing for the Lord with reiterating the talking points commentary they heard last night. Christians were out to do battle with liberals and take America back from the godless. In the process, had we forgotten that after winning every political debate, defeating every anti-christian liberal, and taking America back for conservatism, that our sworn political enemies, even if converted to Fox News, were still as lost and destined for hell as when they were watching MSNBC? Fox News does not equal salvation. When did the Lord or Paul ever advocate the church, or members thereof, waging political warfare against society? While political involvement may not be prohibited by God's word, it is certainly not the suggested course of action for restoring the hearts of mankind to Jesus (1 Pet. 3:1, 2; 11-17).

The transforming power of the gospel is accomplished *through* the gospel and its life-application by christians, and not through political pundits, ballot boxes, boycotts, petitions, or protests. Consider Jonah 3:5-10, where an entire city repented in sackcloth and ashes, or Acts 2:41 where 3,000 souls were baptized. What reformed these people? The word of God. Should we vote? I believe so. Should we voice our political opinions? I believe so. Should we sign petitions? I believe so. Yet, why are so many Christians these days going around with their political guns half cocked, yet embarrassed to even mention the name of Jesus? Further, if we are *redirecting* our energies, finances, emotions, and time *away* from the gospel and/or if our political actions are *alienating* sinners, we have unquestionably missed the mark. Reforming society by mandating morality will not change hearts. Only reformation of the heart, which leads to repentance, will truly change the world (Eph. 2:1-10). Consider the following true story told by an older denominational preacher and retold by his accompanying younger preaching intern,

> I saw in the newspaper an announcement of a meeting of the Gay People's Union, at Stanford University. . . .One of our interns and I went over to the meeting. We found about a hundred young people. . . .After an hour or so . . . I felt that it was time to say something for the other side. So I identified myself, spoke up, and said, "I can agree with much that has been said about the church, but I don't think you have come to grips with the real issue — the stance of Christianity toward homosexuality. The nearest you came was when this young man spoke of Jesus and the woman at the well." "Nevertheless he did speak to her about her condition — having lived with five husbands, and now living with a man who was not her husband. He then offered her release, relief." I said, "I think this is the true Christian position. Homosexuality is very injurious; it destroys people. Jesus understands that . . . he wants to offer to them a way out." As I looked at that roomful of young people, I did not see a room full of lesbians and faggots, though they were calling themselves those names. I saw some hungry, mixed-up, stunted, fragmented, and hurting young people — wanting somehow to find the secret of life, thinking they had found it — but on a wrong track, and destroying themselves in the process. Over and over, Paul's words in Romans about homosexuals kept coming into my mind: "They receive in their own persons the due penalty of their error" (Romans 1:27b RSV) (Stedman, 1975).

When I heard the young intern preacher (now much older) tell this story in 2007, he said that the preachers were actually well-received by most of the attendees. This provided further opportunity for Bible studies (despite their denominational error). Question: Would this door have been opened had the preacher made a *political* statement concerning gay marriage, the homosexual agenda, or organized a protest? What if Jesus had characterized His ministry with political rhetoric? Consider Jesus in Mark 2:14-16. Further, how often do political movements or the "religious right" strike at the true heart of spiritual corruption, which is pride, or popular sins such as lasciviousness, fornication, divorce, adultery, and unlawful remarriages? Finally, aligning with the world on politics rather than on Jesus Christ is not wise, may lead to unholy alliances, and will adversely influence our ability to shine as lights in a dark world (2 Cor. 6:14-17).

John MacArthur sums up the practice of replacing the Bible with politics in this way,

> Political efforts to moralize society result in unholy unions with unbelievers and enemies of the gospel. . . .Moralism fails to understand the true nature of spiritual warfare. . . .The politics of moralism makes those we are supposed to reach with the gospel into enemies. Unbelievers, immoral people, pornographers, homosexuals, and abortionists have become vilified and hated among believers. We tend to regard them as our enemies. *But they are our mission field.* We mustn't become like Jonah, who hated the Ninevites. . . .Many evangelicals today seem to operate with the notion that if we can elevate the morality of our culture, then more people will believe the gospel. They imagine that if we can clean up the country, it will afford greater opportunities for the gospel. *That's exactly reverse of the divine order.* . . .Higher moral standards alone won't earn God's blessing on this country. *Our only hope for that lies in the transforming power of the gospel.* And our calling is to preach the gospel of Jesus Christ to the ends of the earth, regardless of what unbelievers in our nation may do (MacArthur, 2002, pp. 91-97).

VI. Conclusion: Christ Will Be Victorious

Although it may not be in America, christianity will survive inasmuch as the Lord promised that upon Peter's confession that Jesus was God in the flesh, Christ would establish His church and "the gates of Hades will not prevail against it" (Matt. 16:18), and "the Lord knows those who are his" (2 Tim. 2:19). Nevertheless, Peter's bold confession, upon which the apostles would later preach the message of the kingdom on the day of Pentecost (Acts 2), did not secure the salvation of *Judas*, nor of us, nor of *our posterity*, nor of *future generations of Americans*. We cannot take this fact for granted. Look back across the Atlantic to the spiritual wasteland of western Europe, where believers once looked back to the spiritual wasteland of Asia Minor, where believers once looked back to the spiritual wasteland of Palestine. One day, it could be saints in Brazil, China, Africa, the Philippines, or India looking back at the spiritual wasteland of America. God's people, the remnant, will endure. The question is, will we, our posterity and our spiritual offspring, be in that number? If the Lord allows time to continue, America will likely follow suit with every other major civilization the world has known. Eugene Peterson puts it this way,

> Eighteen hundred years or so of Hebrew history capped by a full exposition in Jesus Christ tell us that God's revelation of Himself is rejected far more often than it is accepted, is dismissed by far more people than embrace it, and has been either attacked or ignored by every major culture or civilization in which it has given its witness: magnificent Egypt, fierce Assyria, beautiful Babylon, artistic Greece, political Rome, Enlightenment France, Nazi Germany, Renaissance Italy, Marxist Russia, Maoist China, and pursuit-of-happiness America. The community of God's people has survived in all of these cultures and civilizations but always as a minority, always marginal to the mainstream, never statistically significant (Peterson, 288).

While these are excellent thoughts, inspired writers said it long before (see Matt. 7:13, 14; Rom. 9:27). Let us stir our hearts and those of our children, family, and brethren to the reality that the survival of christianity among us hinges on the faith of the remnant believers. We must be prepared to be unpopular, even among christians, in order to be that remnant. Our desire, hunger, appetite, and "meat" must be to do the will of the Lord (John 4:33, 34). If it really is Christ who lives within us (Gal. 2:20-21), let us be reassured that, in the end, He will be victorious, and we with Him (Deut. 1:21; 20:4; Psa. 44:6-8; Rom. 8:28, 35-37; 1 Cor. 15:57; 2 Thess. 3:3; 4:18; Heb. 2:18, 12:3; 13:5; 1 Pet. 5:9, 10; 1 John 4:4; 5:3-5; Rev. 3:21; 12:11; 15:1-3).

References

Adams, John. *The Works of John Adams, Second President of the United States*. Charles Francis Adams, ed. Boston: Little, Brown, and Co., 1854, Vol. IX. October 11, 1798.

Adams, John Quincy. *Letters of John Quincy Adams to His Son on the Bible and Its Teachings*. Auburn: James M. Alden, 1850.

Box, George E. P. and Norman R. Draper. *Empirical Model-Building and Response Surfaces*. Hoboken, NJ: Wiley, 1987.

Catholic Answers. Forum responses to Jon Ward's article "Gay Bishop Backs Planned Parenthood." *Washington Times*, 16 April 2005. Accessed on 18 Dec. 2010 at: *http://forums.catholic.com/showthread.php?t=50173*

Dawson, Christopher. *The Historic Reality of Christian Culture*. Harper, 1965.

Dyer, Wayne, W. *Your Erroneous Zones*. New York: Funk and Wagnalls, 1976.

Engels, Friedrich. *The Origin of the Family, Private Property and the State*. 1884. Hottingen-Zurich. As translated by Ernest Untermine (1902). Original work accessed online on 7 Dec., 2010 at: *http://www.marxists. org/archive/marx/works/1884/origin-family/index.htm*.

Evans, M. Stanton. *The Theme Is Freedom*. Washington, D.C.: Regnery, 1994.

Feuer, Lewis, ed. *Marx and Engels*. Doubleday, 1959.

Fowler, Larry. *Raising a Modern-Day Joseph: A Timeless Strategy for Growing Great Kids*. Colorado Springs: David C. Cook, 2009.

Gales, Joseph, ed. *Debates and Proceedings in the Congress of the United States*. Washington: Gales & Seaton, 1834. Also, George Washington, *Messages and Papers of the Presidents*, James D. Richardson, ed. Washington, D.C.: 1899, Vol. 1, April 30, 1789.

Harrell, David Edwin. *Churches of Christ in the 20th Century*. Tuscaloosa, AL: University of Alabama Press, 2000.

Hattaway, Paul. *China's Christian Martyrs*. Oxford: Monarch Books, 2007.

Koch and Peden, eds. *The Life and Selected Writings of Thomas Jefferson*. Modern Library, 1944.

Landers, Ann. *The Ann Landers Encyclopedia*. New York: Doubleday, 1978.

Lawson, Steven, J. "The Priority of Biblical Preaching: An Expository Study of Acts 2:42-47," *Bibliotheca Sacra* 158 (April-June 2001).

Lenin, Vladimir. *MATERIALISM and EMPIRIO-CRITICISM*. Moscow: Zveno Pub., 1909. As quoted in *Lenin Collected Works*, Progress Publishers, 1972, Moscow, Volume 14, pages 17-362.

_____. *A Caricature of Marxism and Imperialist Economism*. 1916. Collected Works, Volume 23, pages 28-76, August - October 1916.

_____. As quoted by Wikipedia on 7 Dec., 2010 at: *http://en.wikipedia.org/ wiki/User:Imperator_Honorius/Quotes*.

Library of Congress. *Lesbian, Gay, Bisexual, and Transgender Pride Month, 2010.* Accessed on 29 Dec. 2010 at: *http://www.loc.gov/lgbt/.*

MacArthur, John. *Can God Bless America?* Nashville: The W Publishing Group, 2002.

_____. *The Vanishing Conscience.* Nashville: The W Publishing Group, 1994.

Marx, Karl, As quoted by George Lucaks in *History and Class Consciousness: Studies in the Marxist Dialects.* 1972.

Marx, Karl, and Friedrich Engels. *Das Manifest der Kommunistischen Partei (The Manifesto of the Communist Party),* 1848.

McIlvain, Bill. Personal communication. December, 2010.

Obama, President Barak. *Presidential Proclamation—Lesbian, Gay, Bisexual, and Transgender Pride Month,* Released on 28 May, 2010. Accessed on 29 Dec. 2010 at: *http://www.whitehouse.gov/the-press-office/presidential-proclamation-lesbian-gay-bisexual-and-transgender-pride-month.*

Penn, William. *Fundamental Constitutions of Pennsylvania,* 1682.

Penner, Glenn. As quoted by Paul Hattaway in *China's Christian Martyrs.* Oxford: Monarch Books, 2007.

Peterson, Eugene, H. *Christ Plays in Ten Thousand Places.* Grand Rapids: Eerdmans, 2005.

Piper, John. *Brothers, We Are Not Professionals: A Plea to Pastors for Radical Ministry.* Nashville: B&H Publishing, 2002. As quoted by Swindoll, 2010, pp. 29, 30.

Platt, David. *Radical: Taking Back Your Faith From the American Dream.* Colorado Springs: Multnomah Books, 2010.

Pollard, Jeff. *Christian Modesty and the Public Undressing of America.* San Antonio: The Vision Forum, Inc.

Rush, Benjamin. *Letters of Benjamin Rush,* L. H. Butterfield, ed. Princeton, NJ: Princeton University Press, 1951. To John Adams, January 23, 1807.

_____. *Essays, Literary, Moral and Philosophical.* Philadelphia: Thomas and William Bradford, 1806.

Stedman, Ray. "The Child in Our Midst: Mark 9:30-50" from the series, "The Ruler Who Serves." A sermon presented on March 2, 1975. Accessed on 18 Dec. 2010 at: *www.raystedman.org/new-testament/mark/the-child-in-our-midst.*

Steiner, Bernard C. *The Life and Correspondence of James McHenry.* Cleveland: The Burrows Brothers, 1907. In a letter from Charles Carroll to James McHenry of November 4, 1800.

_____. *One Hundred and Ten Years of Bible Society Work in Maryland, 1810-1920.* Maryland Bible Society, 1921.

Swindoll, Charles, R. *The Church Awakening: An Urgent Call for Renewal.* New York: Faith Words, 2010.

Tocqueville, Alexis. *Democracy in America* (Arthur Goldhammer, trans.; Olivier Zunz, ed.) Des Moines, IA: The Library of America, 2004.

Then Again. 2010. Letter from Julian the Apostate to Arcasius. Accessed on 16 Dec. 2010 at *http://www.thenagain.info/Classes/Sources/Julian.html.*

ThinkExist.com. Karl Marx quote, 2010. Accessed on 7 Dec. 2010 at: *http://thinkexist.com/quotation/the_first_requisite_for_the_happiness_of_the/186768.html.*

Torricelli, Robert G. *Quotations for Public Speakers: A Historical, Literary, and Political Anthology,* 2001.

Trotsky, Leon. *The Russian Revolution,* 1930.

_____. *The Last Testament of Trotsky,* 1940.

Ward, Jon. "Gay Bishop Backs Planned Parenthood." *Washington Times,* 16 April 2005.

U.S. Securities and Exchange Commission. "Mutual Fund Investing: Look at More Than a Fund's Past Performance." Accessed on 12 Dec., 2010 at: *http://www.sec.gov/investor/pubs/mfperform.htm.*

Washington, George. *Address of George Washington, President of the United States . . . Preparatory to His Declination.* Baltimore: George and Henry S. Keatinge. In his Farewell Address to the United States in 1796.

Webster, Daniel. *The Writings and Speeches of Daniel Webster.* Boston: Little, Brown, & Company, 1903. Vol. XIII. From "The Dignity and Importance of History," February 23, 1852.

Webster, Noah. *History of the United States*, "Advice to the Young." New Haven: Durrie & Peck, 1832.

Wolfgang, Steve. 2007. "Footnotes," *Truth Magazine*, 51(11):8.

World Christian Database. Accessed on 21 Dec. 2010 at *http://www.world-christiandatabase.org/wcd/*.

www.ingramcontent.com/pod-product-compliance
Lightning Source LLC
Chambersburg PA
CBHW031832090426

42741CB00005B/220